TREES T
MOUN

The Journey Mama Writings: Book 1

RACHEL DEVENISH FORD

Other Books By Rachel Devenish Ford:

The Eve Tree: A Novel

First published in 2013
Copyright © 2013 Rachel Devenish Ford

Cover art by Chinua Ford
ISBN-13: 978-0989596190

Small Seed Press LLC
PO Box 7775 #48384
San Francisco, CA 94120-7775
racheldevenishford.com

For Chinua, who is better than
I could ever write him to be,
and for Kai, Kenya, and Leafy,
who taught me to be a mother.

TREES TALL AS
MOUNTAINS

INTRODUCTION

I started keeping my blog, Journey Mama, in the summer of 2005. I had just moved from San Francisco to the Redwoods in Mendocino County, California. I had been working on my first book, dogged and determined, for about eight months, but when I moved, my living situation changed in such a way that I found it pretty much impossible to continue writing my novel. I didn't have a clear space to write every day, I was living in a one room cabin with my husband and two kids, and I was pregnant. I set the novel aside and started to write a web journal. It was much simpler for my poor abused mind (pregnancy seems to suck the creative juices straight out of my bones) to find interesting ways to write about my day than to continue creating the world I was trying to create in my book, and I didn't want to get rusty from not writing.

The other reason I started the blog was that I had descended into a sort of morbid victim mentality, a self-pity that clouded everything. I had been struggling with depression for years, and I felt like my life had sort of plopped on top of me and wouldn't get off. I was twenty-five, I had a three-year-old, a one-year-old, and I was pregnant with my third. I was an artist working in a job at administration and the utter servanthood of mothering. I felt cheated. None of our kids were planned, and I loved them to death but I felt, well, like a victim, like all the little things that happen in an ordinary day were making me crazy. So I started to write about my life, and in writing stories about my days, I floated to the top of them, I stood at the crest and looked down on my daily happenings, and I laughed. I made other people laugh, too. I became an author in my life, rather than having everything read to me. I felt like I was driving the car.

A bit of background: My husband and I work and live in an intentional community that helps people on their path in their relationship with God, at the time namely young people who had been living on the streets of San Francisco or other cities in the U.S. Chinua and I had been working with this community since before we were married and it was a wonderful, wild, messy life.

Just before our time at the Land from 2005-2007 we lived in a flat on Haight Street in San Francisco with around twenty other people. Every room had a loft built into it to expand the space vertically under the fifteen foot ceilings. We slept with our two kids in one of these rooms and—with a shudder— I remember how often I climbed up and down the ladder to nurse my daughter or take care of my son in the middle of the night. We shared bathrooms and the one small kitchen with those same twenty other people, elbowing our way past each other in the mornings, all the sleepy parents gathering around the breakfast table with the kids, taking turns with the highchair, just hours after the last late nighter singles had left the kitchen. Community was our life, it was all we knew and we were still working out the kinks of growing families within community. Our shared lives were chaotic and amazing. We had so much fun, we made a lot of mistakes, we loved a lot of people. It was from here that we moved to the land, in 2005.

The Land was an old resort with wooden cabins deep in the Redwoods, hours away from any big city. It was on the Eel River—a quiet place with trees and needle strewn paths, falling down houses, old vehicles in the field, large vegetable gardens. The Land was a place for people just starting out on their journey of Christian faith to learn about life with God. It was a place of teaching and work, a place to live among other believers and grow. There were a lot of people who came along with drug or alcohol addictions. At the time we lived there, it also became a welcoming place for travelers— a sort of faith inspired haven where people—travelers, seekers—could come to stay and sing worship songs around the fire.

At the time of our move, I had just begun to put the pieces together and realize that I was struggling with anxiety and depression. I had a name for what was hurting me for the first time, and I wasn't sure what to do with it. But I was writing my way through it, as well as writing my way through the questions and struggles I had with young motherhood. After hiding how I felt for a few years, I made a complete switch and decided to have honesty as my road and my horizon. I was almost ridiculously honest, vulnerable, open, and it changed me. Before, I felt that I was in a box, alone with a brain that wasn't always safe for me. Though I lived with so many people, I felt unable to communicate how I really felt about parenting or the darkness that sometimes had me reeling. But as I wrote honestly I discovered that isolation was half my problem. And people identified with the things I was writing, letting me know again and again that something I wrote spoke to them or for them.

People have told me that they have gone and read through all my archives. I can't even imagine the amount of clicking and loading pages one has to do to achieve that. But last year, looking back through the shoeboxes of my blog, I saw just how much I had written—so many words, so many thoughts. My life as a writer can be seen so clearly in the sentences that have been added to one another slowly through the years.

I have combed through the shoeboxes and found the best posts to compile in this book. I picked the ones that most accurately showed my life at this time, as well as the ones that lifted me and made me laugh even all these years later. This first chronicle spans the time between first moving to the Land, and leaving with my family to move to India, nearly three years later.

Now, when I read through these old words, what first comes to mind is that I was so young! I was unsure. I was overwhelmed by parenting young children. I want to take my young self, sit her down with a cup of tea and tell her, "Love, it's going to be okay. Go easy on yourself."

But in my writing I also see a story of a girl who is trying to make sense of difficult things and find humor in them. There are funny stories in here, joyful stories, stories of the serious anxiety I was fighting. There are stories of love and grief. Telling stories about our days is a way of showing love to our lives. I believe in the power of honesty and vulnerability to bring light into dark places and to break through the darkness of isolation. As you read, I pray that the chronicle of my life during this time would entertain you, inspire you and keep you, maybe make you feel that you can join in your own life, that whatever you are going through, you can tell stories that will help you find your way.

THE FIRST YEAR

In the first year I discovered the joy of writing stories. I saw that I could take my days, and by writing about them, make them my own. I could tell stories about embarrassing or humiliating things, and the stories would make me (and others) laugh. By writing about the humor and beauty that was in my life if I looked for it, I was giving love to the wonderful and sometimes difficult life I'd been given. Writing about my life was shining love into it, writing about my days gave them a new softness. In my depression and anxiety I had begun to feel that the days that stretched out in front of me were a dark, terrifying wilderness. As I wrote about moments along the way, everything looked more friendly, and I discovered that the days are only days. I received and gave love as I untangled my thoughts through the act of writing, and discovered something wonderful. Truly, life was funny, surprising, and beautiful. I told myself the truth, again and again, and I began to believe it.

august

August 16, 2005

Lately I've been thinking about life in the woods. I suppose the term "the woods" could be a euphemism for more than just living in the redwoods, because I've been struggling on and off with depression now for almost four years, and in a way it has been like walking through a deep forest— sort of a secret one— a dark place hardly anyone knows about. As in any forest, patches of light shine through here and there. Sometimes I walk into a clearing.

Life in my woods— my depression— is darker than life here at the Land. My woods are cold, all the time, and cheerless. Also, lonely. The Land is hot at this time of year. There are people all over and it is full of mirth and companionship. The sun shines through the trees everywhere you look, creating delightful variations of green and gold. It is a place of alternating patches of shade and sun, a place of constant light and breeze. When I hang my laundry on the line I can see the river far below me, flashing silver through the trees. This is the physical reality of the place where I live. Why, then, are these woods I walk through in my mind so bleak?

I suppose the main thing that hits me when I step into a particularly dark patch in my woods is panic. The light is gone, and with it has gone the memory of returning light, of a path that eventually will reappear in front of me. This is a poetic way of saying that I simply lose it. I lose it and don't regain it until I somehow find some calm. Which can take, well, hours. I tend to rant and rave, mostly to my husband, who does his best to keep his head above water. It is the panic that leaves me huddled at the base of a tree, afraid to walk any farther.

It is the panic that causes me to question my life: my usefulness, my calling, my ability to be a mother or a wife. It is the panic that causes me to say stupid things.

I need a new bag of tricks. Since I became a mother, my old tricks for calming and re-centering no longer apply. I can't spend hours sitting in the tub, or reading some kind of sword-swinging novel that takes me into another world. (Actually, I do still read sword-swinging novels, but I read them mostly at night, when I really should be sleeping). I can't write for hours at a time, can't sit and think for hours. You get the picture. I need tricks that don't take a lot of time, that bring me back into the sane world in time to put food in the babies' mouths.

I guess finding this bag of tricks could be considered a mission to keep me sane. I have been thinking about it a lot today, this depression business. The question of sanity. Why I sometimes temporarily lose mine. And I've been questioning things: Is this what I really want to have define the first few years of my married life? Of my life as a parent? This deep forest that surrounds me? Can I fight out of it? Is it too thick? Are there sunny fields to break into? Or should I walk along in peace, willing for it to remain dark?

Maybe I will find a silvery stream to follow, which will take me to larger places. God has always been with me, through these difficult times. The most life-giving thing that I've learned in this time is that God still loves me, no matter how much I despise myself for failing, over and over again. He will never despise me. He will set my feet in a spacious place. The roots of these trees can't keep me.

August 17, 2005

After yesterday's entry of depression and darkness I want to say that we are all still here. Everyone is fine, and I am finding healing in the water sounds that make their way up to me from the sun-speckled river. Every day I hang laundry. Every day I drink tons of water and herbal pregnancy tea.

Right now it is nighttime and the kids are sleeping in our one room cabin. I am sitting on our couch, listening to them sleep. I am quietly happy. I have two favorite possessions. Well, maybe three. Number one is my doorway to writing— my computer. Two: my couch, a love seat, really. The place where I sit to read and write. Three, my little red kettle. I just bought it, and I am having so much fun boiling water in it. There, you know my secret. I am a complete nerd, and I get excited about boiling water. But it is part of the tea fixation, and there is really nothing that can be done for it.

I just ate a third of a pint of Ben and Jerry's Mint Chocolate Cookie Ice Cream. I can never eat more than a third. Maybe a half. But never, never, never the whole pint. It's my teeth. They are far too sensitive for such shenanigans. The layer of protection over the nerves in my teeth is made of saran wrap.

It was a good day for healing. A breezy, not too hot sort of day. A day in which I didn't lose my cool with the kids. I puttered around our little cabin, sorting things out, organizing. Slowly but surely everything is coming together. I think a lot of the healing of the panic of depression will simply come from being quiet. From not trying to be anything other than exactly what I am right now. And that is the kind of day that I had today. Rejoicing in my little home. Boiling water for tea. Hanging laundry. Reading Goodnight Moon to my kids.

I remember that it is okay to be nice to myself, because God is always nice to me. And because He is nice to me, I can be nice to other people. There is enough niceness to go around. Sometimes being nice to myself means ice cream. Sometimes it means letting myself clean my home, not feeling like I should be doing something else. It means watching the kids sleep, with their little eyes all scrunched up, until I feel that love that feels like sadness. It means taking a five minute shower and then racing into bed and diving under my down comforter. And quietly drifting to sleep, held up by the knowledge of God's tenderness towards a failure like me.

August 18, 2005

I really want to get back to India. This is what I am thinking about, right now, after having got the kids into bed. I'm listening to them breathe: Kenya's soft whiffles and Kai's heavier stuffy breathing. He has the breathing of a kid with allergies. It's cute and sad, all at once, and when he's awake you can tell that he's getting a little too intense by the fact that his breathing starts to sound like a Komodo dragon.

But back to India. What's so great about India? I'm sure lots of people have wondered this over the years, as Chinua and I have gotten a little wild-eyed in our ranting about how much we love India and Nepal. Our love for India is one of the ways that we knew

9

that we were made for each other. We tell the same crazy stories over and over again, in different groups of people. I know that one or two people have heard our stories a few too many times, and we probably are in danger of having something thrown at us in the near or distant future, if we crack open the leper-in-Kathmandu-van-running-out-of-gas-in-the-mountains-and-us-hoofing-it-home-story one more time. It's true, we do have some crazy stories. Sometimes I read those travel anecdote books and I want to say, "Huh. That's nuthin." It's the result of budget traveling in one of the most eclectic and unpredictable places on earth. Crazy things just happen.

On my first trip to India, Chinua, our friend Timothy, and I decided to go on a camel trek. We set out with our three guides into the vastness of the Rajasthan desert one afternoon, on three tall and grumpy camels. Tim's camel tried to bite Chinua's camel on the neck again and again, whenever we stopped for water. Mine was a little more placid, but once, when I was in the middle of clambering on, he stood up, leaving me dangling by one leg, a good thirty feet off the ground. Thirty feet or ten feet. Something like that.

Our three guides were about ten, eighteen, and sixty-five years old, respectively. The youngest boy was a cruel tyrant of a camel guide, whipping his camel with gusto while we protested without effect. My guide, the eighteen-year-old, was a romantic who whispered sweet words in my ears while Chinua tried to keep him in check from his own camel, which was trailing behind. Eventually my elbow in the guide's ribs stopped him for good. The old man was a character. He didn't understand a word of English, and his solution to this awkward problem was to join Tim, Chinua, and myself when we were talking and act as though he understood the conversation. He nodded where appropriate, made noises like "Aaah, aaah, aaah," and laughed when we laughed. We caught onto him after a little while. Since camels are so tall, we were always in danger of being decapitated by the power wires if we didn't duck, so our oldest guide kindly warned us by saying, "Campum!" (" careful", in English, but in his English) every time we got near one. Eventually my youthful and peer-influenced guide noticed that we laughed when the old man said this; "Campum. Campum. Campum," so he turned around and addressed the old man with scorn. "It's not 'Campum,' it's 'Calpool.' To this day, "Campum" and "Calpool" are still just as funny to me. This is why I love India.

Riding a camel is not as crazy and adventurous as you might think. Rather, it's a little staid— plodding, one might even say. We three plodded along, swinging with the camels' wide gait, growing stiffer and stiffer, holding onto our guides who were sitting in front of us. When the sun started to get low, we stopped, deep in the desert. We could tell that this was their usual stopping point by the fact that there were old dried piles of camel dung scattered around. Our elderly guide began picking them up in his dhoti, a thin wrap that is tucked between the legs and tied, a garment which is worn extensively by men in Rajasthan. Then, he put the camel pies in a pile and set them on fire, so that he could cook our dinner. Well, we were used to burning dried poo, it is a smell which pervades India. India would not be India without the smell of burning dried poo. It's a very nice smell, smoky and sweet. But then he washed and dried our dishes with the same dried-poo-handling dhoti, and at that point we were a little grossed out. We are tough cookies, though, we can handle anything.

I had been wondering what we were going to sleep on, or rather in. I knew that the desert got cold at night. So I was relieved when I saw that the blankets that we had been sitting on, all day, on the camel's backs, were our sleeping blankets. I mean, talk about efficient. Almost no packing necessary.

Dinner was incredible. Truly. The stars came out and I have never before in my life seen stars like that. Not even in Canada, in the mountains. These stretched from horizon to horizon and the sky was a perfect bowl. Betelgeuse was as red as a poppy. It was amazing, and we ate our rice and vegetables and dhal staring at the sky. Timothy and Chinua particularly enjoyed a type of bread that the guides made for us— a desert camping bread, I guess— it was made by setting a bush on fire, shoving it under the sand, and then making bread balls which were also buried under the sand. The result was a hard doughy ball that was warm and fresh and tasted a lot like sand. The guys loved them, and had seconds, maybe thirds. I was not so enamored, don't get me wrong, I just don't like my bread to taste a whole lot like the desert floor. I stuck to seconds on rice and subzhi — Indian vegetables. And I was glad that I refrained later, when the guys were in agony after the dough ball bread expanded in their stomachs. It was a sad picture, Chinua and Tim bending their backs as far as they could go, groaning like horses in labor, trying to give their stomachs more room in their bodies because there just wasn't enough room for all that bread.

We drifted off to sleep in our camel blankets on the sand. And in the morning, the sunrise. And a long trek back mid-day, which caused Chinua and I to almost die of sunstroke. But that's a whole different story.

August 23, 2005

Yesterday Chinua and I went to the nearest emergency room with our kids.

We were headed to the ER because after his nap Kai was

12

complaining of pain near his sternum. This wouldn't have been too alarming, except for the fact that he had experienced a pretty big electric shock from an outlet in our room, earlier in the day.

I watch my kids. Really. It may seem that I let them run through the woods like Hansel and Gretel while I sit in my cabin painting my toenails, but this is not true. Actually, while I'm painting my toenails, they lurk over me fighting for a better view, Kai busy trying to touch the wet polish on the toe of one foot, while Kenya tries to step on the wet polish on all the toes on the other foot. It is a cross between a day at the spa and a wrestling match. Not totally relaxing.

Anyways. Kai climbed behind a dresser to retrieve a toy that he had thrown back there. Watching him, I really just thought "better him than me." Bending is not the easiest thing these days, considering my rounded belly. But it just so happens that there is an outlet back there, which had an appliance plugged into it, and it just so happened that the prongs were a little exposed, and it just so happened that there was a long coil of wire (that I only bought to use to try to break into the car when I locked myself out in a parking lot a couple of weeks ago, but that's a long story) and it had fallen off the dresser, ready to bend and touch the slightly exposed prongs when Kai brushed past them crawling behind the dresser.

There was a huge flash of light and Kai came barreling out and he was crying, and his thigh was hurt, and Kenya started fake sympathy crying, and I checked for black soot or burns but there were none, except for the burn marks around the outlet. I kept a close eye on him, and everything was fine. Until he started complaining of chest pain.

We called a nurse and decided to go to the E.R., but about halfway there, Kai wasn't in pain anymore. I felt a little silly as we walked in and registered with my child skipping around like a lamb.

The hospital in Garberville is about the size of somebody's large house, and the E.R. staff appear to have nothing to do. But they took us, and looked at him, and in the end we all decided that he was okay. Which is really really good. I would rather have a false alarm than a real reason to be in the E.R. any day. There was one tense moment, when the male nurse, who has a gray braid down to his waist, said, "Well, I can't find a pulse." And the doctor said, "You can't find a what?" I looked at Kai hopping in and out of the tiled squares on the floor and shook my head. "No pulse, bud," I said. "That's not good." But the nurse tried again, and wow! There it was.

*

Kenya speaks like she's learning to speak English for the first time. (I guess she is!) There are too many syllables in every word. When I'm spooning out avocado for our egg tortillas, she says, "avocabadabodado" and looks at me as if to say, "right?" She has learned a lot about how sweet attention can be, beaming at everyone who enters the room, playing hide and seek and a whole lot of other flirty games with everyone she meets. If she puts two pieces of lego together, she brings them to me, shrieking "Wow! Wow!" until I say, "Wow, Kenya, did you do that?" and she smiles and ducks her head humbly. What a good thing. To bring something to your parents because you feel like you did such a good job and you want them to see it. It's so simple and beautiful that it makes me want to cry.

Kai is also brilliant, and as his third birthday is approaching, he is getting smarter and more creative in his imagination, though his view of reality is a little skewed. He says to me quite often these days, usually after he's been in trouble for something: "When you will be a little boy and I am a mama, and you eat all the honey and break the

14

rule, then you will be in trouble, and I will say, you have to do the right thing."

What does a mama say to something like that?

september

September 6, 2005

Some positive things about pregnancy:

1. I take vitamins. I never take vitamins otherwise. Not only do I take a handful of vitamins every night, I also drink a concoction of herbs that tastes like hay but is brimming with good nutrients for pregnancy and childbirth. And it's no wonder that it tastes like hay. The herbs are raspberry leaf, nettles, alfalfa and oat straw. I've grown to like it, actually, seeing that I drink a liter of it every day. I feel amazingly healthy. I recommend it to any pregnant women out there who think they might have leanings toward drinking tea that tastes like hay (and provides excellent reproductive health). I'm expecting a shipment of six pounds of it on Friday, so you can even come over to my house for a gallon or so, if you'd like.

2. People take things from you when you're carrying them. Even your husband. I mean, I'm used to the single guys around here suddenly exploding into gentlemanliness, but sometimes husbands

believe their wives are so capable that they forget to offer to carry things. It's really nice to be walking along with something like, say, a pillow, and have a man swoop down on you and pluck it out of your hands saying, "Here now, I don't believe you should be carrying that." It's true, though, that this principle can work in reverse. It's the principle of: If you don't act sick, people will treat you like you're well. I have a hard time slowing down, ever, so I sometimes end up sitting and feeling sorry for myself, wondering why no one treats me any differently because I'm pregnant. It's the lesson of my life: *You need to let people know what you need.*

3. You have a little friend with you everywhere you go. I'll be sitting by myself, thinking about bill paying or car registration, and suddenly, tap tap tap. My little inner friend is communicating with me. Of course, this becomes much less desirable toward the end of pregnancy when there just really isn't enough room for both of you in one body. I remember arching my back with all my might with Kai, trying to make just a little more space so he could enjoy his stretching without squishing my organs permanently.

4. There is a special hormone given to you in pregnancy, one that is designed to keep you from yelling at your children because you are so irritable and grumpy. The effect that this hormone has on you is like a big giant dose of giddiness over how adorable and amazing your kids are. You could eat them. You could pick them up and squeeze them until they protest and you ignore them and they keep protesting until you finally listen and give up and put them down. You actually do this. And I am blessed, because Kenya has entered her cuddly lovey stage at the same time, so we can cuddle and cuddle to my hearts content. She likes to get her blankie (she

17

calls it her "bing") and lay on my chest and make contented humming noises. It's great.

September 10, 2005

Maybe, while I'm pregnant, I shouldn't be allowed to go out in public. Just a thought. There are times when it can be a little awkward for other people. Yesterday was a good example.

Chinua and I have had our licenses suspended until we can pay fines that we owe for tickets that we can't afford. Yesterday was my big day to go and represent myself before the Humboldt Superior Court, and beg for forgiveness for the speeding ticket that I received over two years ago. I felt a little nervous about it, since I've never been to court before, and even my immigration hearing was like a cozy little chit chat in my new Vietnamese-American best friend's cozy little office. (He became my new best friend after granting me permanent residence on the spot.) I asked Chinua what he thought court would be like. His thoughts were that it wouldn't be like anything on TV, and that it would probably not even be held in a courtroom. What he said made me think of a nice talk with the judge and a secretary, soon to become my new best friends after the judge dissolved my charges and sent me on my way with a blessing and an admiring word for what a sweet person I was.

This is what actually happened: The court proceedings happened in a large room filled with church-type chairs, (you know, the padded ones) after about sixty other people and I waited in the hallway for the judge to show up from his lunch break. The judge, who was a good-natured and humorous old fellow in a robe, sat at the far corner of the room at his bench, which was guarded from people who had potential grudges by four more padded chairs, facing backwards. This, he said, was to give him time to pull out his gun should anyone rush toward him with a hand grenade, at which time, he said, the rest of us should duck. He really said this. Putting the chairs there was a wise move, since there was absolutely no security in the courthouse. This *is* Humboldt County, after all. (I've faced much tighter security at the Central *Post Office* in San Francisco.)

The Judge read us our rights. He also told us that if any of our cell phones went off a large man with a large stick would come and take them away. Then he proceeded to call us up in alphabetical order to plead our cases in front of everyone. I started to shake a little. Several people had last names that started with letters preceding F. Everyone pleaded guilty to their charges, the Judge would ask them if they could pay their fines that day, and they would say: yes. The most common cases were teenagers with speeding tickets who approached the bench with their parents, pleaded guilty, and had their parents pay for their tickets. I started to sweat. I could see that there was not really going to be an opportunity for me to tell the judge about my life, my kids, my low income, my volunteer work, and various other things I could bring up to get me out of paying the ticket. My plan was backfiring. Clearly I would never be able to drive again.

Finally he called me. I waddled up to the bench in a last-ditch effort for pregnancy based sympathy, then pleaded guilty to the charges. The judge pointed out that the charges were from 2003, being humorous. He was nice enough to take the fine down to only $360, and to say that the cop must have really been scraping the bottom of the barrel to fine me for not having proof of registration in the car (since they have it on their computer system). As he started to question me about whether I could pay, I started to break down. I actually started weeping. I stood sobbing before the entire room of people, thoroughly embarrassed. The judge looked a little alarmed, advised me to find 360 friends to give me a dollar, and then dismissed me.

I cried all the way to the clerk's office, as I went to talk to them about payment options. I cried the whole time I was standing in line. I just couldn't stop the tears. Once a pregnant woman is weeping, it takes a whole lot to get her to stop. All I could think was that I was never going to be able to drive again. I was very, very sad. When I got to the counter, I was still crying. The man on the other side looked a little alarmed, just like the judge. I told him I was unable to pay, and he said he would get me set up with a payment plan. Then, he said the magic words. He told me that once a payment plan was established, they would send a "case closed" message to the DMV, and they would work on restoring my license. My tears started to dry up. The man patted me on the hand and told me it would be okay.

All of this brings me to something I have been thinking about for a really long time. It's about the courts of God. I'm not really talking about the courts in the courtroom sense, but in the royal, kingly sense. Yesterday I felt humiliated, admitting my stupid mistake in not paying a two-year-old fine and admitting my inability to pay. But in the courts of God, I have a voice. Meditating on this has changed my life. I know that I can walk into the presence of the Most High and make my requests known, and he hears me, not just as some pregnant lady who somehow made it into his courtroom, but as his daughter, his friend. Do you see how restorative that is? Everyone wants to be heard. To have a voice. Before Majesty, we do. He inclines his ear to hear us. When I am humiliated, all I have to do is remember that I have a place in the courts of God. And he hears me.

This is what I pondered as I drove home with my friend Elena. The white stripes on the road ran alongside us and the river popped in and out of view, wandering beside the highway, crossing underneath, and disappearing into the distance, only to flash back into view around the next curve.

September 13, 2005

I really need stability in my life right now. Routine. Monotony, even. It's one of the side effects of being pregnant, this whole needing stability thing. It's completely instinctive, like, "I need to make a hole in the ground and bring food to it every day, so that I know when I have my pups I'll have a hole with food in it to care for them in." How about if my family wakes up every day and I feed them and do the chores and bring the kids up to what we call the Big House where someone will watch them for a couple of hours while I do my work in the office and then we'll all go eat lunch, they'll take naps while I do more office work, play for a while, eat dinner, play for another while, and then go to bed? How about that?

Life is never that simple. At least not for humans. And especially humans who work in intentional communities. How about this instead? After Kenya keeps us awake for a good part of the night with her teething, I'll wake up and realize that the sink is still broken because the duct tape has come of the hose that connects it to the shower. So I'll wash the dishes I didn't get around to last night in the shower, and make breakfast for the kids. After we're done eating, Kenya will lay herself down on the floor and cry because she is just so miserable from the teeth that are coming in. Somehow we'll all get ready and head up to the Big House. On my way up I'll have an epiphany. The family is still here. That is, the family who showed up a few days ago, needing help. There is a father with five kids on a school bus, and the mom has become estranged temporarily: they are looking for her. (I want to interject here that with all my heart I really want to help them, and I'm so glad that we're able to do even the smallest thing to help them. But, we're talking about my stability instinct, and suddenly having five kids cruising around on top of your two is not the most stable thing.)

When I get to the Big House I'll find out that the person who usually watches my kids while I work is away picking grapes for the week. This is the first I've heard of it. So, in a last-ditch effort to still get some work done, I'll attempt to put a video on for them. But the TV will be broken. Okay. At this point there's nothing for me to do but find my husband and let him know that I quit, because my job has become impossible. He'll suggest that we find another TV, at which point I'll throw my own self on the floor (metaphorically) and wail that there isn't another TV anywhere. But then my friend Elena will let me know that there is. So Chinua will install the new TV, which has been around since before I was born, while I sit and mutter in the corner. Soon the kids will be happily installed on the couch watching Pooh's Heffalump Movie, (all the kids, including Elena's son Jed and three of the other five) and I'll go to start some work in the next room. Not very far into it, though, Elena will come in holding Kenya, and tell me that she found her down near my cabin, crying her heart out. She must have been looking for me. After my immediate heart attack, I'll cuddle her, thinking, "And they call the TV a babysitter. Ha. Nix the TV babysitting."

Not much will be done, and you get the point. We'll have a few more adventures, like Kai waking Kenya up half an hour into her nap, so the rest of my working day is shot as well, and then Elena and I will chase a stray chicken around for awhile. You can imagine how hilarious this looks if you remember that Elena is nine months pregnant and I am five months along. The visiting kids will prefer to think that I am heartless, rather than believe me when I say that I am working, and too busy to fix the VCR for them. It will be an amazingly routine-free and fruitless day, work wise.

And it is so, so good for me. It is at times like these, when I am torn between sympathy and irritation, that I have to turn to God and say, "Look at me, I'm still a wretch," and he lovingly lifts me up. When I am sick with anxiety over the work I have to do and the impossibility of doing it without help, I remember again that it is all in his hands. I really want to help people, but I still have not found a way to combine office work, taking care of my children, and being fully present for people in need. One requires solitude and order, the others my full attention. Will I ever figure it out? Or is walking my life out more a matter of stumbling from situation to situation, asking God to create stability in my heart, to keep me standing by the sheer strength of who he is for me?

It is so important, because maybe one day there will be an earthquake here, and we'll find ourselves in the same position as the Katrina victims. Where will our stability be then? Not in the earth, because even that can be shaken. Not in routine, not in reliable food, or water. Only in him.

September 19, 2005

Today I returned from a three and a half day trip to San Francisco. I left the Land on Thursday, by myself, feeling free as a bird. The courts had given me back my driving privilege and I flew down the road (under the speed limit) through green trees and the

23

golden hills of late summer in California. I sang and prayed and had so much solitude I could burst with happiness.

The drive home was a little different. The four hours getting home seemed to take about a year and two months.

It's funny, now that I have kids. I'm not completely free anymore. I mean, I can leave, but I'm connected, in an almost physical way, to these two little people who can't even dress themselves yet. (When we ask Kai to dress himself, he suddenly has a really hard time remembering which limb goes where. "I can't get this over my bum," he says pitifully, as he stands in the middle of the room with two legs through one tiny leg hole in his undies.) I mean, kids are really little, but they occupy a big space in our lives.

Chinua and I were talking about this the other day. We're the philosopher-type parents. Our children will probably hate us for it one day, when they're teenagers. "The thing about kids," I said, "is that they are so much. There isn't a lot of space around them, and it's exhausting, but so worth it." And what I learn, from being away, is that now that they take up so much space in me, there isn't tons of room for a whole lot else. It actually leaves me wondering what else there was, before.

I can hang with it, though, for a few days. I really like being by myself, visiting friends and having uninterrupted conversations. I slept in until 10:00 for the first time in four years. I eat food when it's hot without sharing any, and take a shower whenever I want. I sit around. I get work done, in record time. It's amazing really. I can even try to have a few conversations that don't include things that my Superstar Husband thinks or says, or funny things that my kids do. Okay, maybe I can only last a few minutes in conversation without doing this, but I don't think I completely bore my single friends. That reminds me of a funny thing. Some friends and I were

24

sitting around talking, and somehow I brought up the fact that Jed and Kai like to pee through each other's pee streams, if they are doing their business outside. See, even writing that down makes me realize how completely hopeless I am in conversation now, not that I was ever so social. But, one of the friends there (a guy) said, "Oh yeah! Crossies! That was so fun, when we were kids." It was stupefying, really. We were like, "You mean there's a name for that?" It led to a nice discussion about pee.

But back to the point. I can only be away from them for a few days. This time I accidentally overstayed, and the result was that I missed them so much I was almost physically ill. I couldn't think about them. I'd drive along and think about Kenya's cheeks and her little duck lips and almost start crying. And I really am not a fan of spending a lot of time away from Chinua. Just enough for me to remember what it's like not to see him; then it's time to come back. So, there was Chinua-missing and kid-missing, and oh, it was so good to get home, to be with them again and see how happy they were to see me.

September 21, 2005

Some days I feel like I'm being pulled in too many different directions. It's like people have a grip on all of my limbs and are pulling, pulling, pulling... Either that, or my mind is made of a mountain of different colored pebbles and all day long I am forced to search for specific stones. The green stone! The red one! I am scratching and heaving through a storm of tiny details, getting sidetracked on one search by the urgency of another.

I may be a little tired right now.

25

But the beautiful thing that supersedes the mountain of pebbles is that, maybe, for the first time in our marriage, I feel that Chinua truly appreciates me. Not that I haven't felt appreciated before, but that now he really knows. He knows. Because I went away for three and a half days and he tried it. He said, "I don't know how you do it. How do you keep the cabin clean, and wash the dishes, and give the kids baths?" Then he said, (this is after I had been back for a while) "Look at this place! You do it so well. You are really, really good at this."

Can you believe it? I felt all warm and fuzzy inside. And I was also thinking, "YES!" Because, to put it plainly, I've wondered if my beautiful husband understands how much work it is to do all this. We've shared a lot of our parenting responsibilities, and I know I'm very blessed to have him so available, being the best dad I could imagine. But let's just say that when Chinua's hanging out with the kids, he's *hanging out with the kids*. He's playing with them, taking pictures of them but not doing the hundred things I would be doing if I was watching them (with the eyes on the back of my head).

So, I got home to a minor laundry emergency (underscored by the fact that we are still line-drying), a pile of unwashed dishes (which is like returning a video un-rewound) and a beautiful loving family who were missing me like crazy because, to them, there's no one like me. That's what a family seems to be, a team of your biggest fans who are also more work than you could ever imagine. And sometimes they're not your biggest fans. Sometimes your 3-year-old is acting like a sulky 15-year-old who might die if you force him to kiss you or hang out with you. And then sometimes he reverts back to your baby boy and stares at you as if he's in love with you while he strokes your face and says, "I just wanna talk to you, Mama."

So anyways, back to how I do what I do and why I feel pulled apart. I do everything at top speed, as well as with the knowledge that at any moment I might be forced to suddenly switch gears. From say, taking care of my kids, to talking to the insurance company on the phone. Or from kissing my husband to mentioning, "I don't think the goat cheese is working out for the kids, they both seem to have pretty bad diarrhea." Or, and this may be the hardest transition of all, moving from the constant surveillance necessary with small kids to talking or sharing with adults. I'm already enough of an introvert as it is, but the mental hurdles that I have to overcome in order to converse with other grownups make it almost impossible.

I'm sure that many moms identify with the line that runs through my head. It goes something like this: wake up, breakfast, kettle on, oatmeal, cuddle kids, tea (big sigh of happiness), laundry!, wash dishes, break up fight, wash face-nope break up fight, oh yeah-make bed, clothes on "where are the clothes?" And then it's time for me to go work in the office amidst thousands of questions from people needing things.

The surprising thing lately is; I actually love it. I really do. It's challenging enough to really engage me, it all keeps me moving through my day with purpose, and it's humbling enough that I'm always calling out for help from God. And I love it that Chinua is stoked on our home when it's nice and inviting. I wouldn't want to trade, I wouldn't want Chinua's job for anything. It's cool, the roles that we have. God knows what He is doing, although sometimes it takes some refining to get us to see that. I love to work hard, and I've never done anything harder than this. It's wonderful.

Besides, in August I moved out of a house that had about twenty people living in it, and the kitchen sink seemed like it was always full of dishes, so when I'm doing the dishes now, the line that is going through my head is "I'm so glad I'm only doing dishes for four people, I'm so glad I'm only doing dishes for four people..."

September 24, 2005

Today I am a walking bag of anxiety, and I know I'm not exactly a stranger to anxiety, but, really, it's been better lately. I haven't been walking around with my shoulders touching my ears, or kicking rocks with a knot the size of a yak in my stomach.

The funny thing is that my anxiety it has absolutely nothing to do with the fact that an ultrasound on my neck revealed a questionable mass that is now the center of attention of the doctors who are supposed to be paying attention to my wee unborn babe.

I had a two-in-one ultrasound, one being pictures of my baby, two being pictures of my thyroid. I've had what I thought was an enlarged thyroid for years. I learn now that actually, I have a growth, a little cling-on. The ultrasound of the baby went swimmingly, and the technician even went so far as to say that my baby gives very good images (which is another way of saying that he is extremely photogenic, even at his tender age) and when I left, she thanked me for being such a good scan (which I took as her way of saying that she has never worked with anyone as kind and witty as me). It was great, the grainy black and white images of my active baby who rolled around the whole time she tried to catch him with her little wand. He has beautiful hands, I can tell. (We don't know that I'm having a boy, I just say "he.") Chinua, Kai, and Kenya were in the room, Kai watching with a kind of stupefied awe, wrinkling his brow to try to see what exactly we were seeing, and Kenya being generally distracting by turning the lights off and on and pulling on various cords. It was at once very like our first, romantic ultrasound of Kai,

28

and very unlike.

But, as for the lump, I can't say that I'm that worried about it. I mean, I have to be careful not to think about it too much at certain times of the night or day, since my imagination is wild and morbid. As Chinua and I drove home after the ultrasound, the kids asleep in the back of the van, we skirted around and dove into the loaded topics of sickness and death. We talked about how sickening it is to think of dying when you have small children. It seems to be not even an option anymore, although of course it's outside of your control.

Then I had a thought. "It's probably just something I swallowed the wrong way," I said to Chinua.

"Yeah," he agreed, "like a piece of chicken or something."

"Or it could be something I misplaced years ago,"I continued.

"Hmmm," Chinua said. "It's probably a wad of twenties. Or maybe it's your twin."

My real anxiety revolves around something that I have absolutely no control over: Other people and their thoughts or emotions, how they are doing, whether they hate me. I walk around scrunching my forehead over things that I have no way of changing. The ball is not in my court. It's not even on the same block. I may as well worry about whether the river is flowing the right way.

Living here, at the Land, a community for people who are in the long process of learning to walk with God, I worry over the guys and girls who live here with us. Are they leaving? Should they be leaving? Did they leave for the wrong reasons? So-and-so looked sad at lunch —are they okay? Or, I worry about conflict. Is everyone mad at me?

I sound really pathetic. But it's funny that I can trust God with my pretty neck (I like my neck, even if it is a bit lumpy. It's one of my favorite body parts, next to my forehead) yet I feel like the pasts, presents, and futures of the people in my life are on my shoulders. How ridiculous is that?

This is all to say that the futures of my dear friends are in the hands of a gentle Father.

Just like my skinny little lumpy neck.

october

October 2, 2005

The first rain came yesterday, and I stepped out into a tropical breeze when I left my cabin in the morning. The air hung close around and wisps of mist were weaving through the trees. It was surprisingly warm and humid, raining ever so slightly. I hurried to get my laundry off the line and felt perfectly happy, loving the warm wind, which reminded me of Thailand. I rushed to tell Chinua to step outside and breathe it in, and he agreed with me. It was a perfect day.

It was a perfect day in many ways. It was my husband's birthday, and I'm so glad that I've been able to spend so many birthdays with him. The first we ever shared was in Thailand, when he turned twenty-seven. We sat with friends at our favorite restaurant in Chiang Mai and ate sesame balls in honey instead of birthday cake. Today was the fifth birthday that we've spent together.

The only thing Chinua really wanted for his birthday was a set of juggling torches. Juggling torches are a lot like they sound—used for the purpose of—you guessed it—juggling fire. Teaching fire safety to our kids seems almost pointless when they have a dad who throws flaming sticks around as if they were as benign as say, crumpled up paper or something. I can just imagine saying, "Okay, kids, don't play with matches, all right?" They'll look at me as if to say, "Sure, Mom." I'll have to qualify, "Only adults play with fire." Given Kai and Kenya's frantic and persistent attempts to learn how to juggle, they'll want to join in some day. Kai's tries at juggling involve him throwing three or more items up in the air and then running around to try to catch them. Every time, they hit the ground, but I think that he really believes that if he just tries one more time, he'll figure it out. During Kenya's attempts at juggling, though, the toys she's trying to juggle don't even leave her hands.

A bunch of us at the Land pitched in to put enough money together to buy Chinua his torches. I made Chinua look for his present, though, with a scavenger hunt where he searched for clues that brought him to the place where the promise of torches was hidden. (All we had was the I.O.U. card. I would have no idea how to go about actually buying juggling torches, so I left it up to him.) The hunt was really, really fun. Maybe even mostly for me, since I was shaking with laughter over Chinua trying to puzzle out my elusive clues.

Then, oh my word, the two of us actually went out to the big city of Garberville for dinner. Together. Alone. It has been about two months since we've done this, so it seemed like the most luxurious thing possible in life. It's kind of cool to be deprived of something you love, because once you have what you were lacking, it is so sweet to you. My dad used to work all night outdoors in ungodly weather. It would be -40 degrees Celsius with a wind chill, and he would say, "It's not too bad when you're cold, because it's so good when you're warm again." Right.

In San Francisco we had many more date nights. We would put the kids to bed and have someone else who lived in the flat with us listen for them while we crept around the city streets hand in hand, a very sneaky couple. But in the City, we lived in a flat with what was sometimes twenty other people, and it was a little difficult to be alone. We don't have the same problem here at the Land. It is so much more peaceful. (Being one of the people "in charge" does make you prone to being asked for advice at any moment, though, so if Chinua and I are walking hand in hand around the Land at night, and I see someone walking purposefully toward us, my instinctive and primal urge is to turn and flee.)

We had pasta with shrimp and smoked salmon, and I was disappointed that the salmon seemed somewhat cooked. I was expecting the rawer, creamier smoked salmon. It was probably good, seeing that I'm not actually supposed to be eating that sort of fish. I crave it, though, and was planning to cheat in that minor area of pregnancy do's and don'ts. What? It's not like I was planning to chug back a bottle of wine or anything. I think that my pregnant self goes into some sort of world motherhood state, because I'm craving like I'm a Jewish mom in New York. Bagels and lox and cream cheese. Mmmmm. Capers. Mmmmm. Or I'm Japanese. Sushi! Miso! Or Vietnamese, desperately craving Pho Ga. It's seems to be different with every pregnancy, actually. With Kai I was Mexican, eating Mexican rice and beans like there was no tomorrow. With Kenya, it was the sushi. I ate whole packages of somewhat fake California rolls, sitting in the car in the parking lot at Trader Joe's. This time it seems to be the aforementioned food of American Jews.

Our meal was delicious and we had a wonderfully nerdy time discussing food in different cultures and the progression of civilizations as represented by their ability to survive and their interest in food. We figure that the colder the climate is, the less time people could dedicate to their culinary arts. Thus, Thai and Middle Eastern and Indian foods win out over kidney pie and borsht. Chinua and I are made for each other. We really sit around and talk about this stuff on dates. Cultural history is our favorite thing to discuss, next to physics or math concepts.

We arrived home to a painfully obvious attempt at a surprise party. As in, "Honey, will you put the ice cream in the freezer? I just have to "check something." Or, as we were walking up to the Big House from our cabin: "Honey? I feel like I should have the camera, just in case there's anything to take a picture of. I'll run back and get it." Because I always take pictures in the dark. We both knew it was a façade. It was a hilarious Land birthday party, though, complete with a round of our favorite game, Narcoleptic Dog. Chinua made Narcoleptic Dog up, but our friend Amelia came up with the name. It's pretty great. It involves skits and drawings and dances and art criticism. The best kind of game ever. My favorite moments were when Jeff acted out Someone Shooting Arrows at San Francisco, and Derek impersonated a parasitic cow. I've had some of the best times in my life playing games at the Land. It's as if in the midst of all the seriousness of broken lives that God is putting back together, he understands that we need these joyful, hilarious moments to even it all out. A lot of the guys who live here now have had their hearts absolutely crushed, and are being rebuilt from the ground up. And God brings such joy through them. I feel so fortunate to be here.

The crowning moment in the whole evening, however, was Kai's break dancing. Our friend Jesse showed him some moves back in the city, and Kai did a little bit for us, refusing to dance to anything other than the ring tones on my cell phone. We were laid out, .

laughing. He got a super serious look on his face, and then started a
little toe tapping, to warm up. Then the fingers started wiggling.
Then the somersaults, the crouches, the kicks. It's the best thing
ever, especially since he feels the music, you can tell. I'm telling you,
this boy has talent. And he's only three.

October 5, 2005

The days are flying by like the leaves that fall continually now.
We can never keep the porches swept clean. That last warm, tropical
morning feels like a dream now that it has grown so cold, and we all
have stiff fingers and cold noses. It's kind of nice, though, once you
can fully let go of summer and realize that winter really is coming.
Woodsmoke and rain and early nights. I have to try hard to think of
it as cozy, rather than gloomy.

What a week! Our non-profit just mailed out a newsletter, and I
stuck the last left-behind letters in the mailbox today. Yesterday I
organized the stuffing of almost 1000 envelopes, which always
involves about nine of us sitting hunched around a table for hours,
putting together letters assembly-line style. We have good music, we
talk a lot, we have fun, I get really irritated and stressed out, and
somebody inevitably ends up with hurt feelings because of someone
else telling them that they are moving too slowly. Sometimes we get
a little too sarcastic. I'm always so grateful when we are done. It was
a marathon day, since after the letter party we had a staff meeting,
and afterward I begged Chinua to let me go into town by myself to
run errands. (Read: without the kids.) My angelic husband is always
willing to give me time by myself, so I didn't really have to beg, I just
did because that's the way I am.

I felt like I needed some encouragement, so I started listening to

36

a sermon by Timothy Keller. His teachings are incredible. I feel like I've found what I'm always looking for in a teacher. He's clear, passionate, intelligent, and wise. Chinua and I have slowly been listening to a series that he did on the Wisdom of Proverbs, but yesterday I cheated and started listening to another series: Living in Hope.

I was blown away. I've talked before about how I've spent large parts of the last four years really fighting depression. It's affected me in so many ways, and maybe spiritually the most. Hearing the description of living in hope that Dr. Keller gave made me weep. He talked about how a life lived in hope, in the certainty of things to come, is completely different from a life lived without hope. Certainty of a good future causes your whole life to be different. He was referring to the promise in the Bible that we have life to come, life forever, life with God. He talked about a lady he knew who lived in poverty, even though she had quite a nest egg in the bank, because she was paralyzed with fear about touching her money. She was sick and dying because of the fact that she didn't draw from what she had in her bank account.

Listening to it, I sat there thinking: that's *me*. For some reason I don't access the love that I know God has for me, and I don't live in hope. It's almost as if I'm afraid that I can't spend it. But now I feel like I'm waking up. Why let everything that God has given to me freely sit there becoming moldy? Why do I live unaware of the goodness he has for me, so often? I live like a worker bee, conscientiously doing all the tasks that are in front of me, without drawing from the love that will sustain me. As though life is about *work*. As though *Christianity* is about work. And I burn out. I lash out. I die slowly.

Dr. Keller described this as a widespread condition. Have we let ourselves forget what we have? What we are headed towards? It's amazing, really, that we can be so dull, while we are being given so much.

October 13, 2005

Yesterday I was in the hospital, and today I was at the doctor's office. I feel worn out. Of all the things that motherhood encompasses, it's the appointments that really get me down.

Yesterday they did a biopsy of the lump that is perched on my thyroid at the base of my long neck. Or, as Chinua so aptly put it, yesterday I was stabbed in the throat several times. I did pretty well, I'd say, considering that when I was a kid I was famous for screaming down the nurses when they tried to draw blood. I'm a little needle-phobic. So I took precautions as I went in, bringing Chinua with me for moral support. We dropped the kids off at a friend's house, where they were absorbed into the surroundings and pretty much didn't notice when we left. The family that we left them with has a whopping ten children, and the wonderful thing about this is that another two don't really make much of a dent.

I was nervous. I probably would have been more nervous if they had bothered to tell me that they actually needed to take about *six* samples. (The nurses I had talked to on the phone had vaguely described "a sample.") This meant that, including the two shots of novocaine, I was stuck in the neck *eight times*. And, I understated it when I said I'm a little needle-phobic. I'm actually a big huge Needle Phobe. I lay there peacefully breathing until they gave me the first shot. That's when the panic set in. That's when I started to faint, to feel lightheaded and nauseous and cold and then hot. That's when I

38

remembered. I can't do this. I hate needles.

It took everything in me not to panic. To lie there quietly while the nurse (who looked exactly like Jennifer Aniston) put cold towels on my forehead, and the doctor (who looked exactly like Steve Martin) became very informative about exactly how much I was bleeding and the methods he was using to extract the tissues. He used words like "sawing" while he was jiggling the needle back and forth energetically. Pretty much every time they put the needle in, they had to talk me out of fainting. And as I was exerting all my will into not panicking, the pathologist, who was there to ensure that they had the proper amount of samples, said cheerfully when we thought we were done, "Since she's so nice and relaxed there, why don't we get another three samples or so?" They only took one, but it unfortunately turned out to be a doozie. I'm surprised I'm not paralyzed.

Not a pleasant experience.

I used to think, when I was younger and would faint when my blood was drawn, that I was just a big wimp. Now I know better. I've been through two long childbirths with no pain relievers, and I look back at those experiences with awe and nostalgia. My problem is as simple as the fact that I actually just hate *needles*.

And I think I've learned to internalize a lot of things, like the way I hid my panic on that table and the pathologist took it as peace. A good friend of mine told me the other day that I've somehow made what I do (she was talking about being the mother of young children and doing the part time work that I do, which somehow seems to take up all my time) seem easy. That it seems effortless. Graceful. *How can this be?* I guess the turmoil and the craziness are inward. I hide the fact that I've been a mom now for three years and I feel like I've *just started* to figure out what I'm doing, the fact that I usually don't catch my breath until the kids are in bed at night.

Well, I'm glad that it seems easy, because it really is a lot better than they tell you. They tell you that motherhood will take over until there's nothing left of you, but they don't tell you that what comes out when that happens will be a real person. Truly nice, instead of nice only when not messed with.

Like today, when I took the kids into the doctor for their check-up. The nurse told me to get the kids undressed for their physical and I was left in the exam room for half an hour with a naked three year old and a naked eighteen month old running around screaming and pulling open drawers that contained hazardous material. The only appointment they were able to give me was smack dab in the middle of Kenya's usual nap time, and I'm telling you, she gets a little wild. Especially in a room full of sharp instruments and nothing to play with. And for some reason, Kai, her older brother, follows *her* example, rather than the other way around. It felt a little like I was being punished in a very creative way. "Here, sit in the little room with your wild naked children and try to make them behave."

I guess I had it coming. They were so good, yesterday, after the biopsy when we were doing our "come out of the woods and shop, blinking, in the bright lights" errands. And they are perfectly healthy, not anemic, tall for their ages, and bright as sunbeams. Just don't put them into a doctor's exam room for long periods of time. And don't ask me to fill out stacks of paperwork, so that I can only half watch them.

And here I am, now, feeling a lot better after having written this, emotionally exhausted from continually pushing the worst-case-scenarios out of my head. It's not the most reassuring kind of exam, you know. A *biopsy*. But I'm in God's hands, which is the only place I've ever been, the only place to be.

October 16, 2005

Why, exactly, is it so hard to pack for a trip when you have kids? It's like trying to put the carrot back together after you've juiced it. I remember, after I had Kai, thinking that birth had done something to my brain. I couldn't collect my thoughts, couldn't figure out how to get out the door without melting down. Now, three years later, I am mostly better, but let me know that we're leaving for a week and pandemonium sets in. I can leave for the day easy-peasy, (although every so often I get really confident and leave something behind that's as important as, say, diapers) but the longer trips have me stumped.

Chinua and I left for San Francisco earlier today. Yay! We're on a kind of journey. We have work to do in the city, people to meet with, and a wedding to attend and photograph next weekend. Once we were on the road it was great. The kids were angels in the car, with barely any crying, barely any protests like, "Mom, I don't want this piece of the seat to touch meeee..." We set our faces like flint, with the In 'N' Out Burger as our destination. Now that we live at the Land, In 'N' Out burgers are rare treats, with their rarity making them all the more precious.

But, this morning, while I was packing in the rain, I nearly had a panic attack. Chinua had to stand in front of me with his hands on my shoulders, instructing me to breathe. It's a problem I've had for a long time, but over the last few months it's been better. It's the feeling that when I am doing something, I really should be doing something else. Torturing myself this way for hours, I used to wander around the flat in San Francisco flitting from office work to kitchen dishes to laundry in my room. I never felt okay doing anything. It was a terrible kind of guilt. *Something else is more important than what I am doing right now, and I should be doing that.* It is only recently that I have realized that this not a healthy or normal way to live, and lately things have been better. I try to finish things I start, try to be peaceful making breakfast when it's time to make breakfast, paying bills when it's time to pay bills. I try to keep my time with the kids and time in the office separated, so that I'm not doing too many things at once.

Today, though, I would put a piece of kid's clothing into a backpack and then jump up to wash a dish and then brush one tooth, before I realized that the kids were not even dressed yet. And all the while, the mantra going on in my head... WE NEED TO LEAVE WE NEED TO LEAVE. It's enough to make anyone insane.

I really admire the people in my life who have good focus. They seem to get more done than anyone else, rather than less. Like my husband, for example, who is a kind of guitar virtuoso. I wasn't around when he was getting where he was with it, but I know that it came out of obsessive hours and hours of practice. I know this because it's the same way he learned how to juggle. I would wake up at 4:00 AM, alone in our bed, and wander out to the living room to find him. Sure enough, there he was, juggling, wild eyed and exhausted. He gets stuck. It's the reason he plays guitar like a master and juggles fire like a pro.

It's probably good that between the two of us, there's a happy medium. But, after today, I realize that I want a return to the peaceful focus that God has begun to cultivate in me.

October 29, 2005

The last week and a half has been one of the busiest and most difficult times of my life. I have slept in maybe twelve different places. I've driven a total of 62 hours. I've had two crackaccinos (you know, the little cappuccino drinks that come out of the machines in gas stations) even though I'm pregnant and I don't drink coffee, just to stay awake. I've had sixteen meetings, slept in a bedroom with four children and five adults, photographed a wedding and attended a funeral. Chinua and I have both cried, in the last week. This is not so remarkable for me, more so for him. I've eaten at In 'N' Out Burger four times, not entirely by choice. I sat with my family in our broken down vehicle on the side of the highway in the middle of the night for four hours.

And tomorrow morning, Chinua and the kids and I are beginning our drive to Canada for a visit. My home and native land. Now I'm heading to bed, since we're pretty much packed up. Did I mention that all our washers and dryers here at the Land are broken? As a result, I haven't done laundry in a couple of weeks and all our clothes are dirty. So, packing was rummaging through the hamper for the dirty clothes I want to bring so that I can stuff them all, stinking, in the backpack to take to my parents' house, where the first thing I will say to them as we fall through the door blissful and exhausted is: "Do you mind if I do some laundry?"

november

November 21, 2005

We're back from beautiful, leaf strewn Canada, where we raked leaves into large piles and jumped in them, where we soaked in the presence of my parents and sister and brother.

I love living in the trees. I'm afraid that I love it too much. I've been worried that I'm growing a bit agoraphobic, lately, which I think means that I'm scared of going out. Or maybe it means I'm afraid of open spaces, which I'm not. All I know is that the other day I was almost in a panic because I was doing errands and there were too many *things*, too many *people*, people looking at me, people *everywhere*. People looking at me with their beady eyes, buying buying BUYING.

I realize I may not be entirely well.

Walking into Bed Bath and Beyond almost did me in. I needed to buy a special pillow for my gimped neck. I fractured a vertebrae in my neck when Kai was an infant, and ever since, I have to be careful of what I allow my tender neck to rest upon. Unfortunately, the only place that carries the one I need is the psycho household store. Have you ever *been* in that store? Talk about insanity. They've taken vertical storage to a whole new limit. There are fifty million types of garlic presses, stacked to the ceiling. I almost started crying.

I'm laughing about this now, but it was really so bad at the time that I had to do deep breathing and positive self talk just to keep from scratching at my face while shopping. I also felt this intense sleepiness, which a couple of times almost had me laid out on the floor. I didn't lie on the floor. I realized that people would find this strange. I came home to the Land without buying half the things I needed. Sometimes it seems like there is too much stuff in the world and buying stuff hurts and brings me to tears. Maybe I had a touch of the flu.

I feel like hiding in the trees sometimes. And so I love living at the Land, where everything is getting greener with moss by the day, even though the leaves may smother us as they fall. And a few days ago when we were driving through the back roads of Oregon on our way home from Canada, I had the curious sensation of coming home. It was as though I saw all the variety shops and junk sellers and burl wood carvers and felt a kinship. I mean, if you're going to sell *clutter*, you might as well make it eccentric, eh?

November 23, 2005

I don't know the basic essentials of *sleeping* anymore. It's 2:00 AM, my eyes are closed, I'm breathing slowly, I'm trying to let my mind drift away... I'M NOT SLEEPING. Kai is sniffing, he's coughing, he's scratching at the eczema behind his knees, now he's turning back and forth, NOW he needs to get up to pee... I'M STILL NOT SLEEPING. You know, I had a very strange experience the other night, when I was staying in the City with friends, *without*

45

my family. I went to sleep, closed my eyes, and when I woke up... the *sun* was up. I almost couldn't understand what was happening. You mean~ I slept all the way through the night? On the same side of my body? Right now, with a mattress as thick as a piece of rice paper on a bunk bed which causes my husband to have to crawl over my lightly sleeping body to get to his side of the bed, and little elves who snore in *their* beds which are five feet away from *our* bed, well. I wake up about thirty-eight times a night. This is true.

Maybe not sleeping is the reason that I felt like my brain was decomposing all day. Maybe it was the fact that my husband has been sick in bed for three days, and I alternately feel terrible for him and envy him with a ferocity that is ferret-like in nature. Maybe I'm really tired and that's why I said the "D" word when Kai peed in his jammies right after I put him in them. He has this terrible habit of holding his pee until he needs to relieve himself so desperately that he is jogging in place while trying to unzip his pajamas. It doesn't work very well. But is that terrible habit more terrible that saying the "D" word over some wet undies? Probably not. I apologized to Kai, and he asked sweetly, "Are you saying sorry because you said Dammit?" "Yes," I said. "Because that's not a good word?" he asked. "That's right," I said. "Because you shouldn't say it?" he asked. And ON AND ON until I almost said it again.

december

December 8, 2005

The other day a girl gave me a handful of drugs. She's been living here at the Land, and had confessed to me that she had drugs stashed in her cabin. We walked down together to retrieve a baggie full of weed and ecstasy. I was struck by the thought that what I held in my hand equaled time in jail. I could almost see a thick chain attached to it, this tiny bag of trouble. What a terrible thing it would be, especially now that I have children. It was a huge relief to walk to the toilet and flush it all down.

It's so *freeing* to have nothing to hide. There is nothing that makes me anxious when I pass a cop on the road (I may glance at my speedometer briefly, though) and no shudder in my bones when I walk through one of those thief detectors at the store. I spent years as a young teenager addicted to stealing, and as a result walking around like a large intense spider, never able to relax. God mercifully stepped in and I was arrested. In the years since, I have nothing to be afraid of. The law can't touch me because all of me is visible-- there is nothing hidden.

48

It's so hard to remember, though, in my own mental illness, in my willingness to accept the guilt that descends on me daily, that *really* the law can't touch me. One day we will be perfect, but until then, it is enough to live in the Light and be honest about how wretched and small we are. It is enough to watch God. To see the way he does things and to be so happy about how good he is, because he promised that this is the way we will become pure.

Sometimes I get so absolutely sick of my own brain: all the writhing and complaining, the neurosis and the litany of put-downs that come toward me. I get sick of battling myself, my fears, my shame. It's good to know that my heart is always safe with God, because there is nothing waiting at the other end of my confessions but Love.

December 10, 2005

There are some days when I feel as though I've been picked up and cradled like a little baby. And there are days when I feel as though I'm forced to walk when I would rather be carried. Wonderfully, today is one of the former. God has been breathing fresh beautiful air in our direction, in the midst of a few trials. I've been a receiver so many times that I haven't deserved, and I need to express how amazing it always is.

When we were in Canada my sister threw a party for us in one of her busiest times. My parents have given us so much I always feel that I have to be stern with them if they want to give us more. My friend Laura rushes around her house to find more and more clothing that she has that she thinks just might look so cute on me, when I haven't even seen her in four years.

Christy bought me glasses when my glasses were so broken they wouldn't stay on my face and I was so broke I just kept putting them back on. Heather watched our kids for free so that my Superstar husband and I could take pictures at a wedding. People let us use their houses when they go away, people let us borrow their cars when we don't have one to drive. Dori thinks I can do no wrong, and I just need someone like that in my life. (Don't you?) Elena gives me her magazines when she's done with them, feeds my fish when I'm away, and always manages to find something for my kids when she's shopping. Megan and Marc bought me a scented candle just like theirs because I was always exclaiming over how much I loved the smell. Our friends Evelyn and Stephen call us to see if we're going to be staying at their house in the City anytime soon, just in case we didn't want to impose—they want to make sure we have a place to stay while we are there.

Crystal gives me little baggies of chocolate if I'm going away for the day. Lavonne opens up her house for me to have time alone, just to sit and be still. Renee and Eddie beg me to play Settlers with them, many people nudge me out of my shell. People slip us little wadded up pieces of money when they think no one's looking. Hundreds of people have given Chinua and I encouragement, many people have affirmed this blog. Our lives are so enriched by the people around us that it's breathtaking.

Lately life has been a little hard. I've been battling my emotions again, breathing deeply to avoid panic more often than I would like. The newest update on the lump is that it is quite possibly cancer and needs to be removed as soon as possible, but after the baby is born. If they find cancer when they remove it, they'll take my whole thyroid out, which is a health issue that involves using thyroid medication for the rest of my life. I think about a new baby, a surgery, two older children who are not quite two and three years old, some misunderstandings and conflict with really close friends, and renovations on the house that we probably won't be able to move into for about another month, and I'm a little overwhelmed. But I want Christmas to be beautiful, and I want to look forward to my Muffin's birth, not anticipate the surgery afterward.

This is why having friends step in again and love us is so good. And why yesterday, after I drove back to the Land fairly exhausted, it was amazing to find a huge box of beautifully wrapped gifts that had been delivered. Our friends Levi and Jessie wanted to bless us for Christmas. It is maybe the most caring, kindest thing that anyone has done for us in a long time. And that's saying a lot. These are the things that I want to remember when my mind turns against me and I grow suspicious and wary. I want to remember all this love around us that swells like an ocean.

December 10, 2005

Just to elaborate on a brief mention of Lump yesterday, here's the scoop.

My surgeon is a 6 foot 4 inches Greek man. He wants me to call him Pete. So we will. Pete sat beside me for an hour and read all of the reports to me, word for word, explaining every piece of confusing terminology. He let me know that he had requested a larger amount of time with me than usual, with no interruptions, because of the sensitive nature of my case. Pete drew me a ton of diagrams on that scratchy crumply paper that they roll out on the exam table and then ripped it off for me to take home to show Chinua.

All of this is very wonderful and a little frightening as well. I'm thinking, *why* does he want to spend so much time with me? Is it because my case is so bad? In reality it's only because they would usually go ahead and remove something like this right away, just because of the medium probability of thyroid cancer. Pete said it was anywhere from a one in ten chance to a one in four chance. (*What?*) He gave me the choice, but he doesn't want to operate on me until the baby is born. Fine by me. I'm not that worried, seeing as I've had this thing for five years now.

I've been told several times now that if I had to ask God for cancer, I should ask for thyroid cancer because it's so easily treated and 96% curable. Whenever I'm telling anyone about this, I always say 99% curable, because it sounds better. It seems to me that what they're saying is it's better to lose a toe than a finger. And who asks for cancer? Anyone? No?

But I hear from my mom that Synthroid is great stuff, and she should know, since she's been using it for almost thirty years. Actually, I seem to recall her getting great bursts of energy from time to time while I was growing up. Or maybe that was the coffee. I actually feel really good about all this right now. God is giving me shots of grace and I'm happy to be alive and making Christmas cookies with Kai today. He's the best help ever. Kenya? Not so helpful. Good at licking the spoon that I just scooped the baking powder with, though, (to her extreme disgust) and good at scooping great handfuls of batter in her mouth even when I tell her to stop? Yes, she's good at that. I gave them both a beater to lick yesterday, and felt really and truly like a mom.

What I really want to know is whether they can do a two in one and take my wisdom teeth out at the same time. One is poking through and I think they could save money on anesthesia if they just took Lump and the teeth out at the same time.

December 23, 2005

Kai: Let's run to the restaurant together, mama! Your baby wants to run.

Me: (Smiling) Um, my baby is making my body too heavy for me to run.

Kai: But he *wants* to run!

Me: Well, he's going to have to wait a while for that, because it's going to kill me to run right now.

Kai: (Shaking his head with his hand on his forehead) I just don't know about this baby and a mama who won't run.

I've been so happy all day because it is as balmy as Spring here and sunny too. This is after it rained so long and hard that the river rose until I thought it would just meander right up to our cabin and take us away. (*Where to?* I wonder. *Maybe it would be an adventure.*) Rain makes me feel like I have to slouch, like the sky is closing in on me, as much as I appreciate the green, tender little shoots of fern and grass that it brings with it. We already live in a forested valley, so we see little enough of the sky as it is. It is wonderful to have sun and light.

In the past nine years I've only had two Christmases in Canada, which means that seven of them have been without snow. I'm moving to the other side now: Snow? Who needs snow? We don't have snow, but I did get the kids stockings. I am more excited than I've been for a long time about when they'll open them. (Bright and early Christmas morning. None of this midnight the night before nonsense for us.)

*

Paul, one of the guys in our community, has been watching the song "this beautiful day", or "on a day like today," or something like that, by Donovan on the *Brother Sun Sister Moon* movie *over and over again for days.* He puts it on so it will minister to us. I think it's the funniest thing I've ever seen; he'll run into the room, rewind it to the beginning of the song (yes, it's VHS), watch it, and then run back out of the room without saying anything to anyone, leaving me and the other occupants of the room staring blankly at each other. As I said to Derek the other day, as challenging as life can be around here, we never run out of entertainment.

*

I had a spastic get-everything-done-at-once day today and cleaned the Big House as well as doing about eight loads of Land laundry and cooking my famous chicken soup (okay, not that famous) with homemade noodles for supper. Go pregnant girl! I think I'm getting close to the end, now, as a super crazy burst of energy can tell. Although, my burst of energy with Kai was still *weeks* off. I just want this yummy baby to be born so I can kiss his face and milky mouth.

Chinua has also been doing some therapeutic cleaning as he continues to sort through the garage. Today it was buckets of *assorted nails.* Sounds a little neurotic to me, although my dear husband is anything but neurotic.

December 29, 2005

Will someone please come over here and give me a good conk on the head with a blunt object? Please. Really, I'm serious. Not because we got back to the Land and we have no running water. Not because the mountain has fallen on the road in a giant landslide ten miles north of us again, effectively blocking us from the hospital and everything useful. Not even because of the day and night of false labor that I had yesterday.

Well, actually, kind of because of that. Mostly because contractions kept waking me up all night and each time I finally managed to fall back to sleep I woke up again thinking "oh yeah, now I finally really slept," but then I would look at the clock and see that wow, gee, it's only been half an hour. Not only that but I had the stupidest song from a Saturday Night Live skit in my head, and each time I woke it was there afresh in full strength. And I developed a fear that all the hot water tanks were going to explode because they didn't have enough water in them. I was especially concerned for the one in the Restaurant, because not only would it be a bad thing for the whole restaurant to burn down, but our friends who are traveling in India are storing all their worldly possessions in the same room that the water heater resides in. You can see why after a certain point I longed for a simple concussion. It was like my own personal psychotic merry-go-round.

I'm still here today and trying my very hardest for a good day. In candle therapy, this is a five candle day. Maybe we should try seven. How about some hot chocolate? Yup. Soft socks? Yes. Lots of praying, lots of time-outs by myself in the bathroom when the kids have driven me to the very brink. (Really, though, I'm the one driving. They are no different than any other day, so I know it must be me and my sleep-deprived brain.) Who needs water anyways? I mean, we have plenty of river water. The road's out, the water's gone. BUT WE'RE SO HARDCORE HERE IT DOESN'T EVEN FAZE US. YEAAAAH.

My poor Superstar Husband is probably belly-button deep in a waterfall right now, trying to fix whatever went wrong with the pipes. God is always good to us although we are in the midst of a cold, wet Land winter with water problems. When the summer comes, we'll be sitting by the river soaking in the late evening sun. It's something to keep in mind.

january

January 1, 2006

1. Highway 101 going North closed until further notice due to mudslides. Open no sooner than Tuesday.

2. Highway 101 going South closed until further notice due to flooding. They're just not talking about it until Monday.

3. Highway 1 closed South of Fort Bragg. No electricity in Fort Bragg.

4. We are stuck. No going south or north. We could go west, but they have no power.

5. No water. Today was day four. No hope of water until further notice. No hope of water until other guys come to help us, but they can't get here until the roads are open, obviously.

6. We thankfully have power. Apparently all of Leggett is

without power except for us and the Peg House (a convenience store to the south.)

Yay! Power! Let's focus on our blessings. Happy New Year!!!

January 3, 2006

And... we have water again. We got it back approximately an hour before the Superstar Husband and kids and I left the Land to visit with my parents at their timeshare. We were only six days without water. No PROBLEM.

But actually, it's like the saying, "Water water everywhere and nowhere a drop to drink," because really, we had lots of water. We had a whole river that was coming closer by the minute, threatening to carry us away, plus a creek, plus the rain that just kept falling. But, we're 21st Century *wimps* who don't like hauling water. I should say, 21st Century North American wimps, because I've been in plenty of places where they haul water every day.

Like Nepal, where they carry extra-enormous loads of things balanced on their backs by a strap on their foreheads. I think they do it for effect. I mean, Nepali people are mostly *tiny*. I can't tell you the number of times I cracked my head on a doorway in Nepal because it was just too short and I couldn't seem to remember that I should bend double to get through. So it really is stunning to see a Nepali man who is half the size of you—because you're an inch away from six feet tall and a giantess in the land of Nepal—*running* down the road with a refrigerator three times the size of him *strapped to his forehead*, dodging a few dogs and the giant bull lying in the street. I am not exaggerating.

The worst is when you are trekking in the Himalayas and you

never ever thought that you were so incredibly out of shape but now you are thinking over and over, please someone just kill me NOW, as you climb stair after stair, and all these Sherpa porters keep skipping past you up the hill *barefoot* with piles of bricks tied to their foreheads, smiling cheerfully at you as they call out, *Namaste!* Every time. *Namaste!* To every single trekker. Once my Superstar Husband and I (when he was just my superstar boyfriend) saw a group of Sherpa porters taking turns carrying an elderly woman up the mountain to medical help. She was also sitting in a basket, which was resting on one of the porters backs, tied to his forehead. I guess you can bear a lot of weight that way or something.

The point is, we are so civilized that it kills us to haul a little water.

That knowledge doesn't keep me from being very very happy that I:

1. Had a shower today.

2. Gave my kids a bath.

3. May sneak into the hot tub at my parent's timeshare condo tonight.

If we had kept on without any water I may have been forced to do my laundry in the river, like I've seen people do in the Ganga in India. Although it probably would have taken all my clothes away, rushing the way it is. Where did our lovely lady river go? Our pretty green darling? She's gone, and a monstrous mud torrent has replaced her.

One thing I saw a few days ago that I have never seen before: three kayakers cheerfully being swept along. They must have been out of their gourds, as my Superstar Husband commented seconds before he yelled out to them, "You're all gonna DIE!"

"YEE HAAWWW!" one of them yelled back.

January 10, 2006

Really, if I had any more contractions I'd probably just explode. I'm torn between just wanting to have this little Muffin baby so all this can be over and wanting just a few more full nights of sleep. Not that I really sleep all that well.

My new birth plan is to go to the hospital right before I need to push, which will force them to simply catch the baby and we can skip over all the drama. This plan was formed after I was kidnapped and held hostage, strapped to the monitor for two hours while I was forced to listen to my baby's heartbeat in stereo. I love to hear my baby's heartbeat, don't get me wrong, but something's gotta be off when I'm talking to my dad on the phone and he asks, "Who's doing construction over there?" And I have to reply that I'm actually sitting and tapping my feet to the rhythm of my unborn child's heart. It seems a little like stalking.

All I wanted was to have my cervix checked. A strange request, but because of my endless days of contractions and the fact that I happened to be near the hospital, I thought it might be good to see if I had advanced at all. I've been walking around at 2 cm. But they couldn't just check my cervix. I should have known better, known not to even darken the hospital door until transition. But I didn't get it until I saw the nurse avoiding my eyes when I asked when I could leave. I'm not in labor, I tried to insist. I really know I'm not. TRUST me. She seemed to think I was going to have the baby on the side of Highway 101 in Weott, something I would totally never do. Maybe in Myers Flat, but never Weott.

That's when I found out their protocol: 2 hours of monitoring if you even *think* about being in labor. I was pretty furious, since I really believe that I know my body better than anybody. But, not wanting to get the BAD PATIENT rap before the big day even comes, I sat like a lamb and drank apple juice through a straw and listened to the washing machine hammering that is keeping my baby alive.

So, I'll go right at the end, push the baby out, and then the nurses can bring me warm blankets and food. Everyone will be happy.

January 24, 2006

I haven't left my cabin since I got home from the hospital on Saturday, but today I finally emerged. Just for a minute. Soon I'll be creeping back to the relative peace of my little room. The last few days have been pretty momentous and intense and my parents have been absolute angels, taking the kids out so they can get all their crazy energy out while I bond with my little baby.

Salif was born on January 20th at 4:41 in the afternoon. He weighed 8 lbs 6 oz and was 19 and a half inches long. He is beautiful and sweet and the kids love him and I am so happy and sad and overjoyed and in despair. I cry a lot. But I have a lot of people who love me all around me and know that this crazy mess of hormones will only last a while.

January 28, 2006

The other night Chinua put the big kids to bed so that I could do some writing, and when I got Kenya out of her crib the next morning, she was wearing a shirt that says "I'm the Big Brother." When I looked at Chinua with a question in my eyes, he said, "I just thought it was funny."

We're doing okay. By okay I mean that I alternate between feeling like I can't do this at all, I'm going to go crazy and die—*this* meaning take care of these three little kids, in our little cabin, in the rain that pours down day after day without ceasing—and feeling like I am a superwoman, I can do anything, I'm so extremely ecstatic about life and yes I feel great. This type of flip flop is something I plan to work on in this Year of Freedom.

I experienced fairly intense depression after having Kai and Kenya. I've read that postpartum depression is more likely to occur if you have a history of it. Mine has generally lasted the entire time I've breastfed my babies. I got pregnant with Kenya when Kai was ten months old and still nursing, so there was no break there, and then, after weaning Kenya, I suddenly felt like myself again! The old Rae, the one who doesn't become overwhelmed easily, doesn't fall into despair over small things. I became pregnant with Leaf about two weeks later, and hormones once again flooded my life.

Looking into the coming year has had me feeling scared to return to the way I felt after having both of my other kids. That's why I have been inspired to name it my Year of Freedom, thinking that maybe walking beside God through some of the battlefields of my mind will have me freer at the end. I've learned a few tricks since I had Kenya. Like not making my husband into the enemy in my mind. Or like being silent when all that wants to come out of my mouth is a tirade of panic and distress. Or being more gentle with my kids when I am feeling particularly fragile. Or letting myself be loved by God when I feel the worst and hate myself for it.

So rather than being so extreme, in thinking that things will either be perfect or they'll fall apart, today I'll just say that my house is cluttered and my kids are joyful and my husband loves me and I have a headache and my baby is amazing and he slept well last night and I'm tired but happy and I forgot to brush my teeth this morning, and rain is good because it makes the crops grow but boy can it be depressing.

february

February 4, 2006

The Leaf Baby has found his voice. And he is *using* it. Rather than making sweet little grunts and squeaks, now when he wakes up he yells something in baby speak that sounds to me like "FEED ME NOW, MILK WOMAN!" I try to tell him gently to say please, but even after I remind him a few times, he sometimes forgets.

We're doing pretty well, even though we have THRUSH. Thrush just like that, in all caps. Leaf's is pretty much taken care of now, thanks to the wonders of Grapefruit Seed Extract (ten to fifteen drops in an ounce of water swabbed on a baby's tongue works *way* better than Nystatin sugar junk) and my left breast is fine, but when Leaf nurses on my *right* breast, it feels like he's sucking out sand, rather than milk. It really is too painful to even write about any longer, so that's all I'm going to say about our THRUSH. Except that I've dealt with it with two other babies, and I know that "This too shall pass."

He's very sweet and smells like milk. He looks like a combination of his brother and sister and someone else entirely

66

different, whom I guess would be *him*, and sometimes I slip and call him by his brother's name. Today Chinua said, "Kai! What did your mama say about what you're not supposed to do when she's nursing Kai?" No wonder our oldest can be confused sometimes.

The answer, of course, although I'm nursing *Leaf*, not *Kai*, is that the two other little people are not supposed to touch the baby while he's nursing. This is purely for sanity's sake, although there's little enough of that around here. Not touching him includes not wrinkling up his forehead or kissing his cheeks or sticking their fingers in his nostrils, and it *especially* includes not leaning on either of my breasts with their pointy little elbows in order to bend down and smother the baby with attention while I yelp in pain.

The phrase most often spoken around here now? "The baby is not a TOY." Which is why you two can't rock his car seat back and forth really fast or touch his eyes or put blankets on him or mess with him at all. They really are good at holding him, though. Except for Kenya's tendency to push him away when she's had enough, (one good reason never to completely let go of the baby when you are letting a toddler hold him) or Kai's sudden freakish impulse to try to turn him upside down (another good reason) they do well. They really *really* love him. Which makes all my hyper vigilance worth it.

February 10, 2006

I had a lot of big ideas about how much writing I would be able to do once I gave birth to my baby. Being pregnant made me so tired that by the time the kids were in bed it was all I could do to drag my sorry self to the Big House and blog for a while. And it took up so much creative energy to form a little person that I lost all inspiration for writing the novel that I've been working on for about a year now.

Or, I should say, *was* working on, until I was about three months pregnant with the Leaf Baby and just couldn't force myself to work on it anymore. With every pregnancy, creativity has gone down the drain. And then, as soon as I have the baby, I'm overflowing with ideas and inspiration again. The only problem is, well—let me put it this way: when I get around to brushing my teeth regularly again, I'll let you know. Right now I'm typing this with one hand while I jiggle a fussy baby with the other.

That said, I still have a ton of hope for future writing. I've actually started thinking about my book again—the characters, different things I want to change, and either all the awards I'll win when it's published to great acclaim, or how humiliated I'm going to feel when no one wants to publish it and I have to pay to get one miserable copy made at Kinko's. Yes, I flip-flop a bit. (No more flip-flopping, Rae, remember?)

The other day, Chinua and I ran away with the kids for the day in our new van. We drove out through the redwoods to the beach, and it took us hours and hours because of having to stop to feed the baby and change the baby and feed the kids, and oh we need gas, and finally we made it to the beach just in time for the magic hour of light that turns everything into gold. And all I wanted to do was write about it! On the beach we met a kind dry-humored man with an English accent who invited us over to his house to see the rammed-earth structure that he had in his beautiful garden. We took him up on his invitation and made a new friend, we saw his garden, which was filled with all kinds of sculptures. And all I wanted to do was write about it!

The fact that I feel inspired is worth so, so much to me. One day I'll figure out how to combine inspiration with time-management and then I'll really be cracking. Until then, it's almost enough to sit and daydream about painting and stories while I nurse my baby and enjoy it, remembering that he won't be this small for long.

He's pretty amazing. Today some of my friends had a little tea-party/welcome-baby party for me and we had tea and scones and itty bitty yummy sandwiches. There were two other gorgeous babies there, and it really struck me how amazing it is that God formed a mother's heart to be captured by her baby, because no matter how cute I think those other babies are, I really have eyes only for Leaf, and he's the one who goes everywhere with me, so of course that's the way it should be. And I know it's the same with the other mothers there. No matter how much we ooh and aah over other people's kids, in our hearts we all know that ours are the best.

February 15, 2006

I fell off the wagon yesterday. Backslid a bit. The thing is, lately I can almost feel my will to even move flowing out of me along with my milk. I can feel a swirl of hormones from my toes to my eyeballs, sweeping my sanity along with them. I stare off into space without seeing. So, I broke a few rules yesterday, about not making Chinua the enemy, not speaking when only toxic waste will come out, and not beating myself up for small things over and over. It was a terrible day.

It probably was sparked by the fact that Chinua forgot it was Valentine's Day. Big deal, right? I mean, he's not known for his memory for these kinds of things. I know this. I was pretty sure that he wouldn't remember, but I didn't remind him, because part of me was hoping that maybe he had some big thing planned, or some great gift to give me. And I felt like I needed something like that. Life has been a little hectic lately. But I have no call to feel like a tragedy queen over my husband forgetting Valentine's Day because 1. I was almost positive that he would forget. 2. I married a man who is forgetful, and it's not a crime to be forgetful. 3. I chose not to remind him. And 4. I know that he loves me.

See, I do know, because I have friends who remind me, that I have pretty much everything I could want. I'm working at meaningful things in a community I love, I'm surrounded by good friends and I live in a beautiful place, I'm married to a superstar who loves me, and I have three great kids. I know this, I really do. I know that I'm not lonely, I know that Valentine's Day doesn't even matter because I'll never spend another one alone (though I did spend yesterday bickering with the love of my life). But man, what I wouldn't give for a little loneliness sometimes.

I'm like a magnet. If I'm sitting on one cushion of the couch, nursing the baby, then I have two little friends, one on either side of me on the same cushion of the couch. No space. There are space issues in our home. I'm going to start a new show called Everyone Needs Mama. As in, everyone needs mama to hug them, everyone needs mama to feed them, clothe them, wipe the poo off their bums, and most of all, everyone needs mama to be happy and sane. I *know* that this is great, that it's wonderful to be needed, that I'm very blessed, but the result is that one thought doesn't follow another very well in my head anymore. I'm starting to lose brain cells. And I'm writing this at 4:00 AM because I just finished feeding the baby (who pooped all over my pajamas) and I have no time to write during any normal hours. In a minute I'll try to still my mind and go back to sleep.

So, I was raging mad yesterday because I had been talking about how much I loved Target, and Chinua suggested that my ravings were a little, well, ghetto. Low quality. Like, *Rae? Aren't you settling a little?* I probably should have realized that he wasn't saying that *I'm* low-quality, or that I just have terrible taste or low standards, but it set me off because doesn't he realize that the things I get excited about now are diapers on clearance? When was the last time I bought clothing for myself? I think I bought a pair of pants last Christmas. You know? So, Target is a great store, because when you have little means and three children you look for bargains everywhere. On necessities. Chinua totally saw this, of course. But I still made a rabid issue out of it.

Poor husband. Seriously. I was not fun to be around.

Part of that was probably my stress over meeting with the surgeon yesterday, which was the reason Chinua and I were out together at all. He came to be with me at my last appointment before I have the surgery to remove Lump and half my thyroid, which is in two weeks. He is totally supportive and understanding. Even so, a little sulky part of me feels like I am in this alone, like no one really gets how hard this is for me. I'll probably write more about the upcoming surgery, since there are so many emotions running around inside me over it.

On a cheerful note, Leaf is turning into an absolute doll. He was so sweet yesterday, giving me those great open-mouthed smiles that are almost more vertical than horizontal, with a little scrunched up nose. And Kenya peed in the potty for the very first time yesterday. My mom was the one there for the celebratory moment.

And then even though I was such lame company all day, after the kids were in bed my Superstar Husband gave me an amazing massage with this intense cordless massage thing. My old war injury, the fracture that I have in my neck from an old car accident, was acting up, like it always does when I'm under the weather. My old war injury is very painful and in irritation perhaps the equivalent of

71

someone slapping me in the face repeatedly all day. And then telling me to act happy. Chinua helped me out with the thirty-eight huge knots in my neck and I went to sleep blissfully. So maybe it was a good Valentine's Day, after all.

February 18, 2006

Kenya made a nice little poo in the potty this morning, and we had a party for her afterwards, with singing and dancing and animal cookies. On her part I think she was a little puzzled about what the big deal was. Kenya's simple like that. She said she needed to poo, and then she did. So what? Why all the hysteria?

That's one poo and one pee. We still haven't gotten down to any serious training, we're just sitting her down occasionally if she has her diaper off. Or if she mentions that she might have to go. So today, before she got in the bath, she acted distressed and yelled POTTY and so I let her sit there while I bathed Kai in our storage bin that we are still using as a bathtub, and when she yelled DONE, I ignored her at first, and then when she persisted I poked my head around the corner and there it was: a neat little turd in the potty bowl. Ahhh... heaven.

My surgery is set for March 1st. Chinua and I met with the surgeon the other day, and he explained the procedure again, as thoroughly as you could desire. The only new information to me was that they are going to go ahead and take the left half of my thyroid out, to get the lump out without too much scar tissue forming. Pete the surgeon says that the other half of my thyroid will do all the work for my body. This seems to be the way in many things. If you cut an inch worm in half, they go ahead as normal. If you're a mama sleeping half as much as you usually do, you just keep

72

on as if you were getting a whole night's sleep. I wonder if the half of my thyroid that's left will get tired. Will it quit one day? I haven't yet googled thyroid surgery to research it to death yet, but don't worry, I will.

There is only one major risk with this type of surgery, and even it is not so major. The nerve that controls my voice box is right behind my thyroid, and there is a chance that they could damage it. Pete the surgeon says he's never done it. But if he did, and there's always a chance, he pointed out, my voice would be a little damaged. "Damaged?" My Superstar Husband wanted to know. "How so?" "Well," said Pete the surgeon. "Have you ever seen the Godfather?" He left off, with a meaningful pause.

Right.

So, if the thought of having a scar that looks like I've gone over the deep end and slit my throat isn't enough to bother me, then the idea of sounding like a female Marlon Brando might. If I would even sound like a female Marlon Brando. Maybe he was saying that I would sound like Marlon Brando as he is. Male. And old. Maybe I'll keep my fingers crossed for a sexy husky damage, rather than a Godfather damage. Or maybe no damage at all. Just not a pathetic, I can't call my kids anymore or yell at them, so they get away with everything damage. Not a people falling to the floor laughing at my silly rasp damage.

The next step during the surgery, after they remove the left half of my thyroid with the lump attached is when they rush it off to pathology to look for cancer. Then, if they find no cancer, just meaningless lumpage, they sew me back up and I get my scar for keeps. And the right half of my thyroid. But if they find cancer, So long, right half of my thyroid! I will be thyroid-less. And I will have to use Synthroid. Which is not a big deal compared to cancer. The only problem is that I will have to go for four to six weeks without any thyroid medication at all, so they can check me for more cancer. In Pete the surgeon's words, I will be miserable. He said that Chinua would crawl to him on hands and knees asking him to put me out of my misery. Or something to that effect. He said that my brain will be screaming for the Synthroid. And that I will be depressed and gaining weight with no energy. It sounds a lot like pregnancy to me. Times a thousand.

This worries me.

I mean, I'm not going to cross that bridge until I come to it, but if you tell a girl who's already struggling with her emotions and low energy level that you might have to take away her normal hormones which help her with feeling even as good as she does, she might worry. Just a little bit.

But, all that aside, I'm not that anxious. The biggest thing I worry about? My dread of receiving an IV. I think I will faint, I think I will punch the nurse, I think I will throw up. I am such a wimp over needles. And a small part of me does want to throw myself to the ground and refuse to do anymore *anything* because don't you know I might be DYING?

February 23, 2006

I watched "Born into Brothels" the other day and was taken right back to India. It was an amazing movie, a documentary shot in Kolkata about a woman who gave cameras to the children of prostitutes living in the Red Light District. She taught them how to take photographs, and they took beautiful and haunting pictures of things around them. They were so wise for their years. Wise and innocent in the worst of situations. Some of the footage was the best

I've seen of India, capturing the chaos and beauty that exists there.

It made me remember the first time I landed in New Delhi and the way I immediately felt overwhelmed by the problems of India. I was eighteen and had never been outside of North America. Everywhere I looked, there was sadness, people...babies...with hands outstretched. My friend Christy and I decided to wash the feet of some of the street kids one night, right after we arrived, on the streets of Delhi. We bought a bucket and some soap, probably for a few cents, and squatted next to the gutter to wash some of the dirtiest tiny feet that we had ever seen. We eventually had to leave because some men were bothering us, but feet washing became one way we had of breaking our sadness wide-open and doing something that caused people to wonder. Jesus washed his disciple's feet before he died. He must have been overwhelmed by everything he saw; sick people, angry people; and so he made a statement by making dirty feet clean. In India, where bare feet are cracked and dirty, it meant something like what it would have meant to the disciples. It's not much, but it's care, it's touch, it's tenderness. Sometimes tenderness is the last thing people receive, but something they need desperately.

We did it again at a Rainbow gathering at the Kumbh Mela, the largest Hindu gathering ever held, and the largest religious gathering ever held on earth. It was chaos; dust and noise. We were overwhelmed again, by the futility of 80 million people trying to leave an endless wheel of punishment by washing in a certain river on a certain day. We found out later that one hundred thousand old widows were abandoned by their families there by the river. Slowing their families down, they were just... left. We felt oppressed and tired and we used water on dusty feet again to fight back with a small spark.

I remember that it was something that my friend Christy always did while we traveled. She would talk about overcoming evil with good while she sat cross-legged on her bed in our guesthouse room, making small beautiful things for people that she met. She took verses from the Bible and wrote them on pretty paper with butterflies or flowers, the size to fit in someone's palm. And so we wove our way across India, fighting to break open the sense of defeat that often followed us, Christy's butterflies sown in every town we visited. "Overcome evil with good."

It is something I think of now. Not that things around me are truly evil, but sometimes life can be dull, or wearying, or discouraging. Sometimes I can remember to fight back by sowing something beautiful into hard times. That's what this blog can be about for me. Writing a story to keep from feeling victimized by life. You can look at life in so many ways. It can be "Poor me" or "Rich me." The worst thing in the world is feeling like a victim. What could be worse than feeling like you have no control over your life? I heard recently that only in remembering that our lives are being written into a larger story can we take the mundane things that keep coming, minute by minute.

I want to be the kind of person who invites a lonely person over when I'm feeling lonely rather than waiting for someone to call. Or to be like Christy, sitting cross-legged on a hard bed in one of the most intense places on earth, making beautiful gifts for lonely people.

February 28, 2006

I have a hard time knowing how to answer sometimes, when people ask me how I feel about the surgery that I'm having tomorrow. I don't always know how I feel, it seems all mixed up with what I want to feel and what I should feel and what I feel when I'm well-rested with a full belly compared to 3:00 AM with a rumbling tummy and a crying baby. But my dreams show me things.

I've dreamed of doctors and nurses yelling at me. In one dream they were prepping me for the IV and I told them to wait because I was still pumping milk and then I knocked the bottle over and it was glass and it shattered. The nurse turned to me and said, "It would serve you right if you just died."

I dreamed that I was in a motorcycle accident and I came in crying and tried to tell Chinua. He and Derek were talking and they turned to me and Chinua said, "Why are you always so dramatic?" Derek said "Stop looking for attention."

I dreamed I was driving down a steep hill and even with all my weight on the brake I couldn't slow down.

I dreamed that I lost Kenya in a crowd and I spent the whole night frantically looking for her.

I dreamed that I screamed at Kai. I dreamed that I got mad at my parents and yelled at them for no reason.

I dreamed that we were in our old house at the flat in San Francisco and I went upstairs and our landlord was moving us out without telling us. All our stuff was in boxes and we had nowhere to go.

I dreamed that I fell out of a window with the Leaf Baby and the glass went everywhere and someone caught me by the ankle just as I caught Leaf by the ankle. We stopped right before we hit the pavement.

I guess I am a little scared inside.

march

March 4, 2006

There's bad news and good news.

The bad news is that I look a little like Frankenstein. My friend Amy brought up the fact that in the movie *Young Frankenstein* the woman who is in love with Frankenstein calls him Zipperneck. This is what I prefer to be called, from now on.

The good news is that I am not dead. You don't even really want to think about dying, actually, going into surgery—it seems morbid and negative, but I cried when I kissed Kenya goodbye because my biggest fear was the idea of my kids not having a mama. Of course the surgery was actually very safe, and Pete the surgeon told me that chances were higher that I'd die on the *way* to the operation than *in* the operation, but still. You don't want to think those things, but you *do*, when your life is in someone's hands. You know, the way it is when someone is carving at your neck with a sharp knife while you're knocked out and helpless under bright lights.

I was really woozy about the IV and it didn't help that the nurse had to try three times before she got it in. My Superstar Husband was trying to distract me by talking about the beads in my hair. "That's a really pretty one, Rae. I've never seen it before. Where'd you get it? Did Jared give it to you? He's really into giving people gifts." I was following slightly but most of me was over with the nurse, totally grossed out by the fact that she was sticking sharp objects into my veins. The anesthesiologist showed up with a five o'clock shadow at 7:00 in the morning and he was one of those guys who has a thick patch of chest hair peeking out over his scrubs. He told me all about the terrible things he was going to do, like give me a breathing tube, after I was asleep. Why *tell* me? It's not like I'm going to *know*. But they treated me like a star, wheeling me down to the operating room while different nurses that I know in the hospital from labor and delivery or my pre-op appointments waved at me and wished me luck. And then I slowly lost consciousness.

Regaining consciousness in the operating room was one of the strangest experiences that I've had. I was lying there totally out of it, while people all around me talked about me.

"Oh *here* she is! She's really *sleepy*! How about some *morphine*, do you want some *morphine*? I'm going to put some special stockings on you, to keep you from getting a blood clot. Oh! Are you very *tall*? These stockings are so short on her, Betty, do you think that's okay? She must be very *tall*."

"She is, she's 5'11." (Presumably reading my chart.)

"Yes, she's *tall*. More morphine? How are you *feeling*?"

Meanwhile I was fading in and out, and I assume I was making some sort of response to all the questions, but it seemed to come from a place that was very far away.

The day was a haze of sleepiness and throwing up. I faded in and out while nursing, while talking, and in between bouts of narcolepsy managed to throw up everything I ate, including pain medication. It wasn't the most fun I've ever had. I'd even say that I never want to do it again. But I did watch a Project Runway marathon, which was a bonus. Leaf was amazing the whole time. He drank my milk from a bottle obediently while I was in surgery. He lay and kicked his legs in the bassinet that the nurses borrowed from Labor and Delivery, looking like a gigantic six-week-old newborn with a terrifyingly large head. (He's already so much bigger than when he was born!) I threw up in a little yellow tub. Although one time I was nursing Leaf and I told a nurse that I felt really nauseous. She quickly walked out of the room to look for anti-nausea medication for me. It was a little late for anti-nausea medication. I vainly tried to call her back and then was forced to lean over the side of the bed and let it out all over the floor. It was that or on the baby.

Then came nighttime and the Android nurse who lacked emotion entirely. She had no sympathy. She treated me like a drug addict every time I asked her for pain medication.

"What level is your pain?"

"Um, a seven."

"Is it *really* a seven? Are you *crying?*"

"Okay, it's a *six*. Please can I have something before I freak out?"

She gave Chinua a booby-trapped reclining chair to sleep in. It was made in 1951 and snapped shut violently every time he shifted, giving him whiplash and waking the baby up. He ended up sleeping on the floor with his legs in the bathroom and his head by the foot of my bed, since our room was the size of a postage stamp. He snored terribly and I couldn't wake him up. The nurses must have heard something like this:

SNORE.

"CHINUA!"

SNORE!

"CHINUA!!!"

SNORE!!!

"CHIN-UUU-AAA!!!"

Finally I inched my pathetic wounded self down to the end of the bed and started smacking him with a pillow to try to get him to stop. Then my IV bag ran out and the machine started beeping. After about a million beeps Android nurse came in and asked, "Is something *beeping* in here?" She sounded upset and I couldn't help wondering whether she thought I had brought something from home that made terrible beeping noises, just to annoy her. Both Chinua and I had close to the worst nights of our lives. Finally at about 4:30 I was able to hold some pain meds down and I actually slept. After that everything got better.

We left the next day, but not before I nearly passed out while Pete the Surgeon took my stitches out and made some remarks about how I shouldn't play tackle football and take a helmet to the neck. (Thanks for the word picture, Pete.) I'm feeling pretty good. I'm sore and I have to move my whole body instead of swiveling my neck, but thanks to the miracle of pain meds, it's not too bad. We're still waiting to hear back about whether or not it's cancer, but they're mostly sure that it's not. All I can say is it better not be, because they are going to have to drag me kicking and screaming if I have to go back. I can't believe the love and support I have around me right now, though. This winter has been a bit rough, and this is the culmination, but people are so loving. God is so loving.

March 4, 2006

We have decided to stop combing Kenya's hair. The reasons are

81

numerous, but most of all because she will have the prettiest head of dreadlocks that any of us have ever seen. A close runner up reason is because I have spent more time now doing Kenya's hair than I have spent on my own hair in my whole entire life. I just have to ask myself: Is this *quality* time? The fact that she is often screaming and crying and throwing herself on the ground and if she could cuss she would, suggests not. I know that my blended race daughter is only experiencing what young black girls all around the world experience: super kinky hard to deal with hair, but fortunately in this family we love dreadlocks. I have them, Chinua has them, and now Kenya will have them.

Her hair is perfect for dreadies. I will probably miss the little braids and twists and all that, but adding a newborn to the mix has shifted me over to the locked up side. Elena pointed out that I will be saving a ton of time by letting her hair dread up. It's true that I spend probably half an hour on it every day. Time that I will now spend picking up toys. Those feet stabbing dinosaurs are a big pet peeve.

The other big piece of news around here (other than the fact that I really don't like this hole in my neck and can't wait for it to heal) is that yesterday my Superstar Husband bought his airplane ticket for Turkey! A member of this family is going on a journey. A long and far away journey. He'll be gone for three weeks in April and he almost reconsidered when it hit him that the kids will *change* while he's gone. Especially the little Leaf baby.

We'll miss him, but I'm so glad that it's settled that he's going. He *needs* it, you know? He's headed for a peace gathering, and it's going to be a raging adventure.

March 6, 2006

Today I slipped into feeling a little sorry for myself. A little like *I'm going to die because this wound in my neck hurts and it itches like crocodile pants and my daughter just punched me right smack in the middle of it.* Everywhere I went (because I stupidly went into public places today) I was sure that people were staring at me and thinking that I was a psycho drug addict. Did you see *28 days* and the guy who gave himself a tracheotomy? I thought that they were assuming that I was like that guy. I became very suspicious. I thought everyone felt sorry for me. I wore this scarf around my neck so that people wouldn't have to look at my unpleasant two inch gash, but it bothered me, so I kept taking it off, and then putting it back on because I felt people looking and plotting about how to get me back into the mental ward.

Why didn't you just stay home? you may be wondering. And that would be a good question. I guess I never know when enough is enough. I thought that all I had to worry about was my energy level, which actually hasn't been all that bad. I didn't realize that after surgery I would feel so vulnerable, that I would feel like hiding. I feel opened up and exposed. The cool thing is, I've realized once again that the community I live with feels like a family. Because I'm not afraid to be around them. It's funny, we went out together today to a church we don't usually go to and after had a very California style Mexican potluck. We hung out and small-talked with the people around us. But we also huddled together a bit, kind of like penguins. I think we just like each other's company. That's what being a family is like.

It's not that we're all that much alike. I think it's just the fact that when you work and toil away and live with people you begin to wear different grooves into each other until you're a bit like a big puzzle.

There are so many friends that I have like this, all around the world, people I've lived with and worked with. We've worn grooves into each other. We fit together in ways that feel empty when we're apart. It's sad. I miss those other friends, the ones I'm far away from now.

But it's good to know that there are a lot of people out there that I wouldn't mind feeling ugly around. More than a few people have actually seen me break down and freak out. Some people are here with me, when I'm so close to breaking down right now, when the stress of having a new baby and waiting for important test results are getting to me. When I can't move my head properly and everything hurts and it's driving me crazy.

I remember about seven years ago I heard someone say that life is made up of sitting and standing. Maybe most of the time you are standing, but sometimes you just have to sit down for a while. And having close friends and a strong community is about the seamlessness that happens when other people can stand up for you while you're sitting. Everyone has their times when they are unable to stand. It's so beautiful to have friends who will be standing around you, especially when you are just sitting there in the dirt, watching ants and eating grass, waiting for your knees to stop shaking.

March 12, 2006

Not cancer. NOT CANCER.

Pete the surgeon walked into the room the other day and found five of us waiting. The littlest could barely hold up his head. "I've got good news," he said. It's a good thing to hear first, unless of course he meant, "I've got good news- we're going to be seeing a lot of each other." Or, "I've got good news- more money for me."

84

But he said, "I've got good news, it's a benign follicular adenoma." And we all, except the youngest three, breathed a sigh of relief. No more surgery, no radioactive iodine, no Synthroid, no six weeks of hell.

Thyroid cancer is supposed to be one of the easiest to treat. But you still have to drink (!) radioactive iodine, which makes you radioactive. For 24 hours you have to sit in your hospital room and only the radiation specialists can come near you in their special suits and so you have 24 hours of solitude, except you can't bring your laptop because it will become radioactive and you'll have to throw it away. So that sounds pretty much like misery to me. Then for ten days you can't be with your kids. Including your newborn.

I'm very, VERY glad that I don't have to go through all of that. I'm full of thanks and praise that I will be able to keep nursing Leaf, and that I won't be crying every day that I can't see my kids. I'm so glad that now I can let all of the worry go and just recuperate, wait for my neck to heal, feel better and better as my baby gets older and hopefully starts sleeping a little bit longer at night.

Here's a confession, though: I'm just the teensiest bit disappointed that I won't be able to write about being radioactive.

That is so sick. What is *wrong* with me?

In other news, we've been having freak snowstorms for the last couple of days. I honestly didn't know that it even *could* snow here. The weather has changed its mind every few minutes. One second it's raining, then hailing, then these big soft snowflakes are drifting down, and suddenly it's hard rain again.

Good weather for community rounds of Killer Bunnies: the card game that makes us all mad at each other.

*

Leaf has crossed the threshold into Adorable Baby country. He smiles and laughs and lies on his back cooing. More than either of the other kids when they were his age, he seems to really want to talk to me. His little face is so intent, as though if he just thought hard enough, he could make some real words come out. He loves the strangest things: A dark sock hanging off the edge of the white metal posts on the bunk-bed gets half an hour of cooing and smiling out of him. We call the lamps his "friends" because he loves to talk to them and listen as they talk back to him. "Who are you talking to, Leaf?" we say. "Are you talking to your friends again?"

Life is good. My neck is healing and I can move it again, I don't have cancer and my family is amazing. Our house will be done by the end of the month and we'll have more space. The fact that it's snowing can't change the fact that it's the middle of March and Spring has to come sooner or later. So... why do I feel so depressed?

March 25, 2006

Now that Kid A has flown full swing into make-believe, life is always interesting. And frustrating sometimes, too. We may be eating dinner in a perfectly normal fashion (which for us these days is with up to ten other people on couches in the Big House) and suddenly it takes a turn.

"Kai, please eat your spaghetti."

"Dinosaurs don't EAT spaghetti."

"Okay... what do dinosaurs eat?"

"Leaves."

"Well, if you can pretend you are a dinosaur, you can pretend that your spaghetti is leaves."

Lots of things are like this. If I tell my three-year-old that he can't stand on the arm of the couch, he'll explain that there are ALLIGATORS in the water and if he gets off, they'll eat him. Obviously, I don't just let him get away with all his reasoning. He WILL eat his spaghetti, and he WILL stop standing on the arm of the couch. But it's not just arguing to him. He really gets so caught up in his imagination that he finds it hard to break out. Almost all day I'm saying "Earth to Kai, FOCUS, put your jacket on, put your shoes on, let's put the toys away... Hello?"

Hmmmm. This reminds me of someone. I can't for the life of me think who... OH!

"So then I was thinking that we should find that number and make sure we call her back... Hey! Are you listening to me, Honey?"

"Hmmm?"

"Chinua, did you hear what I said?"

"Sorry, I was gone for a minute there."

"Where did you go?"

"Fighting aliens."

It's like Madeleine L'Engle says. We are made up of all our ages. I'm a nine-year-old, a sixteen-year-old, a twenty-five year old. Good to remember when I feel like pitching a fit in the middle of the night when Leaf won't go back to sleep for two hours.

april

April 4, 2006

1. My Superstar Husband flew to Turkey today.

2. I'm crazy for saying, no, I don't mind if you go. I think I was still experiencing the euphoria of prescription pain medication when I said that.

3. I like to torture myself by making decisions and then changing my mind when it is too late

4. I aired all my apocalyptic fears while the poor man was trying to pack yesterday.

5. I don't deserve him.

6. It's mostly hard because Kai's whining is making my hair fall out and Chinua is the good and patient one in the family.

7. But today went okay. Kai whined a lot but banging my head sharply against the glass door a few times made me feel better. I accidentally dropped a mason jar into the toilet, where it broke. I spent a few thousand minutes cleaning shattered glass out of toilet water. I played the no-nap game with the baby. I took care of some property tax issues. I fed my daughter sliced meat for a snack to keep her happy while I was on the phone with the property tax people.

8. The kids kissed me lots because I told them not to (what am I teaching them by extorting kisses through reverse psychology?) My mom folded laundry for me. Both my parents worked on painting my new home until late tonight.

9. We won't have to walk in the dark with the kids ever again until next winter. Thank you reverse daylight savings time.

10. I'm really very glad that Chinua flew to Turkey today. It's just sad to be without him.

11. I'm joking about banging my head on the glass door.

April 5, 2006

It's no use arguing over whether the little lizards that the boys are finding all over the Land are newts or salamanders, because it turns out that they are pretty much the same thing.

Except when they're dead, in which case I freak out. Elena came to collect Jed today and when the boys showed her their lizards she said, "This one looks dead to me," and then I had to suddenly turn and run quickly up the hill, shrieking. Not too many things make

89

me scream and run away. Dead things. And people waiting in the dark to scare me. That always makes me scream. I remember one time in Berkeley my friend Eddie ran up to me and growled, "Gimme all your money," and I screamed so loud I must have given everyone within a ten block radius simultaneous heart attacks.

Today it was two dead lizards in one day. Two is too many. One was huge and we think a cat got him, and just thinking about him makes me want to get up and run out of my cabin.

Speaking of dead things. Why are all the hens dead? We have one hen left, and one rooster. Skunks have killed the rest, despite a valiant effort to keep them safe. Not valiant enough, apparently. Those dastardly skunks. Killing what they don't even stick around to eat. It's heartbreaking, especially since the hens were just about to start laying again.

Today was Day Two of Chinua's absence. Today there was no glass in the toilet and a minimum of whining. The Leaf baby took amazing naps all day. Our hot water heater was fixed (I think I neglected to mention that it's been broken for awhile) and I made soup and biscuits for the community for dinner. I always love cooking for everyone because it feels like such an accomplishment and I so rarely get to do it.

I woke up with excitement, thinking about Chinua arriving in Turkey, feeling almost like I'm arriving in a new country.

April 6, 2006

Today Kenya did what I had hoped that no child of mine would do. She stuck a bead up her nose, a big round bead. And I didn't even notice for probably an hour or so. We were sitting and watching Little House on the Prairie, while I worked on her dreadlocks, and she turned to me and very mildly said, "Uh oh," pointing to her nose. So mildly that I thought that she was maybe slightly distressed over being a little snotty. It took me a minute to notice the big purple bead wedged in her nasal cavity.

So I did what every parent would do, after freaking out for a moment over the possibility of a trip to the emergency room, I worked it out of her little nostril with patience and much snot-touching. It was one of those moments when I saw myself from the outside and thought, "Who *are* you? And what have you done with Rae?" Similar to the moments I spent cleaning glass out of the toilet or poo out of the bath or even, the other day, standing in a parking lot wolfing ravioli out of a can in the rain. That deserves more explanation. I was starving like a nursing mother can be, and all I could find was a drugstore. My Superstar Husband could tell you that I don't make the best judgement calls when I'm hungry, and I didn't want to smell my friend's car up with canned ravioli smell, so there I was, in the rain eating nasty cold ravioli with shaky hands. Who *is* that person?

It was probably the hardest thing about becoming a mother—losing some pieces of identity that were important to me. And it was possibly the most important thing about becoming a mother—learning not to be defined by what I do. I used to be known as an artist, a painter, and after I had Kai I really struggled with the fact that a lot of people I was working with had no idea that I painted at all.

I don't really struggle so much with that stuff now, it seems that the edges have been slowly worn off me. I'm like a piece of beach glass, now. Motherhood has softened me, and I don't even really care about my identity anymore, or how people see me as much. Not to say that I don't care about *art*, I still care as much as I ever did.

But I love the absurdity of taking care of small children, of having no more than moments for yourself in a day, of doing totally disgusting things because being a parent means plucking a bead out of your daughters runny nose or straining poo out of a bathtub.

April 8, 2006

Today Kai leaned over the side of the couch and whispered conspiratorially to the Leaf Baby, "Your daddy's dead."

"Kai!" I exclaimed, horrified. "Don't say that! His daddy, I mean, your daddy, isn't *dead!*"

"Oh," Kai replied. "He's in Turkey?"

This confusion between whether Daddy is dead or in Turkey isn't a wild question out of the blue. It all originated in the (gasp) *Little House on the Prairie, Collection Edition, First Season* on DVD. Elena loaned it to me, and I thought—Wow, it would be cool to watch some together before bed every day, while Chinua's gone. We don't have TV here, and I figured that *Little House on the Prairie* is about as innocent as you can get. That is, until the little boy's pa exploded in a rock quarry.

"Wow, uh—whoops, what happened?" I flustered, and then tried to fast forward past the part where Laura's Pa has to tell the man's wife and son that he was dead. Tried, but managed to un-pause it just at the point where the little boy says, "Now that my Pa's dead, I've got a lotta work to do. A *lotta* work."

I watched as Kai's eyes got bigger and bigger, and then, after it was over, as they started to glisten. "What are you thinking about, Kai?" I asked. "I'm thinking about how that little boy's daddy *died,*" he said, in the saddest little-boy voice ever, and the glisten turned into a couple of big tears that still managed not to spill over.

We talked about it a little. Kai was confused about why the boy's dad died. "Was it because he was *yelling?*" he wanted to know. I told him no, it was just an accident. Then later, as we were getting into bed, and we were talking about Chinua, and crossing off another day on the calendar to show that it's getting closer to when he will be home, Kai said, "Is *my* daddy going to die?" Again, in the saddest little-boy voice you've ever heard.

"No," I replied, end of story, because you can't even leave room in his mind for something like that. Not now. And we talked about how exciting it will be when we go to pick Chinua up at the airport. The next morning he woke up talking about how "issited" he was to get Daddy from the airport, and I thought, phew. But today, the confusion persists. Is Daddy dead? Or in Turkey?

As if it wasn't enough that he wonders daily about whether a big rock is going to fall from space to kill him, like it killed the dinosaurs.

I don't think that he really thinks his daddy is dead, but it was possibly the first time that it has occurred to him that a parent could die. Curse you, *Little House on the Prairie*. It's not that I want Kai to be in the dark forever about loss and sad things that happen in the world. But it seems like slightly bad timing, during Chinua's longest absence from the kids.

Kai's funny, the way he takes things in. He's a lot like me. We both personalize everything. If something bad could happen to someone on TV, then something bad could happen to me. It's the reason that I can't even think of the plot of *Flight Plan*. Waking up on a plane to find your daughter has disappeared? ACK. No, can't think about it, la la la, I'm not listening. I've la la la-ed my way through a lot of movies in my life, walked out of even more.

We'll just have to take the next two weeks day by day, crossing off calendar square by calendar square, sorting out the confusion between "dead" and "in Turkey."

April 14, 2006

I will not feel sorry for myself.
I will not feel sorry for myself.
I will not feel sorry for myself.
I will not feel sorry for myself.
I will not...

...Oh dang.

April 19, 2006

My parents left yesterday. I feel a little lost. I was so amazingly blessed to have them here, for three and a half months. I was spoiled by their help and love. Now, with Chinua gone, and them suddenly gone too, I feel like that halo of family care has been lifted, and I am alone.

Except that I'm totally not.

I have the most amazing family around me: my friends here at the Land, and no girl with her husband gone for three weeks ever had it better. At the very least, I have people to talk to, and often I have hands around me to help.

But there is something about the love of parents, or should I say grandparents? My parents love their grandkids with the fervent intensity of devotees in an ashram in India, making their Darshan gleefully. No one else feels this way about my kids. Except, perhaps, me. Maybe.

What grandparents have that I don't have is distance. They have distance from the time in their lives when they were raising their own kids. They have distance from a lot of the parental fears of messing up. They have a lot of freedom. They also have the assurance that they can always hand the kids back to the parents.

I've loved seeing the relationship that has grown between my parents and my kids. Having my mom and dad staying here at the Land has taught me a lot. A few things are:

1. That I am sinfully independent. I would rather pull myself up a sheer cliff with my teeth than let someone help me. This past winter, after giving birth to my third child and having surgery, I've been forced to accept help from people who possibly love me more than anyone in the world. Pure torture.

2. That I am terribly controlling. Kai told his grandma the other day that she "does a lot of things wrong" because she put the juice in the cup *before* the water (yes, I dilute our juice) instead of the other way around. I'm not as bad as *that*. I just don't like it when someone does dishes for me and the dishes are in the dish rack the wrong way. You know, *important* stuff.

3. That grandparents are just as much family as parents are. This should be obvious. It's just amazing to me, how much the kids thrive on the love of their Grandpa and Grandma.

4. That my parents are two of the most giving, loving, flexible, incredible people I've ever known.

April 21, 2006

I'm in LA right now, meeting lots of new people and hanging out with my friend Sheri. She's a great host. Some highlights:

95

1. Well, this actually happened before I even left, but as I was driving down to San Francisco from the Land yesterday I was having a great time. Spring has finally come, it was actually sunny and warm, the scotch broom is blooming, and I even caught sight of some lupine. I felt liberated, as I began to drive through the vineyards north of Hopland, like I hadn't even known I was caught in the prison of winter until I happened to step outside.

I may have been driving a WEE bit over the speed limit. I was coming to the crest of a hill when a friendly soul gave me the ol' "flash of the lights~psst~ there's a cop on the other side of this hill." I slowed down and sure enough, just on the other side, there he was. Whew. A narrow miss, but for a little while I imagined how our conversation would have gone.

"Ma'am, do you realize that the speed limit is 55 here?"

"Yes, but, Officer, it's so HARD to drive only 55. The road is so straight. And the Scotch Broom is blooming."

"Ma'am, this is a stretch of road with several vineyards and wineries along it. If you hit one of Sonoma County's best winemakers and knock him off, Napa will be all over us in an instant. We can't jeopardize our grape-growers."

"Are we in Sonoma? Or Mendocino?"

"Uh~I'm not sure, but I do know the speed limit. I'm issuing you a citation."

(I fall out of the car door) "Noooo. Please."

"Ma'am. Please take your hands off of my ankle. Ma'am."

2. This also happened before I got here. I was in the airport, waiting for my plane to board.

Actually—back up—getting through security wasn't so easy. I was carrying Leaf in my wrap-around carrier, and the officer told me I'd have to take him out of the carrier. And then she said I had to take the carrier off. But I can't do that with one hand. And then she said she couldn't hold him for me. What was I supposed to do? Lay my three month old on the floor? Put him in one of the trays? I ended up enlisting the help of the people around me, asking a complete stranger to hold my baby so I could untie my carrier.

Then my phone rang. A strange number. I answered, and the most beautiful melodious voice in the whole world said, "Rae?"

"Chinua?" I said. My heart leapt into my throat and I almost started crying, right there. Actually, maybe I did cry, a little. It's amazing what a short absence does. Like the way I check my email these days, the way I did after we first met and we corresponded for a year. Both of us were crazy about each other, but neither of us were admitting anything. We wrote nice and deep and sweet emails for a year, and checked our boxes thinking "Did he? Is there a letter.... no." Or, "YES!" It was so good to hear from my Superstar Husband. He'll be home on Monday. It's almost over.

3. It's weird. After living in San Francisco, LA seems kind of thrown together. The buildings don't seem to go together, and the signs are rag tag. It seems kinda... shabby, in a cool sort of way, but I think I prefer the well-ordered buildings and amazing hills of San Francisco. Although it may be hard to judge, after only being here for a day. I definitely feel more at home in Northern California though. In So-Cal I always feel a little bit like I landed from a different planet.

4. Yesterday I went to a recording studio on Sunset Blvd where an old friend, David, was recording his new album. I was there to hear the music so that I can get an idea of what I'll be working with

next month, when I paint for the live recording. I'll be doing art as worship, something that I love, something that I feel born to do. It was a little loud for the Leaf baby right in the studio, so I was hanging out in the lobby and ended up getting a tour of the kitchen and hanging out with the cook, Curtis, for a while. He chatted with the baby and told me about all the places he's been and lived: Chicago, Alabama, Louisiana, Georgia... and on the list went. Another of the workers bragged about all of the bands that come and record there. "Next week it's Sheryl Crow, today Van Morrison's here, sometimes Maroon Five, Weezer..." He went on, too. I didn't ever see Van Morrison. Just his gear. The studio was funny. They're obviously pulling in a lot of money, so why do the carpets look that way? It was very LA shabby cool, I suppose.

5. Who needs to be a star when you have a baby? Everywhere I go, people point and smile, stop and talk. It's great. I forgot about this part of having a baby. It's like it opens people up. They trust you. They feel warm. And Leaf smiles back and talks to them, rewarding them for all that openness.

April 25, 2006

Chinua is home and we met him at the airport with fanfare and squealing. I stood clapping my hands and smiling like a complete moron while I waited for the rest of my family to come over to the legal side of the line. I was trying to keep the kids from running under the barrier at the international arrivals lobby. You know, the barrier that looks like it's made of seat belt material or something. They were pretty good about it, although Kai could not understand why on earth we couldn't just go looking for Daddy. Once he showed up, though, they darted through like naughty puppies and it was fine. No one's going to get angry with a couple of love-struck preschoolers greeting their daddy. I stayed on the proper side, though, bizarrely clapping, just clapping and clapping. I couldn't stop until I could hug my Superstar Husband.

He looks good. He looks like he was out in the sun, a whole lot. Which he was, in the mountains of Turkey. We've been watching some of his video footage, and it looks amazing.

Kai can't stop talking to him. He wants to tell Chinua every single thing that has happened since he left. Speaking of Kai, I'm glad to see that by marrying one another, Chinua and I haven't diluted the absentmindedness gene a single bit. Today Kai wore two pairs of undies, since he forgot to take one pair off before putting the other pair on. I was so busy getting us ready to drive the four hours to the airport that I didn't notice.

April 28, 2006

Sometimes I struggle with anxiety that is so strong I feel paralyzed by it. When I'm like this I can't even have a normal conversation with my husband without being nervous and scared. When I'm like this I'm so tense that my neck and shoulders feel like iron. If you knocked on them, they would ring like bells. When I'm like this, I try so hard to just get my mind to stop, stop, STOP already. When I'm like this, I start to panic.

Anxiety often seems to overwhelm me when I feel like I've been doing really well for a long time. I feel like I've become free of it, like I can participate, now, rather than just watching other people make normal decisions without feeling like the end result will be everything in life crumbling around them. And right when I'm participating with all that's in me, when I feel like I may even get a ribbon, it hits me. And I'm startled and confused.

It always makes me feel as though I've lost all the ground I gained.

I think I was holding a lot in, over the weeks that Chinua was gone. I felt strong because I needed to be strong. I felt victorious. And then he came back and I turned into the little girl, the small one. All the weakness that I'd been keeping under wraps came stumbling forward and I found myself no longer able to think clearly. I was apologizing for every word, every thought. Everything made me afraid. I had a really bad day yesterday, which ended with me driving home at 10:00 at night, my van full of Land groceries, crying uncontrollably on the phone to my husband while he tried to calm me down. The lady at Winco had yelled at me, had told me that my check raised "red flags," had made me feel stupid in front of all the other customers. It was just too much, after a day of trying not to listen to the "Destined to Fail" speeches in my mind all day. I fumbled my groceries into their brown bags, and wheeled myself and my baby out the door, crying.

On days like this I turn into everyone's teenaged step-daughter, angry and defiant at all of my step-parents. The lady at Winco is no longer just a grumpy late shifter, she now gives me identity, gives me definition, and she has decided that my checks are no good. Not only that, she has implied that I'm a liar. She must know. She must be right.

Everything is confirmation of what I've always feared. That I'm not going to be able to participate. That I'm not a good girl. These ideas I can usually fight off. But sometimes, when anxiety grips me, it's like my white blood cell count has fallen drastically. And the viruses win.

This is when I am utterly flattened. Sitting shapelessly and wondering if I'll ever stand back up. They asked, speaking about Jesus, "Can anything good come out of Nazareth?" But this is what they forgot, that God likes people from little tiny shabby places, that he makes broken things new. At times when my mind is so cluttered that I can barely see through the weeds, this is about all I have to stand on. And it is enough.

April 29, 2006

Imagine living in the most beautiful campground that you ever went to in your childhood. It's your home. Now imagine being there year-round, walking from building to building in the rain, shivering in the dark. Imagine losing your running water for hours or days at a time, imagine poorly insulated buildings (which we are working on, hooray!) and small fires in stoves that may or may not be maintained. Imagine a lot of wetness, rain day after day, and a lot of darkness, using a flashlight to get from dinner to bed. Imagine that it is still wonderful to live in this campground, even during the long wet winter, because you get to live with your friends and play games and it is beautiful even in deep dark shades of gray.

But now imagine that it's summer again and the sun is shining and everything smells green and living. Imagine warm evenings when the kids are in bed. Imagine feeling giddy and liberated, wearing short sleeves in the warm night air. Watching the green river, knowing that any day the weather will be warm enough for you to swim. Listening to music and dancing your way around the wide paths.

It's heaven. I feel like a little girl.

I love pulling out the kids' sandals, looking for shorts in second-hand stores. I love seeing more of them; their little brown feet, the little legs, their chubby knees. Today we went on a picnic and just lay around like cats in a patch of sunlight in one of the Redwood groves just up the street. We had so much fun; walking on huge fallen trees, watching a snail, trying to climb a giant boulder. Kai was so cute and little/big boy as he confidently tried to scale it and then ran back to me, shrugging, "Nah, I don't want to," as he climbed into my lap.

Kenya's been sick and it's so sad. She's not her usually spunky self. She's been clinging pretty close to me and when we're in the cabin she follows me around whining, "Mama" over and over again. She's getting better now and we're all glad.

I love Kai's curiosity, the way he makes things up. I asked him about a bruise he has on his leg and he told me he got it running up a tree.

I love that Kenya has named one of her feet "Mama" and one of them "Daddy" and that she makes them kiss and talk to each other in squeaky voices.

I love that Leaf is turning into an adorable chunky baby who drools incessantly and is what you would call jolly. He's got this big wide smile and is very "boy." (All of him, even his gigantic feet.)

Yes, I'm feeling a lot better. We're getting ready for the festivals this summer (where we'll sell art and photography) and I've begun my painting marathon. Last night Chinua finished putting the kids to bed and I listened to music and painted and painted... and painted!

may

May 4, 2006

I have a little room at the Land that I've been using to paint in.

I like to call it my "Studio", even though it's a very temporary place for me to use to make art in. Calling it my studio helps me paint better. It's not a glamorous spot, but I have a new love for life since I've been painting again, so to me it's a loft in the Presidio of San Francisco. Painting even helps me be more fun with my kids because it fills me up. I think that art is what I was born to do. One of the biggest treats that I can give myself is to go to the art store and buy a new tube of paint. An Ultramarine Blue, or a Cadmium Yellow. If I'm really feeling crazy, maybe a Permanent Violet.

Not gray, never gray. In my opinion, gray is the biggest waste of money in the paint world.

Summer came to us swiftly. It doesn't even feel like spring, with 80 degree weather everyday. Today Jed and Kai were playing in the kiddie pool on Jed's porch. One minute we were freezing in the rain, the next minute all our heaters are off and we'll be saving tons on our gas and electric bills. Sweet.

I've been hanging out with Job, our tree climbing rooster. Well, I guess he doesn't climb, he flies. Job is a survivor. He has survived two major massacres, when both sets of his wives were killed. In the first massacre, he was the only man left standing. That's when he received the name "Job". Then he got some new wives and they have been slowly picked off this spring, by vicious and nasty skunks who can apparently chew through chicken wire. Job has one wife left, and they've got the spring love bug, which can be a little embarrassing. Keep it in the coop, guys.

May 17, 2006

Rooster Wisdom:

It is not wise to feed the local friendly rooster out of your hand on your porch, since this may cause him to come calling at 5:30 in the morning, looking for more whole grain bread. And he may call and call, looking through the glass door, possibly waking your baby up, causing you to curse him and your husband to stumble out of bed and throw stones in his general direction.

It may be wiser to feed the local friendly rooster on someone else's porch. Someone who needs to wake up earlier. Someone, maybe, like my friend Renee.

june

June 2, 2006

Tonight I've been thinking about how I probably won't remember too much about the hard stuff of having small children, once they've grown older. The poo, everywhere, in diapers, out of diapers, poo on the floor, on the wall, in the crib, on me. Or the amazing number of times that Kenya has vomited after over-eating. Or the fact that I never ever seem to sleep very much anymore and I always feel exhausted.

I'll probably remember their brown feet in sandals, the way their skin smells after they've spent the day in the sun. The sweet strawberry smell of a nursing baby's breath. Little hands on my cheeks, the elusive and overwhelming kisses. The compulsive smiling of four-month-olds, the funny waddle of a year-old baby. Kenya mispronouncing everything, Kai pronouncing everything perfectly except for poached eggs, which he still calls "proached".

You know, the good stuff.

June 8, 2006

Although I try to be as honest as possible on this blog, I obviously refrain from writing about some things. Some things aren't meant to be read by all. Some things are too deep to be written about, some things are too despairing, some are too complicated, some are too personal.

And all the things that have been rolling around in my head lately are those kinds of things. This, combined with my extreme busyness (which has me running from the moment I wake up to the moment I go to sleep) in preparing for our Booth at the Festival this weekend, has kept me from posting as much as I like.

I could write about the daisies which are the new poppies, springing up everywhere: down the highway, on the hillsides, in the neglected garden.

I could write about my exhaustion again. (Lucky you.)

I could write about how hard it is to get prepared for something like this festival when you live so far away from all the supplies you need. How Chinua came home from the City on Monday only to drive away for the day on Tuesday, preparing, only to have *me* drive away for the day *yesterday*, picking up more stuff. Are we crazy? Yes, maybe. A little.

But I need to go, because we're heading out to set up camp in five minutes.

Life is sometimes hard, and sad, and that passes, but sometimes I can't even find anything funny in it, and that is when I know that it's been a little harder than usual.

June 14, 2006

I am trying to recover from one of the most disastrous weekends

107

that I've ever had. Chinua and I are so exhausted that we might decide to implode.

Scenario One: Thursday.

We leave for the festival feeling bright and chipper, although a little late, in a caravan of two vehicles. Derek warns me before we go that the van has a tendency to overheat. He warns Chinua. We forget to warn Renee, who is driving. The van overheats, on the side of the highway, as we are on our way with the three kids. I decide to drive down with the baby in the other car so that I can register for our camping. The others will wait for the van to cool down and then follow.

Except that our beloved old red van became a little too hot and will never drive again. Chinua sits on the side of the road for five hours with Renee and the two kids, until Derek is able to come and rescue them. I wait in the cold car, shivering and wishing I could eat a gallon of crème brulée to help myself feel better. They reach the campground, (a gravel RV lot) at 1:00 am. We proceed to pitch the tents and lay our weary heads down. Maybe tomorrow will be a better day, we think.

Rest in Peace red van. You were good to us. 18 years and 279,000 miles is a good life. You were even stolen once and then recovered. But I think that this time it really is goodbye.

Scenario Two: Friday

We are a day behind now. The guys pick up the stuff they need to construct the booth, while Derek, Spencer, and Renee and I sit around trying to amuse young children in a gravel parking lot. The kids do really well, falling down a little more than we normally advise, but mostly entertaining themselves fabulously, throwing rocks at cars and stuff. Next, it's my turn. Renee and I run about a thousand errands, picking up business cards, mats, and prints, and buying food. We return. Chinua starts to look through the photography prints that we will be selling.

A little while later, he calls me over to the van. "This isn't good news," he warns me. Basically, the printer did a terrible job. The prints look like a five year old did them on a printer made in 1985. They are unsellable. Fortunately, he didn't have them all ready, so we didn't pay for them yet. Unfortunately, we now have thirteen prints to sell, prints we had done previously at a shop recommended to us by a friend.

We are doomed. I cry myself to sleep. Lesson learned. Always test a printer, even if they have great equipment and show you great samples.

Scenario Three: Saturday

Chinua is able to bring the prints back, and in showing him the difference in quality of several prints from the same files, helps the guy to understand why we can't pay for what he's done. I feel really really badly for this man, but he does need to learn.

We work feverishly at framing the prints, and have the booth ready just a little bit late, not too bad considering our breakdown in the red van. Another friend has brought her paintings, and I have one of my own (we had originally intended to have my paintings and prints for sale, but due to a lack of time had settled on selling only Chinua's photographs) so we manage to fill the empty space with those. The booth looks really, really nice.

We sell absolutely nothing.

Nothing.

Nope, not even one.

Nothing.

All the vendors are doing terribly, although I hope none did as terribly as us. One lady said that her hat business did the worst it had in sixteen years. I think it was a combination of having too many vendors and the extremely high price of the festival.

I don't cry anymore, although it does feel a bit torturous to sit at the booth and continue to sell nothing.

Lesson learned: we won't be doing this again.

Scenario Four: Sunday

Sunday is pretty much the same as Saturday (more sitting at the booth not selling anything) except that now I know that my children have Coxsackie's virus. They have sores in their mouths, although they have no fevers, and this isn't all that bad except that it makes them absolutely miserable. Crying, tantrums, lying on the grass and weeping inconsolably. It's pretty horrible. Kenya is affected more than Kai, since she soothes herself by sucking her fingers, and this is painful. She feels miserable, and she can't comfort herself. Lots of crying ensues.

We break up camp and come home, a little poorer, a little more humble, a little shaken. Poor, poor us.

On the EXTREME upside, I am right now at this very moment sitting at a table. In my HOUSE. IN MY LARGE FRONT ROOM. The kids are sleeping. IN THEIR ROOM.

Today we moved across the Land to our new house. We feel a little nostalgic. This little three and a half year era of sharing one room with our family has come to an end. We've gone from 280 square feet to almost 900. It's crazy. Chinua said, as we were walking across the Land, "This is the only good thing that has happened to me in a long time." It's truly a very good thing.

June 16, 2006

Why is it that things all seem to happen like fruit flies popping out of their eggs? All at once, with no warning, suddenly the country that is your home is invaded and you are no longer alone with your fruit. Your fruit comes with friends.
Maybe there are too many bruises on the fruit. Bruises like forgetfulness and tiredness and a need for a long, hot bath.

I'm pondering fruit because today, on my way back from the city I locked Renee's keys out

of

her

car.

Yes, I know. Whatever you have to say to me, I know.

I have an excuse. We stopped so that I could nurse the Leaf baby, (who, by the way, can say ba ba ba now) and I left the keys in the ignition while I nursed him. Then we blissfully hopped out of the car and into the dollar store to buy stickers for Kenya for our upcoming road trip.

The mistake was in not taking the keys out before we got out of the car and locked all the doors.

A couple of hours later, after some very fun adventures that involved asking lots of people for help, we were on our way. The people from the tow company that came out (no, I don't have AAA, and yes, I think people like me should) were feeling jokey. They noticed that Renee had bought me ice cream to make me feel better, since I was obviously on the verge of turning over the tomato cart, and said, "There's an up side to everything! You got to have ice cream!" I just glared them down, and said bitterly, "Yeah. $50 ice cream."

Anyways. I told them this story, so I thought I'd write it down:

One time, in the City, the community red van got stolen. (The same one that just took its last drive on the way to the festival where we didn't sell any art.) We don't really name our vehicles. It's red van, blue van, blue car. RV. The red van had a little problem with the ignition, which means that pretty much any key could start it. I can write this on the internet now because our van is in a junkyard. Apparently this lack of key discrimination happens to a lot of old Toyota vans, and thieves in downtown San Francisco happen to know this. Because one day, it was just... gone. Bummer. We filed a police report.

A few weeks later our great friend Jesse turned to Chinua and smacked himself on the forehead.

"Chinua!" he said. "I totally forgot to tell you something!"

"What?" Chinua asked.

"You're going to be really mad," Jesse said. And he told him this story: "I was skating downtown, near the Civic Center, and all of a sudden I saw our van. I mean, I wasn't sure, but then I saw the In'N'Out sticker on it and I was sure it was ours. So I skated after it and I got the guy to stop. He looked pretty nervous, but I just said, 'that's our van,' and he said, 'oh—my friend had it.' I told him it was stolen and he said, 'I can give it back, but I just need to drive to Daly City because I'm picking up a friend and he's waiting for me.' I said, 'sure, bro,' so he gave me his phone number and I let him go."

We were pretty blown away by this, but then Jesse told us that this had happened a week before. He... forgot to tell us. Anyways, to make a long story short, the police eventually recovered the van and we got it back. Crazy, huh? Jesse's pretty nice. Nice enough to make sure that one of the guys who stole our van is able to get to his friend in Daly City and pick him up!

*

Right now what I'm really supposed to be doing is writing a reference letter for my friend Curtis who is going to get a job as an EMT. He and his wife Elena are leaving this weekend. Moving away. I can't say how sad this makes me. It's hard for me to even imagine this green place without homeboy and his lovely wife. I'm thinking that maybe if I just write a really bad letter, he won't be able to leave.

That will probably backfire.

I'm going to write the best darn letter I can.

June 18, 2006

The road, she calls us... We leave in a few minutes for our road trip to Colorado for the annual National Rainbow gathering. I've had all sorts of emotions about this, from resistance to elation to "I'm going home right now." But, I think I've set myself on going, so now I need to zip the lip on complaints and death threats. We are taking our RV, with six adults and three kids. We didn't mean to have so many people in our little RV, but somehow we forgot to do a head count.

Ahhh, there is always more to write about this way.

july

July 6, 2006

I'm out of the woods. And I have LOTS of stories to tell. But, today I walked three miles in the dust and sun with a baby on my front and a toddler on my back and a preschooler holding my hand, so I'm a wee bit tired. And I need a shower. I smell like campfire.

July 9, 2006

Here's a story:

One night as we were on our way out to Colorado, I was driving the RV and I realized that I could not drive any further. I pulled over at a rest stop to switch with Chinua. We were all joking around, and as Chinua was getting settled, he said to Derek, "Why don't you take care of this trash, Trash Boy?" I don't know why he called him Trash Boy, or why it seemed funny. Please remember that this was on day four of our road trip, after one breakdown and a whole lot of errands.

So Derek said, "Well, since we're here, I'll jump off and throw it in the trash at this rest stop."

And I said, "Since you're going to do that, I'll get myself something to drink from the vending machine. I'm parched." And out we went, through the door, *having communicated that we were leaving the vehicle.*

Except it seems that we were talking to ourselves.

A few moments later, I was standing at the soda machine, kicking it because it ate my money, (I never even got a soda out of this) when Derek walked over to me and asked, "How long do you think it will take them to realize they've left us?"

He said he dumped the trash and then stood watching in utter disbelief as the RV re-entered the freeway. In Utah. At about 11:00 at night. Of course neither of us had our cell phones on us.

It occurred to me that it could take them a really long time to realize we weren't there. They would assume that I was in the back with the kids, who were drifting off to sleep, and maybe they would think that Derek was in the bathroom or something. The only people in the RV were the kids, Chinua in the driver's seat, Chris in the passenger's seat, and Paul, who was sleeping in the compartment above the driver. Not being in the most observant of moods, Chris and Chinua might never turn around. I came up with a plan to call a friend collect and get that friend to call my cell phone.

Lavonne was pretty amused about the situation, and she did call and get through, except that when she called and asked if anyone was missing, they had already discovered their big mistake.

Kai was the hero. Chinua says that he ran straight up to where they were and said, "I want Mama!"

He said, "Well then, go in the back, where she is!"

Kai wailed, "She's not back there! You left her!"

At this point, Chris turned around and said, "Where's Derek?"

Then he started to moan, "Oh man, oh man, oh man... where's Paul?" "Paul! Paul!" they cried, until Paul spoke from the bed above the driver's seat and said, "I'm right here."

Chinua described it as horrific. We had disappeared. We simply *weren't there.* They hadn't even heard us leave the RV, so they had to assume that we were back at that rest stop. All the exits in this country section of Utah were amazingly far apart, so they had to drive a long way to turn around, drive past the rest stop exit, drive another long way to another exit to turn around again, and then come and get us.

Leaving your wife at a rest stop at night is ill-advised. I don't recommend it, but I do recommend profuse apologies and exclamations of horror over your mistake. Which is what Chinua did, and another example of why he's a Superstar Husband.

July 11, 2006

1. I really, really should be in bed right now. Oh why am I not in bed?

2. I am sorry for everyone who doesn't have the Leaf baby. He is amazing. I could hang out with him all day long. He drools and smiles and creaks out some song and I just don't want this time to pass.

3. We spent a lot of time at the Rainbow Gathering trekking up and down new trails. We hauled gear, I hauled babies, sometimes with a little one on my front and a big ol' long girl named Kenya on my back. Miles of walking, miles of lifting. We are now so ripped that we could pose as bodybuilders. Thankfully all the walking was

through amazing vistas of hills and mountains with tall aspens and pines, a stunning valley with a creek, and wildflowers everywhere. I loved getting out of my tent first thing in the morning and being outdoors immediately.

4. I did nine loads of laundry at the laundromat today. All the guys hauled stuff out of the gathering for two days—in the mud that was created by the rain that Colorado was praying for and unexpectedly received. Mud everywhere. Wetness in clothes and blankets and sleeping bags. Laundry. I've always loved coin laundry. I even wrote a poem about it once. I think that laundry is my favorite chore, although that is seriously getting tested with the amount that I'm doing these days.

5. My kids love dust more than they love Dora and Diego, more than chocolate rice milk, more than putting small round objects in their mouths. They may even love dust more than they love whining. They love to sit in it, to pile it on their clothes, to rub it into each other's hair. They would take baths in dust if they could. This was their primary occupation for the two weeks that they were at the gathering. Playing in clinging, dirty, nasty dust.

6. I dropped a pot of boiling water on my foot while getting ready to cook oatmeal over the fire. I was adding more wood to the fire, standing in the beautiful celtic trinity knot-shaped fire pit, when I accidentally knocked the whole boiling thing on my poor self. Thankfully I was able to run over to Chris very quickly and scream at him to pour cold water on me. But I was definitely burnt. While walking barefoot to try to let it heal I split my toe open on a root. These things both happened to me as punishment for mocking

Chinua about his tendency to trip as he walks without watching the ground.

July 23, 2006

Yesterday my brain melted. It was 111 degrees here and I couldn't help it. It just melted.

I shouldn't be complaining, though. Megan holds the record for the all-time best attitude shown by an almost 8-month pregnant woman in 111 ° heat. Our favorite time of day is around 4:30 in the afternoon, when the sun isn't as dangerous and we walk down to the river and then we just sit in it. We have a great piece of river here, and some parts are shallow, while some parts are deep enough to dive into off of the large rocks that line it. And we sit, Megan and I, and talk about how good we feel in the water. Marc and Chinua swim or dive or play with the kids, but Megan and I just let the water treat us like old friends.

Last night at about 3:00 AM I woke up feeling like I was going to suffocate in the still, hot air, and I had to get up and pour myself an ice cold bath. I splashed it all over myself until I became really cold and felt like I was having a heart attack. Only then did I get back out and go to sleep.

One more thing, and then I'll stop complaining. The hottest weather that I've ever been subjected to was in Varanasi, India for five days in the hot season. It was 46° C, about 126° F. Chinua and I and our friends got stuck there when the police declared a curfew on the whole city because of Hindu-Muslim violence. The power went off periodically all day long, and we spent our whole time there moving between our guest house and the one restaurant we were allowed to visit, five doors down, which for some odd reason is called the Mona Lisa. We ate Sapagiti (Spaghetti) and Rice Pudding, Boll Ramin (Menu English for a bowl of Ramen) and Banana Porridge. We lay staring at the ceiling fans with longing during the frequent power outs. We soaked our sheets in cold water at night, to try to make our beds cool. We mainly stayed out of the heat in the middle of the day, except for me when I ignored a warning and went out for a walk at noon, only to develop heatstroke and a fever. We didn't have to take care of children. We didn't have whimpering, sweaty little babies. We didn't do dishes. I didn't have office work. We hung out and tried to stay cool, talked to our fellow prisoners—a man from Hong Kong who grew up in Britain named Koon Ming, and a Japanese boy named Hiro—and waited to catch the first train out of there.

Yesterday it wasn't far from being as hot as it was there. We don't have a/c here either, although so far, thankfully, the power has not shut off.

I love being in the river with my kids. I love how Kenya hugs me and how she looks in her little orange life jacket, how their wet kisses feel, how excited they are to be there. This is the first summer that Kai has liked swimming, and yesterday we even brought the Leaf baby in, since the water was so warm. There's nothing to improve your spirits on a wickedly hot day like holding a little naked baby in a beautiful green river, with the tall trees rising up around you.

July 25, 2006

I feel like I always come back to this place. The sad place. The anxious place. The "I'll never be different" place.

It's a stupid place. A muddy hole, just big enough for me to

119

stand in by myself, unable to get a good enough grip on the edges to climb out. You probably have a hole of some sort too. Maybe your hole is deeper, or more shallow, or muddier. But we all probably agree that the holes suck.

There are some things that I know now about the hole, which is good. I know a little bit about how I got there. I know that I won't stay there. And I know that it is not my home.

How did I get there? Well, it was a little over two years ago that someone asked me why I walked around with my shoulders so high. And at the same time I'd been having stomach pain everyday, like I had swallowed a roll of quarters. Through the advice of my sister and some friends, I saw that I was having problems with anxiety. And as I started to look into it, started to try to pinpoint the things that made me anxious, I began to see that almost everything in my life gave me anxiety. And that the problem was not with my life, it was with me. (Well, my life was a little crazy at the time too, but still.) I also realized that the hormones that are delivered to my body when I am pregnant or nursing, like a shot glass full of insanity, intensify this. I have been pregnant or nursing without a break for four and a half years. But I can look back and also see that anxiety has never been a stranger. I just didn't know that it wasn't a normal way to be.

What is normal? Well. I realize that a lot of people may feel anxiety, or even struggle with it a lot like I do, but I don't think this is the way we were made to be. And there are words in the Bible that say, "Be anxious for nothing." So, you know. As in, not anxious about *everything*.

I've been working on it. It's been working on me. This blog has been part of it. Writing is cathartic to me, it gives meaning to things, it makes me laugh. I can tell when I've gone too long without writing. It feels a little like bladder pain on a long car ride.

So, lately, as I've broken all of my rules*, I've been sensing the man with the bag creeping up on me. At some point along the line he caught up with me, threw the bag over my head, and stuck me in the hole. I'm almost out, I think, which is why I can even write about it. At my worst, I can't hold a normal conversation with my Superstar Husband. If you pressed mute, you might think it was normal, but if you could hear, you would hear things like this.

S.H.: "I'm going to clean off the top of the refrigerator. It's gotten a little out of hand."

Me: "I was JUST going to get to that! What are you saying? I'm a SLOB? Don't you realize how much I have to do around here? (I give The List.) And I'm not even sleeping at nights!!! Why don't YOU try nursing the baby? Huh? Or how about that time you left me at a rest stop? I know that has nothing to do with this... but it proves that you're not perfect EITHER. What? I don't know what I'm talking about. I just want to die."

That's at my worst. When anxiety keeps me from focusing on anything and I have a vague sense of dread following me around. The depression that comes with it makes me want to crawl into bed forever. So the combo is a little neurotic. They're like bad teachers or the kind of bus drivers that yell at you, or like having street cleaners every other day. Do I park the car? Or not park the car?

At my worst, I'm really confused and trying to come up with a reason to not be anxious. At my best, I'm doing okay, and it's below the surface, I'm stepping on it's ugly little head but I can feel it back there waiting. Today I'm a little farther out of the hole, but waking up feeling overwhelmed made me need to write about it and gain a little more ground. One of my favorite Psalms has a part that goes like this:

If I should say, "My foot has slipped," Your lovingkindness, O Lord, will hold me up.
When my anxious thoughts multiply within me, Your consolation delights my soul. **

So here I am, mind racing with scaly thoughts, and God has a way to console me. And to hold me up. A consolation even for me, even for anxiety. Even for a crazy mama who has a hard time breathing sometimes. There is goodness here, there are wide open spaces.

* These are the rules.
1. Get enough sleep
2. Take your vitamins
3. Wash your face and brush your teeth
4. Eat regularly
5. Don't be too hard on yourself.

** Psalm 94: 18+19

born: *a poem*

Born

I was born to walk long roads alone
and I have done it. one in particular I remember
and dream about: the gray pavement with a long
white line stretching until it disappeared in a small point
like the line I was born to trace around
a canvas, measuring the slight barrier between
who I am and who they are.

the slight barrier, the permeable border.

I was born to cry into my paintbox
take handfuls of paint out and crush
them onto dry surfaces, breathe paint fumes deeply.
there are so many things in this world to weep about.
the children alone. so few to see and weep.
so few willing to make colors into dreams, pray murmured
words over faint photographs.

a painting becomes a name, the right to have a name.

I was born to string words onto a thin thread,
like beads. one after the other, making long trains that
tie up my life, keep it steady. muttering always, frowning
away. words bring life, the spoken word creating,
the written one a record of the creation.
life becomes visible.

the perfect word will set me free.

I was born to give birth, to labour long and intensely.
to have utter joy at the first breath. the slippery body,
warm skin. the perfect comfort of the breast, new eyes
squinting into bright light. that first meeting,
we look at each other and love without knowing.
soft speech, but mostly we just look.

this part I do well.

I was born to find my love and comfort him. to be
comforted by him. has there ever been any love like ours?
our dark nights, the words that should never be said
forgiveness like deep waters. light comes into the room
when he does, his voice finding me lost,
bringing me back.

I never was beautiful until he saw me.

I was born to look for hope until my eyes sting
with the strain. to wait and watch through the night
to shrug off gentle tries until finally I am broken
clearly unlovable. clearly loved. this is what I was born for:
to finally stop fighting and listen. to be soft. to thaw.
God beside me takes my clenched hands and opens them

this is the way He is, broken things are made new.

THE SECOND YEAR

In the second year I continued my way through the ups and downs of my emotions, writing about everything under the sun. It was a year of loss and joy. One notable thing about this year is that I finally woke up and realized I was struggling too hard against anxiety and panic. I needed help. I went to my doctor and she prescribed medication, a serotonin uptake inhibitor that is good for depression, but also effective against social anxiety.

I still remember my reasons for asking for help. I read the book *Love Walked In* by Marisa de los Santos— it's not really about self help, but in the story a woman lamented the fact that her mother didn't take the steps she should have taken to protect her children from her illness (in her case, alcoholism). Reading that was like someone opening the door to a closed up room. I was waiting for someone to rescue me from the darkness of my mind, but really, I was the one. I was the one who could ask for help and protect my children from my illness, because it was affecting them. It can't help but affect your children if you are having fits of panic with toddlers underfoot.

128

In May I started taking medication, and I can so easily read in between the lines of my writing and see the difference it made to me. I had always been worried that medication would make me a different person—it's probably why I waited so long, tried so many other things— but in reality I felt like Rachel again, for the first time in years. *Oh!* I thought. *I forgot what it was like to be me!* Not the me that was shrouded in darkness, even on the sunniest of days. But the me who could see long distances, who laughed in the sun, who will perhaps never be completely lighthearted, but who can find her way through sorrow.

august

August 3, 2006

Kai is getting his Real Nose.

You know how all kids are born with noses that look like Cabbage Patch Kids' noses? You know, squishy and soft and all cartilage? And then there's a point when they have their real noses. This is a real scientific thing. Only, there must be a point when they are metamorphosing from having the Cabbage Patch nose to having the Real nose. And there is no cocoon involved. So why don't we talk about this more? Because really and truly, I've been noticing a lot of change with Kai's nose.

It's longer, for one thing. And when he makes that annoying sniffing sound that he does when he has a cold, you can see some definite boniness in the bridge. It's no longer as squishy. I take this as a sign that he's growing up. He's turning four next month, and he also always wants to know what highway we're on, and whether we need to turn onto any other roads to get where we're going. He notices things like the fact that the sun is getting low, and there's going to be a sunset soon. And he's getting his Real nose. It's a big

130

step.

Of course, in my family, there are three stages to the metamorphosis. My brother and sister would be the first ones to agree to this. We have the Cabbage Patch nose, the Real nose, and then dum da dum dum... the Puberty nose. The sad thing about the Puberty nose is that when it first emerges, it is too large for the face it is occupying. I mean, we all still have largish noses, but in those first days it was really shocking. I remember crying because a boy in my math class remarked in an incredibly loud and obnoxious voice that I had a huge honker. Boy, what a huge honker Rae has! Hardy har har. The Puberty nose is the reason that I spent all my rides to school on the City bus scheming a way to sit in the best possible seat for nose concealment. The very very best were the two back corner seats. It's still habit, I always will pick those seats, though now I couldn't care less about people seeing my nose. You also have my full permission to look at my large feet, my crooked ears, and my sharp tooth.

I remember, though, those teenage years, when the nose seemed overwhelming and I looked at pictures of me with the cabbage patch nose and thought, "What happened? You started out so great."

The Puberty nose, like other aspects of puberty, comes a lot slower for boys than girls, so we thought that my brother had pretty much missed it. I traveled for the greater part of a year when I was eighteen and he was fourteen, and I remember how he opened the door when I got home and I looked at him standing there, fully in the throes of the first stage, the one where it doesn't fit your face. "Oh Matt," I said, "you GOT it. I'm so sorry." Of course, now Matty's face has grown into its nose, and I would challenge any of you into a handsome brother duel if you so desire, but it was a sad time for poor Matty.

131

So Kai is getting his Real nose, and though I really hope for him that he takes after his dad and doesn't get the Puberty nose, I will be right here to help him through it if he does.

August 5, 2006

You've probably heard enough of my incredibly crazy shopping marathons with the kids in tow, but I just have to say a few more things about this one:

1. The first thing that happened to me was that I needed to use the bathroom, so I took my Target cart and my three kids into the bathroom with me, and proceeded to break the button off of my pants, absentmindedly thinking that the button was a snap. You know, I went to unsnap them, except that there was no snap, so the button broke off and went flying across the room. Does this happen to anyone else? So I walked around with button-less pants all day. Once again, just sweetly trying to affirm everyone's preconceived ideas about frazzled mothers.

2. It happened. My sweet little undemanding boy has started to ask me to buy him things. I LOVED that he never did this. He was the kind of kid who would point at things and say sweetly, "Isn't that a nice Cookie Monster balloon" and then smile and be happy and just hold that picture of the balloon in his heart to be cherished. But some little bird landed on his shoulder and told him that maybe he could have that balloon. That maybe it wasn't enough just to like it. And maybe if he asked for it, I would pull out my magic papers and buy it for him. And so yesterday he thought he'd try it out. On many things. We're going to have to start talking about money and

socio-economic brackets and the fact that this family doesn't just walk into Costco and buy a freestanding basketball hoop. We're at Costco to save money, not spend it on a box of Glade scented candles. We buy lettuce, son. And those big bags of onions, potatoes, and spinach. Also laundry detergent. And garbage bags.

Okay, well, maybe I'll leave all that stuff out, but still. I'll have to help him understand about his own buying power.

3. Okay. Grocery carts. Grocery carts were made with the idea that you might have a more sane child spacing thing going on than I do. The littlest kid rides in the cart, and the older ones walk. Or, at Costco, the two littlest kids ride in the cart, and the oldest one walks. This assumes a lot. It assumes that the kids who are walking have the maturity to do so without causing harm to themselves or to others in the store. Which isn't so much the case with us. My favorite part of the day was when Kenya was lying on the floor on her back and Kai was dragging her down the aisle by her arm. Or maybe when Kenya was doing the army crawl in the freezer section. The bottom line is that Kenya shouldn't be unrestrained in the grocery store. Although, actually, she does really well for a two-year-old I think. But Kenya really shouldn't be unrestrained anywhere when she hasn't had a nap.

I guess I just need to get used to my new way of life. Grocery shopping involves a lot of fierce whispering, and sometimes a lot of fun. Like when I was heaving the Costco sized pack of paper towel rolls onto the cart and Kai burst into action. "I'm SO strong! I can help you! I'm like SUPERMAN I'm so strong."

And then there was when we were finally home eating Renee's fabulous tacos with the fixings and Kai inexplicably yelled, "Wait a minute! Did I eat *ashes*? Because my belly really hurts." Hmmm.

133

And there was the Leaf baby. He is a perfect angel sent from heaven. I mean, the child doesn't cry. He got cheated on practically every nap and still, all day he simply stared lovingly into my eyes. So, there's that. And there was the end of the day, when I was getting the kids into bed (Chinua is away for a few days, to sing at his friend's wedding) and I pulled a Dora the Explorer and asked them what their favorite parts of the day were and Kai said driving, and I said that story about the paper towels, and then I asked Kenya and she echoed "towels" and then we sang and we prayed and I felt this burst of happiness, like finally we were on top of the day, and the day was not on top of us, and all the craziness and my sadness in missing one of my best friends who moved away faded into the night, and then the kids were sleeping and the house was quiet and I sat down and checked all my working parts and found that everything still worked and then I just listened to the quiet.

August 7, 2006

Over the weekend some very kind people came to the Land to do some work on various projects we have in the mix. They were mostly men, except for one tall and fabulous woman named Nancy who is housemates with one of the most amazing women I know: my friend Amelia. Amelia of the fudge and knitting and PG Tips tea. Also of the sushi and Wendell Berry and hours of listening to me talk. Also German pancakes on Christmas morning with orange syrup. Ahhh Amelia. Anyways, although I don't know Nancy as well, I always love to sit and talk with her when I get the chance. We end up talking about tall girl stuff.

The rest of the crew were men. They had manly trucks and manly five gallon buckets with tool belts strapped to them, and they

134

installed wood stoves and fixed plumbing and split firewood. It was great.

They took to calling Kai Max. "Hi Max!" they would all chime, when he came near. He hated it. "No, no, no!" he would exclaim, making little chopping motions in the air with his hands like he does when he's really sincere. "I'm NOT Max!" They laughed and said, "Okay, Max."

This kind of rough uncle teasing is not my favorite approach to kids. I mean, when Kai asked me the other day if we could play "goofball" (instead of foosball) I tried my best not to laugh at him. But I figured, if these incredibly kind guys found this amusing, probably other people who wander in and out of Kai's world will tease him in the same way. In the past I have asked people not to tease him ("Eddie, please don't pretend to put him in the cooking pot on the stove...") but I figured that Kai is getting old enough to learn how to deal with teasing.

So, I took him aside at one point, when he seemed to be getting really distressed, and told him that he should just say something silly back to them. When they called him Max, he could say, "Hi Zizzer zazzer zuzz" or he could just call them Max right back. He brightened immediately and walked back over to where the guys were working. "Hi Max!" one said cheerfully. Kai looked up. "My mama says that I should call you Max back."

It was like that for the rest of the day. I couldn't explain to him that he should just say, "Hi Max," back to them, because he always would say, "My mama said..." And it was so sweet, because he's so little, and I'm a hero to him.

It was a good example though, of something I've been mulling over, which is how to deal with people who don't always have the script that you want them to have. I've learned that in my own life,

135

but now, with my kids, it's a challenge again. I'm used to people making comments about my dreads, and I'm used to what used to happen before I had dreadlocks, which was that old ladies would approach me and tell me that they paid hundreds of dollars to get their hair to have the ringlets that I had naturally. But what I'm having to get used to is all the comments that I get when I'm out with my kids.

"Are those YOUR kids? Wow. They're so beautiful."

"Can I touch her hair?"

"What a gorgeous little girl."

"They've got the good skin, huh?"

"Wow, look at this hair. Are these YOUR kids?"

And there's the now famous, "How much do you get paid for two?" That was what a lady asked me when we lived in San Francisco and I had Kai and Kenya at the playground in the Panhandle Park where mostly nannies hang out with their charges in the middle of a weekday. So I can excuse her. I told her that I wasn't getting paid, and if she found someone who wanted to pay me, could she please contact me? She was flustered and said, "Oh, it's just that they're so... beautiful." Polite people say "beautiful," instead of "dark-skinned," but what they really mean is, "You're white, and these children are people of color. Are they really yours?"

But, although I don't usually mind comments about our family, or the things people say, it is starting to bother me a little. Maybe because the addition of a third child has upped the ante and more and more people have started to approach me in grocery stores. Part of this can probably be attributed to the fact that we look a little like a circus act, with Kai doing handstands and Kenya doing her best impression of a tightrope walker.

I was complaining to my Superstar Husband about this on the

phone the other night, all the questions about whether I really was the mother of these children.

"Rae," he said. "You're really going to have to find a way to deal with this, because you'll be dealing with it for the rest of your life."

"Yeah," I said, "but it's just that they ask if they can touch Kenya's hair and stuff."

"Welcome to my life. Welcome to the rest of our life. You'll just have to come up with a good response."

So, just like Kai, I'll have to come up with a "Hi Max" of my own. I'm just not sure what that will be. Or I could say, "My husband told me to say..."

August 16, 2006

It's been a long time since I wrote, which is not good. It's not good because what happens is a sort of traffic jam in my head, which causes me to get absolutely stumped, wondering what to write about.

What to write about?

Well, I could write about why I haven't written in so long. About the fact that my family is on vacation, and how there is nothing in the world like spending some time alone with your family. And I'm not really saying there is nothing more blissful than spending time alone with your family, (although it is much-needed time, I will add, since I live in a community and rarely spend a day alone with my family) there is just nothing *like it*. It is blissful, at times, frustrating at times, as my Superstar Husband and I begin to decompress and then attempt to communicate the long overdue stuff with one another, which is like getting the ketchup out of the bottom of the ketchup bottle. Having a deep conversation with this particular wife

137

is also a little like conversing with Ali Baba and the Forty Thieves: there are a lot of us in here. I do want to talk about it, I don't want to talk about it, okay, now I do again, now I just want to snarl at you, now I'm picking an outright fight, okay let's talk nicely again, okay happiness! we're talking! we're working things out because everyone knows that marriage is long raft ride in a lovely green river, with rapids here and there that need to be navigated with care.

It's just that I feel sorry for Chinua, that he has to be in the raft that has the crazy person in it, sometimes paddling, but sometimes trying to hit him in the head with the oars. And sometimes even stabbing the raft with a pencil on purpose, just so we have to sit on the bank for a while with a patch kit.

And that brings me to something else, something I can barely even write about but really feel like I have to. I noticed somewhat of a theme, as I went back over my previous writing. There was a suspiciously large amount of entries about me crying in public or freaking out in stores because people were looking at me, or getting upset because the checkout lady was talking to me in a mean tone of voice. And there is a lot of writing about anxiety. And you have to understand, that there are many many things in life that I am never anxious about. For example:

Germs. (Go ahead kids, eat those crackers off the ground, seven second rule.) This is one reason that I do so well in India, I believe. People like me were MADE for travel in countries like India which have, let's say, *issues* with sanitation. I'm going to be ridiculously open here and confess to you that as a kid, I ate a lot of gum off of the ground. My poor mother was always asking me what I had in my mouth. "Nuffing," I would say as I tried to hide a large wad of someone else's watermelon gum under my tongue. Obviously I regret this decision to eat gum off of the ground as a child, simply because it's a little embarrassing, but really, I never, ever worry about germs.

Money. Most of the time. I've lived a life of faith for so long that I'm pretty good now at relaxing and allowing God to take care of us. We work pretty hard for no pay, and somehow God always brings us what we need. Like this place to rest, a place that Jessie and her husband Levi offered to us and we receive joyfully because God always likes to work through people. He rarely showers mountains of money out of the sky, but there seems to be a different way of living, an economy made of people who give to each other in different ways at different times. Now, I have had times of near heart attack with money, I'm not going to lie, such as when our community lived in this crazily expensive flat on Haight Street and I was in charge of collecting rent and paying bills. (If there is any job in the entire world that I should not be in charge of, *ever again*, it is collecting rent.)

Disaster. I'm not super fearful. I travel a lot, have been in fairly dangerous circumstances a lot, and yet don't find that I'm really all that worried that something bad will happen to me or my family. I find it easy to believe that everything will somehow be okay. I know that we could be in danger, that things could heat up here, that one day in India I could be put in a bad position, but I also know that God often doesn't give us the ability to go through hard things until we need it.

I don't lie awake worrying about money, sickness, danger, or potential disaster.

I do lie awake worrying about *people*.

I have a lot of anxiety when it comes to people and social situations. At the best I can be a good friend, listen to people, be in public and not be terribly self-conscious, and go to sleep at night easily. At the worst I flinch when people look at me in public, am afraid of talking to people, and am knotted up inside at night, worrying. After a conversation I may go over what I said obsessively, wondering if anything was wrong or upsetting or offensive. I'm coming to think that I need to seriously address this.

But how?

It is the hardest thing I have ever faced in my life. Why am I so afraid? What am I afraid of? I guess I'm just going to have to continue to write it all down. I think I could seek a diagnosis, and probably find one, but I'm reluctant to do that. I don't want to be contained within an illness. There are many parts to a mountain: there are the trees, the rough patches, the old stones, that dirt underneath. There is the sky, coming all the way down to touch the dry earth, the occasional wildflower and there are wide-open spaces. I am not made only of the parts of me that are sick and hiding, and I hope that healing is more than surgery, more than medicine, more than a bandaid. I don't know why I am so afraid of people being angry with me, I don't know why I feel a sort of constant judgment humming underneath the ground. I have seen those open spaces, I know that there are many trees to climb through, to get there, and I know there will be the small flowers in the trees, the glimpses of blue sky to help me through. God is a true Friend; He neither allows me to escape this, nor allows it to break me. And there is my Superstar Husband, who, when I am wild with fear over the days ahead of me, the people I will disappoint, the mistakes I will make, looks me in the eyes and says, "You only have today. You only have this moment."

August 26, 2006

If you ever want to juggle fire on the beach, and you're hoping for a crowd, just park yourself next to a bonfire with many many teenagers standing around it. They will not be able to contain themselves, and you'll find yourself surrounded by awed, cheering fans who will either shriek and scream in delight (OH MY GOOOOOD!!!!), if they're female, or say, "Oh dude, that's sweet. Check that OUT," if they're bros. Teenagers are so great. They almost always make me tear up, partly because I remember what it felt like to be a teenager, how I was almost coming out of my skin with ideas and humiliation and the wonder of the universe, and also because there is nothing quite like the paradox of a teenager, how self-conscious and free they are. They're all like, ohmygod, someone's looking at me, and then screaming in exhilaration as my Superstar Husband catches the torch by the flame (ouch!).

Seriously, though, Chinua is amazing, and he did gather quite a crowd. It was really fun. And the great thing about Southern California is that everyone is so laid back. The fire department showed up to keep an eye on things, but no one asked Chinua to stop.

*

My son, while trying to eat a hot potsticker, said very seriously, "It's not hot on my white teeth, only on my gum teeth." I am very proud to be his mother.

Yesterday we went to Mexico, and it was a combination of being the best experience that I've had in a long, long, time, and being a day of me trying to get away from myself.

I was looking around and loving where I was, loving my beautiful family, loving Mexico, loving the beach and the taco stand

141

and my husband. Chinua can get along well enough in Spanish with a good enough accent that people take him to know it fluently, and the train of conversation takes off, with him clinging to the sides. I loved Mexico from the first day I was there, seven years ago, and my innocent, pre-India self was amazed and intrigued by the messiness of the streets and the pinned-together houses. Chinua and I, longing to leave America for a while and travel, drank it in yesterday like thirsty sailors.

But there it was, the anxiety, that knot in my gut that never left, the tension in my neck that curled around my spine and yanked, the sick feeling that had me in tears a few times. I hate myself like this. I don't know how to love myself like this, and even worse, I don't know how to believe that God loves me like this.

And then I went swimming, by myself, while the kids and their Superstar dad made a sandcastle on the beach. I stood in the waves and was knocked off of my feet again and again, and I thought, *yes, this is how it feels, this is why I never catch my breath*. I pretended that the waves were my fear and my loneliness, pretended that if I could just stay standing I would beat all this, that I would feel like Rae again, like that teenage self who can scream and shriek in delight. And then I let myself be carried for a while, and I was tired, and I wondered if I could let go enough to let the waves of this great fear hit me, yet still see the sunset, like I was seeing it around me, the sherbet colors, the sparkly horizon. And I rested, and I breathed deeply and watched the silhouetted fishing boats with their circles of birds.

september

I remember the first time that I ever saw Chinua. It was summer.
I had turned eighteen that spring. He was running down the steps to
open the gate for me at the old community house on Ashbury
Street, in the Haight district of San Francisco. I saw him open the
door and jog down the stairs and I thought, *Um*. He was gorgeous.
There wasn't a buzzer at that house, we always had to open the gate
manually for every person who stepped inside. At the time I didn't
know there would ever be a "we". I didn't know that I would live in
that house, would walk through it with my husband, right before it
sold, or that Haight Street would become my home.

My friend Heidi and I stepped inside and joined some people
who were standing around in the kitchen. Chinua and I started to
talk about Canadian politics, a subject that I knew nothing about,
but I'm sure I made a few things up. We had come to see another
person, someone we wanted to talk to about maybe doing a little
volunteering around the Christian house. The Christian house was
in the Haight and existed for the purpose of loving kids on the

street, being Jesus love for them, having them over for showers and food. The lady we were looking for wasn't there. So we left.

A few days later, Heidi and I helped out with some people who were serving a meal for people in need in a church. Chinua was there, with his guitar, playing worship songs while everyone ate. I was serving salad, and the older lady beside me had two things going on. 1. A bit of a control issue about the size of the scoop of salad I was giving people, ("That's too big," and "No, not so small!") and 2. Quite the crush on Chinua. She went on and on about how he came all the time to play at that meal, and that she just loooooved his voice, had I heard his voice? And there was just something about him. Since Ms. Perfect Salad Scoop beside me was talking about him so much, I did watch Chinua a bit, and I did listen to what she said about him and I know this is going to sound like the silliest thing in the world, but what I really thought was, "I know him." Except that I didn't. I had just met him.

That was all, we left town and went back to Canada. But about eight months later I ended up volunteering at that same house in San Francisco for a week.

I was a shy and gawky girl, growing up. In social situations I was completely self-conscious. I had a few rules for myself, like, never let your true feelings be known; when in doubt: be silly; and above all, never, no never, let a boy know that you are interested in him. I had some pretty good force fields. On that trip to San Diego I had come to the conclusion that there really was no one out there who was interested in a girl like me. I was traveling with five other girls, and we met a lot of guys, guys whose eyes glassed over when I started talking about books or art and God.

A few things happened during that week. The first was that when I came running up the stairs in the upper part of the house one day, Chinua was walking out of his room and said, "I like it that you're tall, like me." My height had been such a thing of consternation for much of my life, and this was the best moment of height that I had ever had. Aaaahhh, I thought, this moment is what it was all for: my Social Dance class in the ninth grade, when I was already 5'9" or 5'10", I don't remember, and it really doesn't matter, because my dance partner was a boy from Hong Kong named Helmut who was prematurely gray and hilarious, a great friend, but still half a foot shorter than me. Or all the boys I knew who were my friends and always stood on tip toes around me to make themselves the same height or taller. It all suddenly seemed insignificant when I was standing beside Chinua, who was 6'2" and liked it that I was tall.

The second thing was that somehow it came up that I really liked poetry, and Chinua gave me one of his books, a compilation of e. e. cummings poems. Note to boys who like girls who love poetry: ALWAYS give her a book of poems, preferably by someone like cummings or Rilke or well, anyone at all. It will make her feel like a queen.

The third thing was that he asked to see my own poems and then we sat on the stairs and he read them, while I read some of his. I will remember the way those stairs smelled for the rest of my life, it was a good smell, and after that I could never walk inside that house and smell its housey smell without sighing with happiness. I had no idea at the time, but it is a testament to how smitten we both were that 1. he told me that my poems were epic, that they were better than everything he had ever read, better than cummings or any great poet and 2. that I believed him.

The fourth thing was that he took my friends and I out on a tour of the city and we went hunting in North Beach for this little jazz club he had been to, only we never found it. And the beauty of that night was this: we were silly. We were silly and we had so much fun that at one point Chinua fell down on the street laughing. On the corner of Columbus and Broadway he just lay down and laughed. Of course nobody even so much as glanced at us. And then we played at the playground in Washington Square and spoke in silly British accents and I have never had so much fun in my life. And then my friends and I left, the next day. The whole time it had been dawning on me, that if we were standing in a group, Chinua would stand next to me. He seemed to like to talk to me, he seemed to favor my company. It was shocking to this awkward, gawky girl.

Looking back, all the signs point to smitten, but Chinua and I had what I like to think of as the perfect romance, because it was a year and a half later, after many letters and many phone calls, with him traveling around India and Nepal, and me traveling around the States and Canada, and then at the very end of that time traveling in India, Nepal, and Thailand together, a whole year and a half later that we ever talked about how we felt about each other. It was always there, right from the beginning, but we just didn't open up that can of worms. And built an amazing friendship first. Eventually we had all that, we had the romance, we had the proposal, we had the amazing wedding.

Which was good, because we need that now, as we are celebrating our fifth anniversary with three kids, the youngest still only seven and a half months old. We had three kids in four years, and took on some serious responsibility within our community. We've gone through money stuff, kid stuff, my postpartum depression three times, we've traveled together, lived in tents and an RV, lived in two towns and a big city since we were married, been lied to numerous times by people that we've cared for, had things

147

stolen from us. We've written songs like "Everything's gonna be all right, everything's gonna be okay, everything's gonna be alright, no matter what they say" that we sing to ourselves to feel better, we've lived in small spaces, we now live in a beautiful big space. We've swum in rivers, lakes, the Gulf of Mexico, and a few oceans (warm and cold) together. We've been through flooding, storms, and mudslides, we've sat in several broken down vehicles together. We've danced, we've sung at many weddings, we've tag-teamed as photographers, as parents, as community directors. We've tried to juggle together, we've eaten many different foods, been guests at many different homes, driven down countless roads. We've filled our tank with gas many, many times. We've spoken words that shouldn't be said, we've cried (mostly me), we've been immature and petty. We've made up. We are solid and we are in love and we've been through a whole lot and I can honestly say I've never known anyone I esteem and respect as much as my Superstar Husband.

September 14, 2006

Kai walked out of his room today and announced, "It's not 'pants', it's pant," while shaking his head in amusement. I smiled.

"Well, no. It sounds like it *should* be 'pant', but we say 'a pair of pants', so it really is 'pants'."

Kai shot me a derisive look. (As derisive as a four-year-old with brown eyes the size of tea cups can be.)

"No," he said. "It's pant." I don't drop these kinds of things anymore, because really, the kid has to *know*.

"Well, you're almost right, because almost any other word wouldn't have an 's' sound on the end like that, but it's 'pants'. Trust

148

me."

"No, it's pant."

This is when I had to pull out the old standby.

"Kai," I said. "Who's four years old?"

"Me!!!!" (BIG smile)

"And who's twenty-six?"

"Kenya?"

"No. Me. Who knows how to read?"

"You do? You know how to read, Mama?"

"And who has been through school? Me again. So you can trust me. It may not make sense to you, but I know that the word is pants. You may call your pants 'pant' if you want to though."

I've found that this tactic works well for other things, too, like when Kai tries to instruct me on driving ("You were supposed to stop back there, Mama!" "Kai, do you even know what *city* we're in?") or cooking or other things. Except that I may say things like "Who's been driving for ten years?" and "Who's not tall enough to reach the pedals or see over the steering wheel?"

It helps us all remember where we stand.

September 25, 2006

Ever since Kenya became one of the speaking members of our family (it seems that it always consists of speaking members and non-speaking members, although the only non-speaking member right now is the Leaf Baby... and our pet rats, I guess) she and Kai have found the strangest things to argue about. They really can argue about anything and everything. Listening to them argue makes me want to lock myself in a sound-proof box, it is even worse than whining, and it showed itself right after I said that whining was the

149

most annoying thing I'd ever heard. Arguing is worse, particularly because it usually culminates in shrieking from Kenya.

It can be pretty funny, though.

Yesterday we were all sitting on the couch, and Kenya was staring dreamily out of the window. (If I wrote in Kenya's dialect you wouldn't be able to understand a thing, so I'll write as if she speaks with more than two consonants.)

Kenya: That's Mama's sky and Daddy's sky and Leaf's sky and Kenya's sky and Kai's sky!

(I'm thinking here, how beautiful! What a sweet girl I have. You always wonder about what your kids are going to say when they finally start talking. And then Kenya says something pretty like that. We can only see the tiniest glimpse of it through the window, too, since our trees are so, so tall.)

Kai: IT'S NOT OUR SKY!!!

Kenya: IT IS OUR SKY!!! IT'S Mama's and Daddy's and Leaf's and Kenya's and Kai's.

Kai: NO IT'S NOT!!!

Kenya: (Bloodcurdling sound that shouldn't be heard within a closed space because of the danger to the baby's eardrums.)

Me: Kai, it is kind of our sky. And kind of not, too. Besides, she can say that if she wants to.

Kai: It's NOT. It shouldn't be our sky. It *shouldn't* be.

Kenya: IT IS OUR SKY!!! (More blood curdling ensues.)

Me: Okay, kids, we are NOT TALKING ABOUT THE SKY ANYMORE.

Kai: (whispering) It's not ours.

Kenya: SHRIEK!!

Me: NO MORE SKY.

Do you see what I'm saying here? About the soundproof room?

Maybe I could just invent some kind of soundproof head. I could walk around with my soundproof head all day and smile all the time, because I can't hear the madness.

october

October 5, 2006

Fourteen and a half ways to improve your spirits (A note to myself.)

There has been sadness this year. Thankfully, these sadnesses are the light kind, no deaths, no major sicknesses. But sometimes they seem to pile up, and they threaten to overwhelm me. I thought I'd write a helpful list for myself to mull over on a day like today, when it seems like I'm followed by a sadness cloud that is tied to me by a strong piece of twine.

1. Riding a scooter will do the trick. For a short while, anyways. My Superstar Husband recently had a birthday, and one of the things I plotted was a motorbike ride through San Francisco with him. It wasn't too hard to figure out, either. We were already going to the City for a meeting, we have an amazing friend named Amelia who watched our kids and lent us her scooter, and she had helmets for both of us.

In my black leather jacket and big, visored helmet, I looked like a superhero from the seventies. Chinua was wearing one of those little helmets that don't cover your face, and because the helmet was made for a small woman, and he is a large man with plentiful dreadlocks, it was perched on the top of his head like a shiny hard kippah. He was our black, Jewish scooter driver.

We zipped down Market in deepening twilight, then drove over to North Beach, the very place we fell in love way back when. We had pizza at a seedy urban pizza place, then sped back over to the Mission in the dark to pick up our kids. It was amazing, everything I had hoped, and even the fact that the idle was too low on the scooter, and Chinua had to restart every time we were at a stoplight, even that was perfect. He was perfect in his shiny kippah, and I held him around his waist and his shoulders and I laughed at the dark.

2. Listen to Radiohead's *Hail to the Thief* album. Sometimes it will lift your spirits just to be really, really melancholy, with lots of angst.

3. Talk to the Leaf Baby for awhile. He'll make a combination of faces and sounds that make you laugh until you've shaken all that sadness right out of you. He'll make dolphin sounds, raspberry sounds, squinch his eyes up, and wrinkle his nose. You'll want to hold him forever.

4. Read *Harold and the Purple Crayon*. Especially the line about the "very hungry moose and the deserving porcupine". That line makes you laugh every time.

5. On that note, read *One Fish Two Fish*, by Dr Seuss. Go play a

game called Ring the Gack. This makes you laugh too.

6. Listen to your silly husband in the car, people watching. He'll say, "Where are you going?" to a woman walking by in a big rush, not so that she can hear him, of course. Or, "You got some foooood?" to a woman carrying a casserole dish down Market St. Or, "What's in your little green bag?" to a business man carrying a tiny green bag with handles alongside his briefcase. All of this is only loud enough for you to hear, sitting in your van in traffic, and cracks you up to no end.

7. Laugh at Kai, secretly, when he manages to say the oddest things you've ever heard. For instance, when he yells out, HEY! and you turn to look, only to see that he's talking to his pita and hummus. Or when he calls out from the back of the car, "I burped, and it tasted like my yummy bubbly juice, and now I'm sad that it's all gone."

8. Buy yourself a new book.

9. Make plans for an upcoming trip to Canada. Okay, so this might actually stress you out quite a bit, but focus on the positive: you'll be in CANADA. Your home and native land. You'll be able to hang out with your parents. And Becca. And Matty. And go to your brother's wedding. And smell the air that smells so different.

10. You would normally eat some chocolate or ice cream but now you are finding out that sugar has a very bad effect on you, and that it gives you a false high that brings you right back into the pit later. Too bad. Eat healthy things and feel happy about it. Think

about cells being regenerated and your brain cells being replenished.

11. Mull over that scooter ride again and think about the time that you and your Superstar Husband rode scooters on tropical Havelock Island in India. Okay, maybe don't think about this too hard. Especially not with that gray sky looming.

12. Listen to Kenya laugh. Get a kiss from Kenya, or a hug, or a touch of any kind, because this will give you great happiness.

13. Clean your house. This is calming and methodic.

14. Sing really loud at a gas station. This makes people look, but spreads joy around. Maybe. Depending what you're singing and how well.

And a half: Drink half of a forbidden cup of coffee, just because.

October 12, 2006

I don't think you can ever know how having a new child will affect your family. How could you? The small person that is your child shines and darkens in ways that have never appeared to you before. Sometimes there is a spark of recognition, a piece of your childhood, the smile of your sister or the eyes of your husband. But this person is new; new to the world and to the small village that is your home.

With the birth of each of my kids, I died a small death and awoke to new love. With Kai, it was the death of my independent self, a self that spent hours reading and writing and painting, a self

155

that jumped in the car without checking lists or shoving shoes on tiny feet. With Kenya, it was the death of having only one baby, the concentrated affection, the passing back and forth of one child. And with Leaf, it was even more imperceptible, but it was the transition of Kenya being my baby girl to being my middle child. This is what felt like a small death to me. It's what made me cry, during that first week.

But the awakening! The new love, the kind of love that you never have for anyone else, not even your spouse. Love for my husband is constant and huge in me, but how many times have I watched my children sleep and felt that clutch of pity, the fierce protection that brings tears to my eyes? I've never felt love like this before having these children. It has made me intensely vulnerable, easily shaken, and yet as solid as the hills.

I've also watched each of my children's hearts expand with love as our family has grown. They open and blossom in care for one another, and this is what forms them, in addition to the love they receive from us. Leaf has never known a life without a brother and a sister. Kai has received each of his with joy.

In all the craziness, the dullness, the frustration of parenting, love binds. Love takes a family and makes them a small force in the world. In all the ways I've changed since my first son was born, the biggest are that I am more loved, and that I have more love.

October 23, 2006

The day didn't start out so bad, yesterday. We were driving on one of the loveliest sections of highway in the country, which was made even more beautiful by the fact that the poplars have turned yellow. Bringing the car around curves, I was presented with beauty that soothed all the crazy parts of me. We drove through the dark forest where the sun shot through trees of the brightest yellow and out into vineyards and peace was all around me and the kids chattered in the back seat. The orchards and vineyards in Sonoma were turning as well, and there were soft hills of fiery little trees spreading in every direction.

We're leaving for Canada this week, and I'm hustling to get everything taken care of before we go. Chinua has a flight to Israel from Seattle on Thursday, and we'll be gone a little over two weeks, which means that we need to pack and prepare, STAT. I had some bookkeeping work to take care of, close to the City, so I zipped down and did it yesterday, taking in some psychological trauma as well, just for kicks.

I had the two older kids with me. In trying to configure who would take care of which children when both of us had great swathes of work to cut through, I settled on taking Kai and Kenya, thinking that they'd be the best for the seven hour round trip, while the Leaf baby would be the easiest, relatively, to take care of while working at home. Those big long naps are great. (By relatively, I REALLY mean relatively. It's funny how you get to saying, "Wow, this is so easy, I only have the two kids to take care of today." I imagine in the larger families they say, "Shopping was a cinch- I brought only five of the kids along!")

We just had to make one, brief stop at Target. Can you hear the creepy music?

I don't know why so many of my life events happen while I'm on shopping expeditions. I guess it's a comment on the nature of parenthood, the weekly forays into the wilderness of Costco, the way my whole life seems to be reflected in one little shopping trip. I mean, how many times can you walk through Costco without going absolutely freaking insane? Oh, they have their Christmas display up again! Wow, has a whole year passed already? What's that, for Halloween? A MAN-SIZED SCARY FIGURE? Oh, Costco, what will you think of next?

I've also shopped at practically every Target on the West Coast. Living in the woods means that you stock up when you can, so we shop wherever we are, north or south, east or west, this town or that town. Yesterday I was in Novato (a town to which I will now never return) and all I needed to buy was long underwear, socks, pull-ups, (for Kenya, who by the way is now a whiz at the potty) and a Dora the Explorer DVD for the kids to watch while I was working. (They have ONE, which they've watched seven hundred times, and I figured that I was pushing my luck by trying to keep them occupied with it again, while I worked.) I picked it all up in record time, didn't go near the clearance racks, and checked out. We were on a tight schedule.

Then I walked out to the parking lot and realized that I didn't have my car key.

After this, a lot of stuff happened, including me retracing my steps seventeen times, searching on floors, under displays, in the bathroom, in the bathroom trash, and in the trash at the entrance to the store. I caught some looks, let me tell you, and I realized that people saw my shopping cart with two kids in it and assumed I was looking for food, or cans or something. I started to make little remarks, standing there with my arm shoulder high in trash, messing around with the melting ice cubes in the bottom of the bag, desperate to find my key, like "I really have to find that key!" and "Oh, kids, I hope we find it soon!" to let people know that I wasn't looking for leftover hotdogs. (Seriously. As if I would ever score food from the Target trash cans. The dumpsters behind Whole Foods are a thousand times better.) My Superstar Husband says that my mutterings probably didn't make things look any better.

I hassled guest services until they were ready to throw me out, and called all of the locksmiths I could find in the Yellow Pages. They were all closed on Sundays, except for one 800 number where the lady told me that new keys started at $120 AND UP, and that they wouldn't be able to tell me how much it would cost me until they got there. I don't want to mention how, but I've had a key made before, and it was $80 and I didn't want to pay any more if I didn't have to. (Okay, *okay*, it was an incident involving the beach and the vast expanse of sand at the shore as well as shallow pants pockets and my little car key, but that was *years* ago.)

In between trips to guest services, my kids took turns falling apart. I walked around with a worried, stressed out look on my face, with two kids in my cart who were pulling hair and generally losing their minds. It was nap time, for Kenya, and after three hours, my kids weren't even trying to listen. I wasn't holding out to find the key at this point, I just couldn't even locate a locksmith. I was literally stranded at Target, and at one point I looked at the man at guest services and asked him to please show me the way to where they kept all the bathroom trash once they emptied it. They started to think about calling security. On me.

As I was calling the police, a last ditch effort to find a local locksmith, an angel in the disguise of a Target team member ran up with my key. I have never seen anything as beautiful as that girl, standing there with her red shirt and khaki pants. We left, in a hurry, since we had been there for *over three hours*, and we didn't exactly have three hours to spare when we left that morning. We drove the rest of the way, I worked, the kids were delighted with their new DVD, and I was ecstatic that we didn't have to pay money that we didn't have for a new key.

You might think this is the end of the story, but you'd be missing the part where we finally left, hungry and tired, to drive the long drive home. We stopped to get gas and...

...I couldn't find my wallet. It was gone.

I'll give you some hints. I located it in the very same store that my keys had been lost in earlier. The very same boy that I had been hassling about the key handed my wallet to me in a polite and embarrassed-for-me manner. I cracked some joke, tried to get him to believe that this wasn't an everyday occurrence for me, and scratched the Novato Target off my list of places that I can show my face ever again.

The list is getting shorter and shorter.

October 31, 2012

If you walk into a coffee shop in Canada, and order a coffee, and then meander over to the counter where you doctor your coffee up, you won't find a container of "half and half" like you will in the States, you'll find a container of "cream." What Americans call half and half, Canadians call cream, and heavy cream is called whipping cream.

What Americans call a stocking cap, beanie, or various other words, Canadians call a "toque". It's French, like serviette, which a lot of Canadians say instead of napkin.

On a sign that indicates a place to use the toilet, you'll see that it's called a "washroom" here in Canada. This has caused a lot of confusion as I've asked for washrooms in department stores in the States and they look at me as if to say, "You want to take a bath?" Now I know to ask for the restroom when I'm in the U.S.

The sofa in your living room may or may not be called a chesterfield if you are Canadian. This word is fading with progressing generations, but every Canadian who speaks English as his or her first language will know what you mean if you say, "The magazine is on the chesterfield."

Canadians take out the garbage. Americans take out the trash.

When an American says he's pissed, he means he's mad. When a Canadian says he's pissed, he means he's drunk, really really drunk. For angry, he'll say pissed off.

I'm in my musing, sort of melancholy, philosophical world of being in Canada, trying to figure out what is so different about this place that I can literally feel it in the air as soon as I cross the border, and why it makes me so sad to be here. Sometimes I feel like an impostor: I've adopted Americanisms. I say "huh". I do, all the time. I say trash, I say restroom, and I say "Sem-eye" instead of "Sem-ee" when I'm talking about a big truck.

We're in Victoria, and as we drove past the Parliament Building it was night, and the old, beautiful building was lit up with thousands of little white lights.

There is a song by The Innocence Mission from their Small Planes cd, and I'll just quote the whole song here, since it pretty much exactly describes how I'm feeling.

Song About Traveling

A man said Why, why does traveling
in cars and in trains make him feel sad,
a beautiful sadness.
I've felt this before.
It's the people in the cities you'll never know,

it is everything you pass by,
wondering will you ever return.

A sweet and sad song, and add to that the sorrow that I sometimes feel about not living in the country of my youth, and you have how I feel. Well, add some relief and joy over being with my family right now, some adoration of my kids as well as some general frustration about the little crying party they all decided to throw at six this morning, some desperate missing of my Superstar Husband, and some real homesickness for, (can this be?) America— gasp, my home now, my Redwood cabin, my community. Life is so strange, all the little loves and hurts, the way I love my family and I love my community. The way my home and my husband are intertwined, the way I miss Canada, miss British Columbia, but have come to adore Northern California where I met Chinua, where we have our life together.

And then there are those pangs of nostalgia for India, for Thailand. This earth is vast and there are homes everywhere for me. And yet it is not my home at all, and that is why this constant search, under tables, in lit windows as I'm passing by, this search for home is not futile. It's as if God holds my home in His cupped hands.

november

November 20, 2006

I hate not writing. When I don't write I feel itchy. I feel rank and hurt and stupid. So, I write as much as I can, but occasionally there are times when it seems impossible. And there are times when it becomes essential, like tonight, when I am sitting here with my taquitos and cheesecake at ten thirty, eating forkfuls of spanish rice and typing in an attempt to get my mind into some kind of working order.

Do you ever wish that you could see things for the first time? For example, these giant Redwood trees that are all around my home. We drive through them on small highways all the time, and they are as imposing as mountains, and I can't see them. I want to see the trees, see their enormity, take giant breaths of their height. I crane my head and I can't see the tops, and they have become as commonplace as, I don't know, pavement. I want that first gasp, you know? The eyes of a child. I want to drive into the financial district in San Francisco and see one of these trees, rising far above the buildings, so I can finally digest its sheer size. Don't you want that?

164

To see the ocean and feel yourself as a mite in the center of your world, wet and salty, rather than sitting on the shore staring at the horizon? I want to *understand*, to truly grasp my smallness.

But large things are hard to see. Sometimes when I'm driving by a particularly large grove, I see how dark it is on the forest floor. Almost no light makes its way through, but there is the gold; pure sun illuminating one leaf here, a group of leaves there, some mossy roots, a patch of clover. These bits of sunlight break through and I see clearly, just for a moment. I see it, I really see those few leaves, and I may start to cry.

I think I've lived for a long time thinking that if I just did everything right, if I was just as nice as I could be, bad things wouldn't happen to me. If I played my cards right I would not disappoint anyone, and I definitely wouldn't make anyone angry with me.

I'm beginning to understand that this is not so. I still don't want people to be angry with me, but people are. I don't want to disappoint people, but I do. Somehow these are not the things that God is telling me to avoid. He simply hasn't asked me to make everyone happy. Knowing this doesn't make me any less crumbly inside when I do these things. It doesn't make it feel any better when I lose sleep, when I lose friends. It goes so deep, this tearing around inside over the "f" word. I mean f-a-i-l. It's the word that I dance around most, the whispered word in the dark early mornings when the baby is nursing and I can't get back to sleep and there are things racing through my head besides the phone calls I need to make, things I can't just get rid of by getting up and making a list. I only wish I could. Succeed, Work Harder, Do Better, Buck Up, I would write, and then fall into a deep sleep.

In the sadness of these past months, though, I have seen the one leaf illuminated on the forest floor, the few leaves dancing. I wrote a poem a while back, and the last line was, "This is the way He is, broken things are made new." This is the heart of my faith. This is what I have chosen to throw my life at, and this is what I will waste it all on. Broken things are made new. How many broken things have I seen being made new? The first brilliant smiles of the girl staying with us who has been trapped inside herself, the long-legged steps towards grace, lives rebuilt, families restored.

Sometimes you fail even when you mean the best. There is tearing down, and there is hurting, and then from the ash heap comes a light as brilliant and inexplicable as the sun at midnight. This is the story of the whole bible, it is the story of the true Christian faith, it is so important that God couldn't leave me following all my rules, thinking that if I did the tomato cans would all stay on the store shelf. My rules have left me gasping for air, and the tomato cans are all around me on the floor.

One time my Superstar Husband and I were driving with our friend Amelia. "I have to show you something," she said, and she brought us through a deep and dark forest grove. The trees stretched for miles above our heads, and we followed her to a small tree that had needles that were absolutely white. It was an albino Redwood, leaning on a larger green tree, it was a magical snowy fairy tree in the midst of a dark green forest. It was forced to depend entirely on the tree that it was leaning on for its sustenance. It was beautiful and sad and unique, and I've never found it again. But I saw it that day, and I felt its weakness like I feel my own now, when I become offended by the words behind words, or when I hash out old conversations again and again. I am weak now, I am leaning, I have no sustenance other than what I receive from God.

This is how He is, broken things are made new.

166

November 27, 2006

I remember that when I was first stepping into mommishness, and I had my one wee baby, my friend Carol would tell me that the biggest change in her life since becoming a mom was her lack of a *thought* life. She had three children, the oldest nine, and the youngest three at the time. Since I only had a baby, I couldn't really relate yet. Most of my struggles were with being tied to a young creature, night and day, with having really tight cycles of sleep and food and wake time, which are big struggles in the beginning, don't get me wrong, but I didn't really understand what she meant by that lack of a thought life thing.

Until now. Now I understand. It has something to do with waking first thing to requests for juice that grow ever shriller and then sitting at the table sticking to my guns about the fact that everyone is eating their breakfasts and juice can wait until I've finished my own breakfast, for pity's sake. And then on into the day, racing away, breaking up fights, telling stories, of course the ever-present and heroic bum-wiping, and just generally, the living consistently with other talking people who do it all the time. Talk. And talk. And talk.

I like to think. It fills up my writer self with stories and ideas and memories. So I was glad to drive down to the City yesterday to work, a job I do about once a month, although I half froze in my heatless car. It was good to think.

I passed three dead deer, not all together, as I drove. Once, a while ago, I started a poem about the carnage on the highway first thing in the morning, here in the woods. Something about the flocks of carrion birds. It was storming so hard yesterday that even the crows were staying away. It was storming so hard that I stopped to eat to try to wait it out a little. I could barely see, and when I ran from my car to the store it was as though I had stepped into my bathtub and turned on the shower.

I thought a lot. Before I left for the City this morning I ran into our communal kitchen to get something. The kitchen looked as though seven young bulls with dirt on their hooves had wreaked havoc for hours. Somehow in the aftermath of Thanksgiving the kitchen was neglected, partly because a lot of people caught a flu bug going around and were feeling yucky and under the weather, and probably because it got to the point where it was overwhelming. I felt upset. First I thought, *how did this happen?* And then I thought, *why didn't I plan better?* I should have thought to set up a clean up crew for the after Thanksgiving earthquake.

But it's like G.K. Chesterton wrote, after a local paper asked writers for essays on what they thought the biggest problems of the world were. His was brief. "I am," he wrote.

It's all part of a theme that I've been mulling over, in those rare moments when I can mull, about perspective. For instance, I could have continued to stew over the wreckage of the kitchen as I drove. I realized that I was doing it, and understood that it was stealing my joy over what an amazing Thanksgiving we had. I mean, it really was amazing. I had the most fun that I've had in a long time. Friends came from far away, we ate, we sang the Thanksgiving song, we played music, we played games like Mafia and Grand Pooba, Chinua did card tricks, and the guys made a sweat lodge.

Yesterday I stopped along the way to visit with my friend who got really hurt in a motorcycle accident. He's in the hospital, and it's so, so sad to see him there and in pain. He looked gray, like people in the hospital often do, and his eyes were shadowed and pain-filled.

168

He's going to get better. That's the amazing thing. He could have died.

It's crazy, how crumbly we are. There are so many casualties, all the time, like those deer who stepped onto a dark road, like people who fly off their motorcycles because some other person in a car made a bad choice. Something like seeing someone in so much pain really makes you think about casualties. Sometimes we are even casualties of our friendships, of careless words and the sediment of hurts. For me, seeing my friend in pain and his family working through it made me want to say, I'll be a better friend, I really will, to everyone I know. There are small things and there are big things, and I want to focus on the big things.

Don't get me wrong, the kitchen needs to be cleaned, but sometimes I need to look past the dishes. That's all.

december

December 8, 2006

When our community first moved to this Land, nine years ago, the large house that we call the Big House, which serves as our gathering place and office, was decorated entirely in pink. Over the years the pink has been replaced, and the last surviving pink things were the bathroom tiles that the previous owner used to tile the entire kitchen; floors, counter tops, windowsill, everything. As of this past weekend, they are there no more. The kitchen hasn't been used for years, but we're renovating it to make a working kitchen.

No one is sad to see those pink tiles go. No one is even the least bit nostalgic. I tend to be a pretty nostalgic girl, certain smells can make me collapse into bits of memory- unlikely things, too, like the smell of sewage when you are walking by a sewer opening in the city and it wafts out at you, because of how it reminds me of Bangkok, or the smell of smoke from fires because of how it reminds me of the burning cow dung in India— but even I do not feel as though I will ever miss those pink tiles.

We are fighting a battle here, at the Land. Sometimes it feels as though it is a gigantic burden: *What will break next?* we wonder, with trepidation. For example, in one of the cabins the electricity recently went out. Just disappeared. We don't know why. And the wiring around here was all done a long time ago, perhaps before I was born. Electricians often refuse to come somewhere that is so remote. It's a quandary with no apparent solution. And this is just one example. Don't even get me started on the plumbing. Or our largest building, which appears to be listing to one side, has a leaking roof, and has one wall that is folding in. Forced to evacuate, we'll most likely end up tearing it down, making something new.

But still I feel that we will do this. One step at a time we will fix this Land up, we will have our garden going, we will make our buildings warm. We will get rid of the broken pink tiles and this will symbolize a new way of doing things. It's just slow, that's all. We've inherited a bit of a beast in the form of a gorgeous, tree-filled, river-bordering, green fairyland.

We're here to be a family to those who need a family. One guy who is living with us right now told me that *this feels like the first home he's ever had.* Surely it's worth the work to be that. Every family has maintenance, everybody has their stuff, everybody chooses to put effort into something. For us right now it's this sprawling piece of paradise, this broken down resort that is an unlikely place to find a family. Yet people still find a family here. I do.

December 11, 2006

On Saturday I woke up sick. It was a strange sickness, with no symptoms, really, other than the loss of the will to live, a sore throat, swollen glands, aches, and extra sensitive skin. I'm sure that other people must have extra sensitive skin when they get sick. Chinua thinks that I have some sort of strange neurosis about my skin, but I'm sure I don't.

On Sunday I woke up feeling a lot better, but still under the weather. We had plans to be out for the whole day, leaving at 9:30 in the morning and getting back at around 10:00 at night. One thing that I don't really like about my mind is that my rational self never quite catches up to my emotional self. So my emotional self is lying on the floor throwing a tantrum and my rational self is sitting on her sofa, scratching her head and mildly saying, "I don't feel very well. I believe I'm overwhelmed and could really use a day off." I can't hear my rational self, through, because the tantrum-thrower is drowning her out. She's really loud. And crazy, she's crazy.

By now I know that this is what Superstar Husbands are for. While I was stomping around complaining about how sick I felt, mine asked me gently if I would rather stay home with the baby while he took the older kids with him. I couldn't decide whether I felt sad or happy about not going (probably because my emotional self was shouting in my ear that he was abandoning me and I couldn't hear my rational self stretching on the sofa and smiling while she said, "That's great, that'll be just the ticket,") but I decided to stay. And then they left.

It was perfect. For me, solitude is a way of getting out from under the microscope. One of the things that marriage and parenting has brought into my life is a magnified view of my flaws, a view that I just cannot get away from. As a perfectionist, I am sucker-punched in the gut with this view, though it is possibly the best thing for me. My life lesson is that it is not my effort that makes a difference. God through me can do something lovely, but my own tightly held breath and careful apologies won't even be able to begin. Every day that I am with my children, my impatience is held before

172

me like a new magazine. Every day my interactions with my Superstar Husband illuminate my anger and my deep insecurity. It's the best thing for me. I'm not sure that I would ever have known the depth of my need without these mirrors, short and tall, all around me. We have our own private funhouse over here.

But it is exhausting. And yesterday I was able to get out from under the microscope and drink some coffee, read a little, watch a movie, wash my floors. I played with my Leaf Baby, listened to a great talk on cultivating a healthy marriage (which was very inspiring and just what I needed) and sat, and thought, and got better.

Today I'm back where I need to be careful of my words, need to keep my attitudes in check, need to be kind and gentle and take care. I will try not to be self-conscious, though, try to look around at the other things swimming around in here, notice that lovely light, that cell, the pattern that the little hairs on the paramecium are making on the walls. And the amoebas! The amoebas are lovely under here.

December 12, 2006

Last night we were all up in the building that we currently cook and eat in, getting ready for dinner. I had walked up with the kids (I believe that it is about one and a half city blocks from my house to this building, if you could measure it in city blocks) and my Superstar Husband had stopped along the way to do something or other.

On his way into the building, he stopped at the window to make a scary roaring face at our kids, which they started to laugh at... except that at precisely the same moment, we lost power and were smothered by complete and total darkness. After that, there was

173

almost nothing we could do to convince them that Daddy hadn't made the power go out by scaring them. My kids hate complete darkness, and they started screaming almost immediately, while I tried to get over to them to hold them.

We scrounged around and found a couple of candles, then a big sack of tea-lights left over from a party. Renee had made lasagna and apple turnovers for dinner, and we ate happily, illuminated by dozens of tea-lights. It was dark, but pretty.

The silly thing is, I almost never went anywhere in the dark last year without my head lamp. Head lamps are an absolute necessity with us. There are patches of the Land that are very dark at night, and at a Rainbow Gathering you can't possibly get along without one. I LOVED my head lamp. But at the last gathering I loaned it to someone when I left, and when it was returned to me my poor head lamp looked like a horror film for gadgets, wires popping out, pieces missing. Someone did a bad thing to my light.

Silly me, I haven't replaced it. And Chinua didn't have his, either. So, the two of us were in the tight spot of trying to make it down to our house in fairly heavy rain, in complete darkness, with only three tea-lights to help us. We had two little kids and a baby in a stroller. It was not at all easy. We felt like we'd made it into some awkward slow motion movie. *Why is it so hard for us to get to our house right now?*

Crazy thing, sight. Without it, you keep veering into the bushes, heading for the pond rather than down the path. You step into an ankle-deep puddle that you'd normally avoid. Have you ever tried to walk by candlelight? It's not easy. The rain kept putting the candles out, so we'd quickly relight another one before they all went out and we were left there without any light.

We got home safely, got the fire blazing, and lit a bunch of candles. About an hour later, the power came back on. Kai saw some lights go on in my room, and said, "What? It's not possible!" as he ran to investigate. He was so serious about it, he had Chinua and I laughing ourselves into a fit.

Tomorrow, I'm going to buy a head lamp.

December 18, 2006

When I was nine or ten, I ran into a tree. I was running under its branches, chasing a kitten, but I didn't see the thick, broken off branch in front of my face. It slapped me and knocked me onto the ground, where I rolled around holding my swollen nose. The branch had come dangerously close to my eye, but I thought that I had escaped the incident relatively damage-free. However, it has always seemed that there is something... missing.

I've figured out what was damaged, that summer day. My shopping nerve.

I'm lacking, seriously lacking. I don't have the muscle, or nerve, or gene, or something, that other people seem to have when it comes to the ability to shop. This always plagues me, and I mean always, but it comes out most seriously at Christmas. I go into a store with the best of intentions, even a detailed list, and within a few moments of entering, my mind goes completely blank and I start to panic. I begin gibbering to whomever is with me about being afraid, and then the stress begins. Grocery shopping is not quite as terrible as shopping for clothes or presents, because it is more straightforward, but lately even grocery stores have me curled up on the floor, right beside the cucumbers.

Some people appear to enjoy shopping. I don't understand this. I really do think that my problems began with that one maple tree that had it out for me.

December 20, 2006

It's like a candy-making house of horrors around here. I made an ugly batch of fudge two days ago, then yesterday my second try turned into something that can only be used as hot fudge. And it's true, it still tastes good, but failing once is bad enough for me, failing twice is pretty much the end of the world. It has me wondering whether I'm just not good at this. This whole Christmas thing. I mean, I love Jesus, and I can identify with Mary, (about the having a baby part) and I am all about celebration, but I can't see how to pull the rest of it together. And then that has me wondering about whether I'm just not good at this whole mom thing. Do all moms do well at Christmas? From my standpoint (which may be warped, it's true) it seems as though they've all got it under control. But maybe that's the beauty of childhood. All you see are the pretty lights, not the crying in the bathroom over the ruined fudge.

I think I have PMS. Or something.

But back to the fudge. I learned to make it in an old-fashioned girl-to-girl recipe way. My dear friend Amelia taught me to make it, with phrases like this:

"Wash the chocolate with the milk, to get it to melt into it smoothly. *Wash* it."

"Add the sugar and then a glop of Karo. No, not a glop like *this*, a glop like *that*. Just a glop."

"Cook until it's at soft ball stage."

"Place a stick of butter in it, and a splash of vanilla, and then cool it until you can stick your finger in and there is no *impinging*

176

heat." (This is usually the point when we start dipping the pecans in it and eating them.)

"Stir the pecans in and keep stirring until it begins to lose the gloss. This is when you put it in the tins, when it will stack up."

Amelia is also famous for giving directions like, "Shake hands with the turkey. Can you shake hands with the turkey? Good. Then it's done," and "add just enough cream to my coffee to see it bounce back from the bottom.

Last year we made fudge together at her house in San Francisco, drank tea, went out for sushi while it was cooling, and then watched Project Runway after. I'm beginning to think that it's a good idea to plan on doing that, if I'm going to make fudge.

Yesterday I called her, distraught. "I'm sure there was no impinging heat, Amy! I'm positive."

"How firm was your soft ball?"

"Weeeelllll... it was a little melty."

"I don't think your ball was enough of a ball. You probably didn't cook it long enough. It's like chemistry, Rae."

Ugh.

january

What a wonderful way to ring in the New Year, sick as soggy toast, not fulfilling a single one of the almost resolutions I had in my mind this year. Not a single one. It's a *great* start, can I have a start over? A reset? No? I didn't really write them down or anything, but they were a jumbled mess of jogging, getting up early, reading and meditating on the Bible, focusing more clearly on Kai's early homeschooling, working on my novel, and taking vitamins. I didn't do any of them. Not a single one.

It's actually good for me to start the year this way. It's like God saying to me, "Let's just put away any newly formed ideas about that whole Supermom thing to rest right away, shall we? Now that we have that out of the way, what do you want to do this year? I have some ideas."

I'm excited, when I stop standing over my own shoulder with a whip, to think of God's ideas for me this year. When I was younger, I used to think that those ideas would be mostly exciting things that included travel and people telling me that they didn't know what they'd do without me. I'm ashamed to admit it. Now, well, I don't know, but I think that his ideas are more about formation. More about tossing me ingredients and seeing what I'll make. Sometimes his hands work with mine, and what comes out is mostly his own creation, and sometimes I feel like I'm struggling along, messing it up. If it's clay, it comes out cracked and dry, and if it's food, the rice is overcooked and the beans are burnt and tasteless. But while I'm working on what I'm making, he's really forming *me*, which is the important thing. Am I making any sense?

Yesterday I felt like I was thrown a pretty big mess. We left to go to church and spend the day up in the college town north of us. When we woke up, though, my Superstar Husband looked at me with bleary, pleading eyes. He's been burning the candle at every end lately, and fighting the flu that I fell prey too, so I said, "I'll just go!" After some minor issues and a little fun stress-filled tearing around to get everything together, I was on my way with the three kids, and some friends; one visiting, and two friends who live here. About halfway through the day there was a crisis with the girl who came with us, someone who has been trying to get her life together here at the Land, someone I have really come to love in the last few months. At first it felt like something I couldn't handle, like too many ingredients to make anything that wouldn't be a huge mess, that wouldn't take hours to scrape off the ceiling. But then, I heard God's gentle voice urging me to jump in and try, and I did. And I found that a crisis like this brought total honesty, that maybe now I'll be able to help more than before, and then somehow we muddled through the day without anyone getting hurt or lost or too far gone. What emerged was a day of love and honesty, a day of softness with my kids, a day of working through hard things with friends.

I haven't been able to follow any routines this past week. My house has been rather messy, no matter my slow-witted attempts to clean it, and I haven't exercised. But I think I'm starting to see that this year is not going to be the year that I become the majorly sculpted and disciplined housewife, but more like the year that I learn a little more about how to listen. I've been tossed a family, and not only that, but a community, and sometimes I feel like I have nothing to offer, I haven't come out with enough arms to make something of this. I think God is still here, though, waiting to see what happens, offering a hand here and there. He's the one telling me that Yes, I can be kind to my children even when the house is messy and I woke up later than I wanted to. And most of all, he smiles at my efforts, gently taking that whip out of my hands, offering me a shoulder when I flop on the couch at night, exhausted. He urges me that I can be like a child, that this can be fun, even if it's not all travel, even if I'm not seamlessly saving the world. What a Guy. I guess that's mostly what I want this year, anyways. Just to be making stuff with God, in the kitchen, making bundt cake with the Lord.

January 10, 2007

Yesterday I fell in love with my Leaf baby a little more. I don't know why there are some days like this, where you look up and recognize each other and one more brick slides into place; your understanding of each other is a little more whole, you find that your heart can really expand just a little more. I never cease to wonder at the bonding experience with babies. Now Leaf says, "Hey!" to me when I come back into the house if I've been gone, and his expression is entirely welcoming, and I think I need that kind of

180

welcome in my life. No one gives it like a baby, so pure and open.

*

The other day, the crisis that I spoke of got worse. It involved drug use, and the girl in trouble had to be taken to the Emergency Room on Monday night. Everything is okay now, and I think we're at the beginning of a long journey of working through a lot of emotional brokenness with this person, the kind of brokenness that would have her on a binge, totally out of the blue. I still feel so scattered. While Chinua was putting the kids to bed on Monday night, I was trying to break into someone's psychedelic madness and bring sanity. Renee and I tried to help for three hours, until we had to give it up and put it into the hands of doctors more capable than us. We had three hours of trying to communicate with someone who is not in the same world, mentally. Three hours of trying to convince someone not to walk around blindfolded, literally, not figuratively. Three hours of crying on and off, of witnessing heartbreak. And then after we had given it up, after we decided that all that could be done was to take our friend to the E.R., where doctors could give her sleep medication so she could sleep it off, to come back to my cabin and find Kai in the bathroom, asking me to wipe his bum. Suddenly, bum-wiping seemed so normal, so sane.

I'm rambling a lot, I know. I'm trying to make some sense out of this. I've seen a lot of really really hurt people who do things to sabotage good in their lives. And now here I am, with my community in the woods, and I bathe children, I send out tax receipts, I dive into madness, and I fold laundry. I work to keep my house peaceful, and then God asks me to leave that peace and help a person who is without peace, someone who is tormented. It has

181

happened again and again over the years, and it always makes me feel like there are two of me. Different women to do different things. The noise of quarreling kids is a kind of peace, compared to the roar of cold brutality from lies, from madness.

Maybe there are a lot of different parts of me. There is the woman who washes dishes, and there is the woman who wants to write a novel, and there is the woman who says, "take off that blindfold, right now." And this is okay, and I am here to do this, to raise children and affirm them, and to help hurt people. Maybe we are all here for this, in different ways. It is no small thing, to move from one world to another. The bridge is not easy.

January 15, 2007

Last week I may have mentioned something to the world at large about how my Saturdays are absolutely, for-surely, positively going to be restful. I'm just not having it anymore, I said. I need to rest. Can't go go go like this. Dude, I believe in the whole Sabbath thing, day of rest and all. Not legalistically, but it's a good way to live.

Sometimes it's just not up to me, though. For instance, this Saturday, the one that I was so intense about, went something like this:

By 9:00 AM, I had already called poison control because Kai had a moment of out of control sugar craving while he was supposed to be going to the bathroom, climbed up on the toilet seat, opened the childproof bottle of children's ibuprofen, and drank the whole thing. Tom the poison control man was calm on the phone, but I suspect he's always calm. I wondered if they hired him because of his soothing voice. He assured me that Kai would probably be fine, but that I should be listening for any complaints of a sore tummy. "Just don't suggest it to him," he advised, "the idea of a sore tummy."

Kai was fine. Aside from a massive, enormous sugar high.

By 9:30 a new friend had shown up (this was the high point of the day) to do some volunteer electrical work on one of our cabins. He ended up fixing the problem, which was that the entire cabin had inexplicably lost power. By inexplicably, I mean that there is no explanation other than our massively jury-rigged electrical situation here, which includes the fact that the power lines are stapled into trees that have grown around them in a loving embrace. The electrical system here pre-dates us, probably by a hundred years or so. It was probably brought here on the Pony Express, which, other than the fact that the technology wasn't available then, is quite possible, since one of our buildings used to be a stop on the Pony Express.

Our new friend fixed our problem for the time being, which was wonderful, but doesn't nullify the fact that the entire time he was here talking to me about work stuff, Kai was tearing around the house like a three foot tall Doberman Pincher. "Sugar high," I explained, rolling my eyes and shrugging.

By 10:30 I was talking to a fellow community member about what kind of intervention we should have with the troubled girl who is living here.

By 11:00 I had decided to take my poor, poor husband to the hospital. Chinua has been sick in bed since last Tuesday, feverish and delirious many times over. On the fourth consecutive day of fever and chills we decided to pack up the fam and take him to Urgent Care.

By 12:00 we were on our way.

By 1:55 I was tearing into the only pharmacy in town, which closes at 2:00 in the afternoon on a Saturday, and arguing with the pharmacist's assistant over whether my insurance covered the antibiotics for Chinua's strep throat.

By 2:45 I was in the midst of the aforementioned intervention. Think drama, pain, and frustration. And grace, lots and lots.

By 4:00 I was taking a break in an effort to get Kenya in bed for a nap. And by 4:30 I was giving up on an afternoon nap for either of my older kids.

And blah, blah, blahdee blah blah. Sorry for the boring details. I ended up talking with the girl for awhile, talking to about twenty people on the phone, asking for advice, making dinner, and all the other stuff, until:

At 8:30 I absolutely insisted on reading a book and doing nothing else until it was time for me to sleep.

So, I did get some time of rest after all. Thank God. It's funny, and I'm not really giving up, because I know these things come in seasons. Sometimes it is so quiet, and everything goes so smoothly that you look around and wonder what happened, where the turmoil went, why the river is so still. And sometimes all your reserves are called out, and all that peace can serve a purpose.

January 26, 2007

I'm showing up here right now with nothing good. I've been consumed in office work that sucks all my energy right out of me, I feel low, rejected, sad, and anxious. Let down, hanging around... oh wait, did I just step into a Radiohead song? I haven't been posting all that much because I found myself counting how many poopy diapers I had changed and how many loads of laundry I had washed, and I was writing it all down when I got sick of myself and deleted it, all of it, all my numbers and charts and adding things up.

Nothing adds up. I'm learning that I should just stay away from numbers. They don't feed me. What does?

My wood stove. It's purty. And warm.

A big heavy four-year-old boy agreeing with me when I tell him it's cuddle time after he's had a grumpy morning. I could sit with his head under my chin all day. I always marvel at the large skull that has grown from the tiny fragile head he was born with. Not to mention the long legs from those little bowed bird legs.

My Leaf Baby. He tries to make me laugh and he always succeeds.

Collecting stones from the beach.

A beautiful painting/song/poem.

BEAUTY. Oh I need it. In me, around me. Lately I've been rebelling, feeling like such a cleaning lady. I know it's all to the end of creating a beautiful space for my family, but does it have to be so repetitive? Does it have to feel so futile? Or how about other areas in life? Does loving people have to feel so one-sided? Can we get a little rain? Oh, here I am, complaining.

I'll write again tomorrow, maybe the morning will shake some of this out of me. I have things to tell you, I do.

Now I prefer to stew in my misery.

January 28, 2007

Today I flew to Chicago in a sea of pink-tipped clouds, by myself, happy and sad at the same time. I know I should relish every drop of solitude that I can get to trickle out of the bottom of the cup, but one of the paradoxes of being a mother, I've found, is that you desperately need alone time, but desperately miss your kids when you get it. Motherhood is a life vocation, comparable to nothing else, because it is a type of work that is encompassed by love and worry, a type of work that can never be banished from your mind. Sometimes I feel that I will never relax again. Talking this week with another mother friend whose children are adults, I realized that the fears with small children over choking and sickness are replaced with other fears as time goes on.

All to say that I have to learn to trust God more.

And despite saying this, I will not deny that there was a complete ease about checking in for my flight today, a simplicity that was precious, like water in the desert, despite being picked "randomly" (as always) for a special extra security check, and despite having my cream-top yogurt and Mango and Antioxidants drink taken away from me. *Flying has become like paying to be arrested*, I thought, as I was standing in a machine that blew air at me to make sure that I didn't have any hidden weapons or drugs on my person. I can't believe they took my yogurt away. When our kids are grown up we'll be telling them, "I remember the days when they gave us food on the airplane and- oh yes, the days when we were allowed to wear our own clothing, now we have to wear specially manufactured uniforms." It's funny, though, flying without my kids. It's not as if they aren't completely well-behaved in an airport-they're great-it's just that it takes so little effort to move my own gangly body through the line, down the hallway, into the seat. It's amazing. It's nothing like the effort it takes me to wrestle little people into car seats, just to go to the store. And yet every so often I found myself peeking up over the seats at the kids sitting three rows down because aren't they magical? Kids are just the most amazing small creatures, and even when I'm exhausted and finally alone, I'm watching someone else's kids, missing Kenya's hand on my cheek.

I sat on the airplane and read my new book, *"Freddy and*

Fredericka" by Mark Helprin, which so far I am delighted with, and looked out the window. My mind allowed me to have a little glimpse of pure observation, and as we were heading up above the clouds, I thought, *I can't believe I can fly.* Really, we can be above the clouds, looking down at the mountains around Tahoe, catching sight of a frozen lake, marveling at a seemingly endless view of farms in a perfect grid, an ocean of clouds, the sun setting over Lake Michigan. We can FLY. I can be in Chicago, coming from San Francisco, in four hours.

This trip was a sudden decision, and was the only response I could think of giving to a friend's deep hurt and crisis. *I should just go and be there,* I thought, and not surprisingly, Chinua said it before I did. I'll only be gone a few days, and a friend helped with part of the ticket. This is what I love about a community that stretches across the country, that we can say, "I'm here," even when we can't be there all the time, that we can imperfectly love each other. It's got to mean *something,* this stumbling love we share. God has not given us any small task in commanding us to love him and love one another, but the gifts he gives are more than enough to make it happen.

I love the friend that I am traveling to see. She has amazed me so many times, and I think she is still like an unlocked door. We have barely seen the beginnings of the beauty that will come from within her. And she is hurt, and all I can do is say, *"I'll come over."* It feels so small. I begin to wonder, lately, in the midst of so many crises, what it takes to get through.

It's kind of like flying, I think. Everybody thinks you have weapons in your toothpaste, and they take away your yogurt and your lip balm, you have to be in this climate-controlled chamber in order to survive, and it's not exactly effortless, but we're *flying.* It's a miracle. We're getting there.

february

February 6, 2007

Yesterday I fell apart. Limbs were dropping hither and thither, it was crazy. I still haven't found my right arm.

Why are women like waves? Why the drama? My Superstar Husband can cruise along for months without the slightest bit of drama, his emotional path is a solid line to the horizon. I don't understand the point of my ups and downs. As soon as I even think that I'm in the clear, BAM, I'm knocked down by the sheer intensity of my discouragement. The huge and pervasive piece of logic in my head is, "I don't think I can do this." And so, I fall apart.

Because who wants to spend their life doing something they'll never succeed at? Doesn't this seem like the ultimate road to insanity? And this is what gets me, this voice in my head throughout my day that tells me I'm not doing anything at the standard that I want. I think the problem might be my *standards*, as well as that stupid voice. (Shut UP, voice!)

A good thing about these waves is that I am forced to take stock. Often I am speeding along in my little path, not noticing all of the bad information that clings to me like barnacles. It's time for some picking off of the barnacles. I realize that I begin to measure everything with a little measuring stick, how clean my house is, how much work I get done in a day, and then when things crash in on me I look at my stick with new eyes and I'm amazed by this stick. Where did I find it? How did it make its way into my hand? What does this flipping stick have to do with dreams anyways?

Because dreams are very important, and dreams are not standards that crush you. I think the Bible is full of dreams, although it is often used as a stick. I believe that a lot of people are afraid of something as beautiful as these holy words because they're using them as another stick in their lives, and let me tell you people, they will never measure up. And thus, we are afraid of living our whole lives through, never being the thing we are trying to be. Insanity.

Last night I had my first flying dream ever. I think that it was the glimmer that started the thoughts behind this post, because although I've heard of people talking about dreams of flying, I have never actually flown. In my dream I was walking and suddenly the horizon dropped beneath me and at first I had no idea about what was going on. But I was flying, and I've never had such a wonderful dream. Never. During the rest of it, I was trying to show other people that I could fly. And there we were, trudging along our own dusty paths until we were lifted suddenly above it all.

I think that this another way to look at the Bible. Here I am, walking on this dirty road and I read some words, words something like these: "Do nothing from rivalry or conceit, but in humility count others as more significant than yourselves,"* and these words are like my feet being lifted from under me, like that rush of air on my face. Do you see how they are dreams of a different world? How

191

beautiful, a place where we generously bestow significance on one another rather than clinging to it for ourselves. Where we are never rivals. If I make these words into a measuring stick which I beat myself with, I lose the dream, the one which will ultimately change me. These words *lift* me, rather than popping me on the head and forcing me back down.

When we dream, we walk into large fields where anything is possible. Where a world without rivalry or conceit in our hearts exists. This is at the heart of meditation, I believe. We lift our eyes from what we are, we drop the stick, and we dream true dreams of what we actually desire, which is real love, real beauty, and this we find in God. It is a very restful thing to realize that all of the things we so desperately want are found in one Being. There is a place where these dreams are true, which is why we aren't stupid for still dreaming.

This morning, trying to pick myself back up from yesterday's mud, I wrote for a while in my journal trying to work a new pattern of thinking into my brain, and this is a little of what I wrote.

Today is a day when I can be meditative instead of frantic, rhythmic instead of chaotic, positive instead of negative, loving instead of resentful, and a wise child instead of an immature adult. Today is a day in the forest, a day of sweet breezes, a day of clean laundry. Today is a day to settle accounts, to make things balance, to check a few things off of my list. Today is a day to laugh with my kids, to notice them, to call their beauty out. Today is a day to knit with my friends, to listen to words of wisdom, to make bridges between our hearts. Today is a day to reach out, and a day to rest in near silence. Today anything can happen.

It's another way of listing out the things I need to do, my

192

routines, my cleaning, my office work, taking care of my children. I could make a list like a slave driver, and forget the holy ground that I stand on, but I don't want to live that way anymore. Unfortunately I need to be reminded ten thousand times that it doesn't work.

Another way to say what I wrote might be, "Be at rest once more, O my soul, for the Lord has been good to you."

Philippians 2:3

February 9, 2007

<u>I Am</u>

I am five feet eleven inches of vertical space, taller than most women but shorter than most trees. I am the woman who said "okay" when her husband proposed, and then laughed, the one who threw sand on the beach in joy, the woman across from my man at the fire, glowing with our secret future. I am wanted, I am captured, I am wearing white under a large tree on a sunny day beside a green lake, saying "Yes."

I am bare feet among jelly fish in clear warm waters, longing eyes reaching off the back of a rumbling train, watching the giant red sun in an Indian field, shoulders swaying on the back of an elephant, a camel, a rickshaw. I am lost in the Himalayas, walking all day until my feet are raw and I fear we will never be found. I am limp in the heat of a warm Thai rain, waiting for a bowl of noodles on the side of the road. I am standing under a waterfall, I am watching the stars in the desert. I am incense, I am smoke, I am jasmine scented air. I am tossed around the earth like ashes, little pieces of me lost in places I will not see again soon.

I am shared space; it will always be written in my heart that three other people have resided with me for a time, in my own space, the warmth of my body which has grown and nurtured three young wild things, given to me but not mine. I am a mother, needed in every waking moment, my hands are always touching a person needing to be touched. I am the midnight hours, I am giving water, cleaning sick children, going without sleep. I am panicked, not knowing whether I can do this again, night after night. I am doing it. I am chapped hands from washing dishes, bent over picking up toys, breaking up quarrels, I am exhaustion, I am dull from repetition, I am safe, I am blessed.

I am the quiet space between night and morning, opening up the day with a cup of coffee and a pen. I am paint thrown onto a canvas, words wept onto a page, I am always longing, always seeking. I am a camera, I am oils, acrylics, charcoal. I am dancing while I paint, I have never felt so free. I am lonely, I am afraid, I am sad and away from my easel too often.

I am the young child who read for hours, the woman who sneaks a few chapters between lunch and nap time, the girl who told her brother and sister to "Go away, I'm reading." I am a loner surrounded by friends, I am helping, I am wanting to make you happy. I am stormy, emotional, I am too many words when I should be quiet, I am apologies.

I am from a proud gentle northern country, I am a girl who knows black ice and windchill well, chapped hands and lips and frozen toes, who knows Northern Lights and loons on lakes and prairies and forests with great wide space.

I am cupped hands, I am tossed like a flower, a well trodden street, I am known. I am hopeful, I am not alone, I am written on the palms of the hands of God, I am adopted, I am not afraid. I am loved.

Sometimes when life has become a little humdrum (remember that I am addicted to excitement) and things are just SO routine and SO repetitive, one of my kids will come into a season that is just like clouds moving away from the sun and we are all blasted with sparkling light.

This is where Kenya is lately, and I want to record every moment of her existence, I want to write down every single thing she says. She's almost three, my baby girl, and somehow in the last couple of months she stepped into the spotlight, she grew up a bit, she came into her own.

Now she says she loves everything. Yesterday when I was getting her ready for bed she wriggled all over with a happy smile and said, "I LOVE it."

"What do you love?"

"My pull-up."

Kai told me today that when they go to the river she says she LOVES the river, and when we eat chips and salsa she says she LOVES chips and salsa. She has entered the world of her very vivid imagination and naps are no longer any problem (they rarely were to begin with) because she will lie in her bed and make her dollies talk to each other until she falls asleep. This is a typical conversation between her dollies. (Everything is "super" in our house. The babies are super-babies, the dollies are super-dollies, the kids have a super-cat and a super-horse and a super-monkey, and when they wake up they are super-dooper hungry. So hungry that they fall on the ground and claw at my ankles.)

Super-dolly # 1: I love you and love you and love you.

Super-dolly # 2: You're the good girl in the world.

As a result of Kenya's Uncle Matty calling her the cutest girl in the world every day that he sees her, Kenya uses the term "in the world" a lot, although she is a little shaky on how to use it. It doesn't stop her, though, and I don't stop her either, because I like to hear her say it the way she does. I figure she'll get it soon enough.

"I love you in the world." "You're the good one in the world." "It's big in the world."

Sometimes it is very, very rewarding to be this mama in this family.

February 16, 2007

My thoughts are like clouds, driven by a stiff wind.

1. I love to sit and drink an Americano with two shots of espresso.

2. I'm so glad that Elena bought me that little espresso machine. She's prescient like that. Probably knew I'd be using it everyday.

3. The sky is so pretty today.

4. I want to knit myself a sweater with a hood that's big enough to fit over my gigantic head (actually my head's not that big, it's just that my neck is so long) and some socks, and a shawl, and some slippers and everyone I know linen hand towels and cotton dishcloths and soft wool blankets.

5. How long will that take me?

6. I want to write about something kind of intense, but I don't want everyone to feel sorry for me or have sympathy for me.

7. I want everyone to feel sorry for me and have sympathy for me.

8. No I don't.

9. Shoot, that Leaf Baby is cute.

10. I want a burrito.

11. My friend Devon looks so pretty with her new hair color. I wonder if I should dye my hair? Maybe black?

12. Black is a bad idea.

13. I want some stuffed pizza like we had on my last day in Chicago.

14. I hate that a lot of my friends live far away from me.

15. This coffee is really good.

16. I'm proud of myself for writing over 6000 words in the third first draft of my novel this week.

17. My novel sucks.

18. No it doesn't. I love my novel. It's my fourth child.

19. Okay, so the kind of intense thing is this: I've lived in community since I was eighteen years old, which is eight years, for those of you who don't want to do the math. It's all of my adult life. I've never really lived any other way. And when I started out, I had a lot of ideals. I was really starry eyed and intense about loving one another and looking out for each other and considering others before ourselves. And then, over the years, I began to get slightly jaded. And as people wandered in and out of my life, I started to more often have my arms crossed over my chest, to protect myself. And then I started to think things like I'd better look out for myself, because no one else will. And actually, even I can't look out for myself, so I guess no one is. And then I even thought things like I can't tell anyone how I really feel inside. And that turned into I'd rather kill myself than feel like I do. And then, there's no way out. And then something broke, and I started to talk to people more, and my fists unclenched a little, and life looked a little more beautiful, and I started to notice wildflowers again and to feel happy when I was hanging out with my friends, rather than alone. And thoughts of death didn't come so suddenly, and I began to take pleasure in my kids, and the forest was healing to me.

And yet. There are always new corners to be turned, and I have gradually realized that I still have my arms crossed over my chest, and I have completely missed the point, somehow. To put it very practically, I spend very little time wondering how I can turn someone else's day from a speck on the calendar to a brilliant spark on their path. You know, the special things. Above and beyond. I spend my time playing out my role in the community, defending myself and my commitment, doing the office work that I tolerate. But what about life on the mountain? What about washing other people's tired feet, dammit? What about encouraging others, even at my own expense?

I've learned a lot of simple things in taking care of myself when I'm feeling depressed. Remember my rules? 1. Wash your face and brush your teeth. 2. Eat at every mealtime. 3. Sleep at night. I've expanded these to include, 4. Take breaks throughout the day. 5. Write everyday. 6. Get on the floor and play with your kids. And there's more.

But life can't only be reduced only to these things. I had a realization this week that I've begun to think of a community as a place where we co-habitate, rather than a living journey, a walk together where we strengthen each other along the way. And not only that, but have I begun to think of my marriage this way? I've done so many things that are unintentionally hurtful to my husband over the years that I'm surprised, in a way, that he still looks at me with hope.

I have a little sermon that I give about condemnation versus conviction. Condemnation comes from the enemy of our souls and leaves you gasping in the creek bed, wondering whether you should just lie at the bottom until you drown. Conviction takes you to the edge of a vast ocean and shows you a new way to be. It hurts, sometimes, to realize you've been stuck on the land when you could have been sailing, but the beauty of the ocean soothes you and draws you to itself. And that's where I am, I'm not lost in this, I'm afloat, God is beside me. The sky is pleasant and I have years ahead to try again.

But I feel like I need to apologize, to any of you reading who have been a part of my community. I'm sorry. I forgot how beautiful it could be. I don't even know if I'll be able to do any better right now. The old defenses come up so quickly. But I can try.

20. That was hard to write.

21. I like the music that's playing in this café.

22. I need to download some Otis Redding.

23. This coffee is really good.

February 20, 2007

There is no greater happiness than a Saturday afternoon, after I've put my younger two in bed for a nap and I sit on my little couch with a cup of tea and read, or write, or lately, knit. Oh happiness. On weekdays I am very, very busy. As soon as my little ones are napping I am rushing around doing various office work and administrative blahdee blah blah, and I think that the idea of the impending week kills me on Mondays.

But, I can write again, because it's Tuesday and I am not paralyzed with fear and dread anymore, so I can write my way out of it. Like, I can tell you how I'm going to start calling chores "meditations." We will not use that word, chores, anymore. "I'm getting up from the table now, because I have to do the dish meditations," or, "I can't come out and play just yet, I have to do some meditations." Plural like that, because I think it sounds cuter.

I'm not talking about in a lofty, detached way of doing things, but more a trippy, "dude, this soap is really sudsy and it feels soft on my hands" way. You know, noticing. Marveling. Like a kid who loves to use the vacuum because it's so cool.

Think about the way it feels to bathe your newborn for the very first time. You hold them so gingerly, you are a little scared of all this water near their little open nostrils. They are tiny and bird-like and they might cry, if they are like Kai, or smile, if they are like Kenya. But you are so reverent. Then think about the way you bathe your little kids now (maybe this is just me) as you dump a cup of water over their heads and hurriedly wash their hair. You're thinking, "Didn't we just DO this?" I'm saying that I want to bathe my baby slowly, marveling over his toes and how they look more and more like his dad's, aware of the water, my baby's skin, and how intricately he has been formed, what a miracle he is.

So, there you go. I'm just writing over my reluctance to do things I consider mundane (like make the bed for the sixteen thousandth flipping time in my life) trying to tattoo my hands with the words: slow down, be thankful, consider, and above all: give a sacrifice of praise.

February 21, 2007

Today I am getting ready to go visit with my Grandparents, and have to skip off to the office now (on the other side of the Land) to play with numbers (like a child, right?) and documents and endless sheets of paper, so I want to quote something that I find to be very profound.

When I thought, "My foot slips," your steadfast love, O Lord, held me up.

When the cares of my heart are many, your consolations cheer my soul.
Psalm 94 verses 18,19

How many of us have thought, "I'm slipping," and have looked around wildly, trying to find a firm place? I have, I know, many times, only to find that I'm not, really, because steadfast love is holding me up, is holding me together. And how many times have wild anxieties threatened to overwhelm us, only to be answered by the consolations of a gentle Father?

May today find you delighting in your meditations and your consolations.

Update: Later as I was thinking of this again, I remembered a day when Chinua and I sat in a hot little room on an Indian island, trying to write a song with these words in it. I had my little Indian violin, and he had his guitar, and we were stuffed full of papaya, trying to keep cool under the fan. Even back then, maybe six years ago, I loved this verse, and these words spoke to me. I think it was because I can always look back at times in my life and realize: I thought I was slipping, thought I was about to go off the edge, but God's unshakable love always supported me. Even when I couldn't see it.

February 26, 2007

Over the weekend I became convinced that I can't write. What a crazy girl I was to think I could! I've been fooling myself all this time. It made me very, very sad to know this. I reacted by going into town on Saturday, drinking an Americano with a double shot of espresso too late in the day and then sitting in my van, while the rain poured down all around me. I sat there reading a book until the sun started to go down and the light got too dim. Then I turned on my dome light and read some more, until it was really, really dark. Finally I shook myself, bought some groceries, and on the way home I listened to the same two Innocence Mission songs over and over again. Remember that I live half an hour away from town, so they repeated about a thousand times. When I got home I told my husband all about it, about how I can't write! I'll never live my dream! What a sad reality, to want something so badly and never have it! What kind of a cruel joke is this?!

Are you kind of understanding what he has to live with?

Then, yesterday, I was reminded again that I said I would try. And I will. I'll come back and try to make a safe place for myself, from myself, and face a blank page, and write mud that can hopefully be turned into something as radiant as dragonfly wings by the time I'm on the eighth or ninth draft. Just like I'll keep trying to be even slightly graceful as I stomp and stumble around the floor in my West African Dance class tonight. And I'll keep turning out these hand-knitted dishcloths until I'm good enough to make myself the hooded sweater that I've always wanted, with a hood big enough to fit on my head above my long neck.

*

Last week I was able to spend time with my grandparents, two incredible people who have been married to one another for almost sixty years. Sixty years! Not only that, but they've been working together in their store every day until just two months ago, when they finally retired. My grandpa is seventy-nine.

What I really love to see, when we're together, is how they sing together while they wash dishes and clean up. Maybe Chinua and I should try that, rather than throwing water in each other's faces and dishcloths at one another's heads. You never know, we might get more done.

march

March 1, 2007

I came up with a new motto for life on the roller coaster. Are you ready? It's "Give it a year." It works like this:

"I'm totally depressed about how this book is coming along. I think my dialogue is stilted and it sounds like I'm in the second grade."

Give it a year.

"I am the worst dancer in my class. I look like a geranium with epilepsy."

Give it a year.

"I'm trying to be more organized, but my house still looks like my housekeeper is a potato. Where is my wallet? I can't find my keys."

Give it a year.

And what it means is to keep trying and not even think about quitting for a year. Wake up and write, go to dance class every week, try to organize. Because I am an insta-quitter. You're probably going to hear about all of this until you're sick of it, but I'm trying to tie myself into getting over certain aspects of my personality that have kept me from doing things I want to do for a long time.

I discovered something over the last dark, snow covered, powerless week: I love electricity! I LOVE IT. What? The power was only out for about 28 hours? Well, it felt like a week. Especially when, during one long, power-lacking night, the kids woke up three times shrieking their little hearts out because the candle had gone out in their rooms. My two older kids have complete darkness in the "top three most terrifying things that could ever possibly happen" list that they carry around with them. The way they scream, you'd think that they woke up falling out of a tree, rather than just in a lack of light, and if there was ever a heart attack waiting to happen, it's being awakened, three times in one night, by ear splitting screams.

But, yes, I love power. I love lights, I love my computer, I love music, I love refrigerators. I'd make a lousy pioneer, although there are times when I willingly leave my world of light and microchips to go into the woods and sleep in a tent and cook over a fire. But it's one thing to sit around a fire in the dirt, drinking chai and singing along with my Superstar Husband with the guitar, all without power; it's another to sit in my house staring at the fridge, willing it to start working so that I don't have to throw my milk out.

On another note, the snow falling yesterday morning was very, very pretty. Like pieces of ash, huge and light and drifting over moss and trees. Our wood stove bravely fought the cold, and we sat inside watching with wide eyes as our rare, once yearly, snowfall made a light dusting over the forest, at least until the sun won out and it all went away. We are blessed.

March 5, 2007

So, I think we've figured out a solution to the little writing-time crisis that has been going on around here. We've tweaked the schedule a little here, a little there, and I think it's all going to work out. My friend Evan told me a long time ago that life with little kids is all about pinching a bit of time from this part of the day and sticking it on over on that part of the day. He said that while his kids were young they were just constantly tweaking their schedule, trying to make it work better, working in circles. I'm glad he told me that, because he's a pretty wise person, and I feel justified in our endless efforts to make ours work better.

My schedule feels a little nuts to me at times. In hours, I have what is the equivalent of a part time office job, but no childcare. In gray hairs (in the making) and effort and sweat and tears, the equivalent of much more than a part time job—but never mind. So, I run around fitting my work in between nap times and non-nap times, and sometimes I just feel like I am not doing anything well. You might say I'm doing too much. I know my friend Dori did, when I called her exhausted and in tears one day, but it's hard not to at this juncture in life, which is why there is a need for frequent readjustment of the only 24 hours that we are given in a day.

But what else should I talk about? Maybe my nearly perfect Saturday? I puttered around my house, cleaning and folding laundry and cooking and taking breaks in between to read and to knit. In the afternoon, while the kids were napping, I escaped to the river with my knitting and my cup of tea and sat with the pretty green lady who has the most soothing voice. My friend Renee said to me later, not knowing that I had been there on that day too, "Don't you think the river is healing?" And it is, oh boy. There's just something about the smooth rush of it, watching the same shapes streaming over rocks and stones over and over again, and that beautiful sound.

It's second only to the ocean, and maybe even more accessible, you know? You can see to the other side.

But sitting down there, finishing my second dishcloth, drinking my PG Tips, marked a moment for me. It is the beginning of the season which contains a happy trip to the river almost every day, to sit and think, for now, to swim, later. It is the beginning of a season where the evenings will stretch to be longer and longer, when we can sit on our porches until late in the evening, when we can stop walking around all hunched over with cold. Oh, Spring! And Summer is on the way!

March 13, 2007

Under all of the little things and the big things in this last couple of weeks, there has been a constant stream of sadness in me, not without reason. I've done my normal things to overcome it, but today it feels as though I'm losing. And it's the kind that cripples my writing, that makes me want to hide when the phone rings, that makes me want to wear a t-shirt that says, "I don't want to talk about it." That's pretty good, actually, I think I may have that made.

So, all I have to offer is this: Kenya came out of her room yesterday, first thing in the morning, and walked over to where I was writing on the couch. Without further ado, she said, "Mama? Today can I choose Life?"

Talking about cereal, of course, but still. Mildly prophetic, no?

March 14, 2007

Streams of sadness or no streams of sadness, life does not stop for babies. I thought I should let you know a little about Leaf's busy day.

It's only the early afternoon, and already the Leaf Baby has:

-Played in Kenya's potty, after she peed without telling me and then left the door open.

-Stuck his finger in the rat cage and received a little nibble which I couldn't see but still made him cry. (I think this means he's going to turn into a Teenaged Mutant Ninja Turtle or something.)

-Opened a bag of barley and spilled the whole thing over the floor, after which he attempted to eat it-the raw barley that is, which set off a chain reaction of Barnum and Bailey worthy events when the kids decided to "help" me clean it up, and I let them, only to notice Kai swishing the barley into the living room (Space? How do you say that with an open plan?) with the broom and Kenya dumping the barley back out of the dustpan, at which point I took over, causing Kenya to dissolve into tears on my foot while Leaf was still trying to shove raw barley into his mouth, crying, because he didn't like the way it tasted.

-Dumped a whole cup of water on his face which was incredibly shocking to him. Kenya had left her cup of water on the edge of the table and Leaf is now the exact height that he needs to be to pull something like a cup of water towards himself and dump it on his own face, causing himself to sputter and then burst into tears.

-Taken his first steps in succession. He's taken one step before, but today I sat down with him and practiced and he found, to his delight, that he could walk to me.

March 20, 2007

I can't really explain what is going on with me right now, except that it is deep and swimmy and a little froggy. Does that help? I am encouraged and overwhelmed all at once.

Maybe I can just let you know some factoids. Sketch a little picture, so that you can put it together.

I drove some of my friends to the airport yesterday. We drove down to Sacramento on Saturday, then I dropped them off at the curb early Monday morning. It's the first step in their process of moving away from the Land, which makes me very sad. I'm happy for them, but sad for me. Yesterday, as I was sitting at another friend's cafe, my sadness punched me in the gut when she said, "this is good for them, hey"? and I laid my head on her bar counter and cried. I wanted to pull myself together, only there seemed to be nothing to pull together. Over the last two years I have lived through a slow attrition of a community that was tighter than anything I've ever been part of, (I'm being starkly honest here) and though we have hope of rebuilding, it is hard to say goodbye to people when you've seen each other married, give birth, walked through foreign corridors together...

I feel as though pieces of me are trickling away, as people move. I invested too much in my friends, I guess. I don't know how to grieve this properly, I waver between hope and belief and bitterness and a kind of flinging my hands around my head.

It is NOT all about me. I know. This is about a whole village, the movement and shape of a group of people who have grown and walked together, and I see God's shape in it. He is a great orchestrator, an author. Our stories continue. But, I feel hurt. I feel left alone, out here in the woods, where the trees are always tall, where light is green and golden, alternately. I go back and forth, reminding myself of all that I have to be thankful for, and then feeling forgotten and used up.

So. That is one thing.

Another? Well, I have these kids, see, and I know that you know that. But, boy. I love them to death, and I'm also feeling a little overwhelmed by how much they need me. An ebb, if you will. I know you understand.

I have also been encouraged by my friends, heroes of mine who have realized that part of their reason for being here is making choices that give to people around them. While I was in Sacramento, I had the privilege of meeting the new baby girl of some friends of mine. They've been waiting for her for awhile, having decided to adopt their third child, and she came home with them a little over a week ago. She's precious, like a rose, and it's lovely beyond words that they have found her and she has found them.

Another friend of mine has been building into her community for a while now, almost a year, through the ownership of a cafe in Sacramento which supports local businesses and economy. She's also the kind of friend that I would keep in my sleeves if I could, but alas.

Bits and pieces, I know. I guess to wrap up I would say that I see people moving in the kind of ways that are like shadow puppets on the wall, like the something more beautiful than they are. Adopting is beautiful, but there are still diapers. Running a cafe that refuses to make its money off of other people's suffering is heroic, but there are still those bills needing to be paid. What I'm saying, I guess, is that revolution is made of many sacrifices. All of those sacrifices together build something larger than themselves (is that called synergy?) and fling themselves into the face of a great and pervasive evil that broods across our culture, an evil of selfishness. It's the evil I face every day when I don't feel like taking care of others, when I want to sink into laziness. If a battle is going to be fought against injustice, it seems like it begins with the same motions that cause us to wake up in the middle of the night to take care of a sick child. Why do we do it? Because they mean so much to us, because they're our family.

I think we need to expand our family to include more of the world.

March 22, 2007

I'm still here, although I'm drowning in a pool of my own self-pity, which disgusts me, and then that disgust for myself renders me useless. And then I start banging my head on the fridge again. And that doesn't help and it puts dents in my head, so I should probably stop it.

Yesterday Kenya managed to perform a feat that I didn't think was possible. She outdid even the time Kai forgot which way he needed to be facing in order to poop in the toilet. Chinua and I were talking and we could hear her in the background, sitting on the potty in the bathroom with the door slightly ajar, talking to herself about pooping. "You POOPED!" she was saying, in her "big" voice, a voice that is hilarious because of its big smallness. "That's so EXCITING! You're so GOOD! YAYYYYYYY. You pooped in your POTTY!" We laughed a little at her as we talked, so blissfully unaware of the horror that was about to display itself to us. She hadn't called for me to come and help her yet, so I just waited, continuing to talk with Chinua. And then she started crying and we ran to the door and!!!!

She had tried to pick up her potty to empty it, I guess, and then decided to set it back down, only she tripped, and it was flung, it was flang, it was throwed, all over the wall! POO! ALL OVER the

WALL! And the floor and the trash can and just, well, everywhere.

I opened the door and then my heart failed me, I tell you the truth, I chickened out, and not quietly. And my Superstar Husband did the most heroic thing that I think he has ever done and cleaned it up. Oh, love. When your man cleans up the poop wall for you.

March 27, 2007

My parents were in ~~town~~ the woods for the weekend.

They arrived Friday just before noon, after driving down from Canada, which takes them around twenty-four driving hours. I, their unappreciative daughter, had decided to shop with the girls for the day anyway, figuring that food in the house was important when guests are around. Have I ever talked about our weekly shopping days? I can never remember if I'm being repetitive. Or if I'm being repetitive. Due to unseemly gas prices and the strain of eight hours of shopping with kids, four of which are spent in the car, we contrived a day during the week when the kids stay with the dads and the girls shop. It's great, we all look forward to it and we save on gas and fuel emissions, and we all drink a lot of coffee and run into bathrooms a lot. Sometimes we spend two hours in a thrift shop, or an hour in a yarn shop, only to race through the rest of our shopping. Sometimes we have fun and laugh all day. Sometimes we get hit on by men driving by, while we're walking down the street ("So much beauty on one CORNER!") which we attribute to absent husbands and kids. (Renee loves the shopping days because she's single, and she rarely gets us girls to herself. I have to say that Renee is pretty much the most perfect friend a mother could have. She's fun and great with kids, but LOVES to do girly non-mommish stuff. I don't know that I could say that I'm the best friend a single girl

212

could have. I wish.) And then sometimes we are grumpy and we snarl at each other and apologize too much and I flounce around like my fourteen-year-old pouty self. She's still lingering in there, not having entirely grown up.

On Friday we were having a good day, although it was our first Friday shopping day without Candace, something that made us all sad. But I did phone Chinua's phone about five times to find out whether my parents hated me for not being there when they arrived. I had hemmed and hawed and hooed about whether or not I should go, and the food issue tipped the scales, but later I feared that I had made a VERY BAD DECISION. And Chinua reassured me that, no, my parents didn't hate me, not at all, and then at one point my mom called and said, no they didn't hate me, silly girl, not at all. And slowly my anxiety began to ~~lift~~ retreat back to that place under my kidney where it lives and waits to pounce on me.

My parents are not haters. I have parents who are more loving than any parents I could ask for, more loving than I deserve. But I do have this crazy anxiety, see? And I remember that when I began this blog I wondered if it should be a chronicle of trying to overcome this anxiety, but then I thought, no, I'm made of more than the knot in my gut. And usually it's true, but lately (again) it is like it's all there is. Like where's the girl? Where'd the girl go? What's this clenched fist in her place?

I need to find a way to work this out. It is a thread that weaves in and out of my life, and HELLO! There's just too much going on for me to be climbing through obstacle courses all the time. I'm not sure what it is. But for as long as I can remember, my whole life maybe, there's been this turning away inside of me, a feeling of needing to escape many things because *that's* too much to handle, that will put me over the edge.

After freaking out all day Friday, though, I had a really great time with my parental unit. The kids had fun, too.

Yesterday we went to Santa Rosa, just for kicks, we thought, let's drive for a few hours to get to a bigger town. It ended up being really, really fun. Have I ever told you that my Superstar Husband is a little strange? Example: While we were eating, at In 'N Out Burger, the California treat my parents craved, Chinua was doing that thing, you know, the thing where you flip your eyelids inside out? Totally disgusting. Kai calls it the "red eye" trick. I was turned away, since I don't want to imagine the inside of my husband's eyelids the next time I'm kissing him, and he was trying his best to get my attention, apparently not caring that he may never be kissed again. Or maybe so confident of his charm that he was sure he'd be able to overcome his red-eyed stigma. And then the kids wanted to get involved, and Chinua spent the next ten minutes trying to help them *flip the insides of their eyelids out* while we were eating our fries. Am I the only one who finds this a little odd? My mom was laughing away, everyone in the restaurant was getting a good show, and I was trying not to see the insides of my little children's eyelids. My babies.

Then, at the mall (it was rainy and cold out) I emerged from the bathroom with Kenya, only to find Kai standing in the hallway with his overalls on *backwards*. He was not alone, his dad and grandpa were there with him, so I asked, "What happened?"

Chinua said, "He's got his own style!" My dad said, "I don't even want to go there," (since apparently Kai had insisted on taking ALL of his clothes off to use the toilet) and I realized that they were both *totally okay* with letting Kai walk around for the rest of the day with his overalls on backwards. I quietly took Kai into the women's bathroom and helped my poor kid out. Is it just a mom thing? I mean, they don't *fit* that way, there's this bulging thing that goes on in the front and a tightness in the back, and that can't be comfortable.

Then, when we were eating dinner, Kenya managed to spill her water, which is totally normal, for a three-year-old. And we cleaned it up. And then she managed to spill it another three times. The floor was very clean, when we were done eating and left the establishment. We had pretty much mopped the whole place.

What else? We ate ice cream, Kenya opened a few early presents, we bought things, and on the way home we listened to a live recording of Chinua's music from 2002 that someone recently gave us. We didn't even know it existed. And I drove and thought of my parents and how much they love me and their son-in-law and their grandchildren, and how they didn't even hate me at all! And I was glad, and I was thankful, and I was also ~~the teeniest bit~~ quite anxious, as I always am, and when I got home I asked Chinua if he thought that they knew how much I loved them, and he said, "I don't know, maybe you should tell them." So guys, if you don't know it already, I really, really love you.

april

April 3, 2007

I haven't been well. The last week has been incredibly hard, but I want to write about what heals me, because God is always so good, and there are little gifts here and there. My Superstar Husband had a concert on Saturday and Renee was wonderful and watched the kids for me so I could go. And I sat on a leather couch in a well-lit cafe, with a cup of coffee in my hand and watched my best friend play the music that I love. When he was introducing the song that he wrote about me, he said he was married to the most beautiful girl in the room, and I felt awe fold in on me, tearstained, wrinkled soul that I am.

And the drives, lately. The drives. Sometimes we drive around a curve and suddenly there is a view before me that is so breathtaking that I want to hurl myself into the center and drop into it like a stone into a lake. Or squeeze it, squeeze it and squeeze it. It's like the line from the Edna St. Vincent Millay poem, God's World, where she says, "That gaunt crag, to crush! To lift the lean of that black bluff!" When I drove to Sacramento a couple of weeks ago I took Highway 20, through Lake County, and all along the lakes and the hillsides there were these purple flowering trees, so incredibly vivid in the brown and green hills. I rounded curve after curve calling "applause! applause!" to the purple flowering trees, because it is hard to clap when you are steering on curvy roads.

On Sunday we went out to the ranch of some new friends of ours, and again, I was stunned. We followed them home, and we left the highway to drive for about twenty more minutes along a small road that was only paved partway up. We climbed and climbed through the forest and then came out of the woods and we were surrounded by such a pastoral view of wildflowers and valleys and hills stretching off into the distance that we all gasped. There were happy cows grazing in fields, and funny-looking sheep among boulders and you could see for miles. We drove up farther and got acquainted with the house before going on a journey to find the waterfall. The kids and I climbed onto a hay bale in the back of the Kubota and I held them tight as one of our hosts drove us down steep inclines to get to the waterfall. When we got there, we sat on a warm, flat rock and Kenya had a revelation ("The water falls!") and then the kids rolled in the grass and found bugs and worms.

It was such a sweet break, such a warm and comforting day. Grass and wind revived me and I felt healed by the beauty my eyes were taking in. When we all piled into the Kubota and climbed back up to the house, our hosts fed us hot chocolate and popcorn in the sunny dining room and we ended up staying so late that Renee made dinner and we stayed for that too, and drove home tired and happy.

There have been days like these.

And yet there have been days of loss, loss that I don't know how to contain. Do I hold it in my heart, or do I open my hands and let it fly away? I am in the midst of miscarrying a baby so young I didn't know I was carrying him. I found out that I was pregnant about two minutes before I found out that I was also possibly losing the baby, and my heart lifted and then fell, and it has been like that for days now. *We are not sure what is going on with you,* they say. *We don't know how far along you are. We think you are miscarrying. It may be ectopic,* they say. *And that is life-threatening,* they say. *We need to watch you. We need to do another sonogram.*

So they have me coming every other day (driving over an hour each way) for blood work to measure my HCG levels, to make sure they are going down okay, and meanwhile I am bleeding and I am opening my hands, letting him go. It's amazing how much sorrow I feel for a baby that I wasn't planning on having. It's amazing how much my heart expanded in the short time that I prepared myself to have another baby. I would have said I couldn't handle one more thing right now, one more bit of sadness. But I guess I am, I guess I am handling it. And when I drive up to the hospital, the trees and the mountains and the grass hold me. And I see these things are from my Father, just like when people feed me and sun comes through the trees and the future doesn't seem as scary, for a moment.

Sometimes when I'm walking around the Land there will be a big noise, like a pack of wolves bursting through the brush, and it terrifies me, but then I turn and I see that it's only a flock of quail. Why do those quail need to be so scary? I think this is like the fear that overtakes me sometimes. The days ahead are only days, after all. The people are only friends. What I think are wolves are actually quail running from me, scattering from the bush with their hearts beating madly. Neither they nor I need to be afraid.

April 7, 2007

From Chinua:

My wife Rachel is in the hospital recovering from surgery. We discovered that instead of miscarrying, she had an ectopic pregnancy. It had to be removed, tubal pregnancies never result in a live birth and the mother's life can easily be lost. Thank all of you so much for you genuine concern, it is humbling. She wanted to thank everyone that has been so kind, and to let you know that God is answering many prayers.

When I saw Rachel in the recovery room, she was surrounded in white, pale skinned and woozy. Her eyes seemed to stand out, red rimmed but full and clear. I have seen her like this before; I know that this is when she is strongest. Cotton-mouthed and smiling, she said in a simple voice "Jesus has our baby now". It was audacious and shattering to the cold, beeping, clinical and hopeless room. It was very much like her.

In most times of tragedy, it is hard to understand what happens as you pass through them. I feel a small echo of how I felt when my mother died. There is a harmony to the ebb and flow of emotions that resist any simple description.

When you lose a pregnancy, you naively assume that it means you will simply sit around and be sad until you snap out of it. In reality (as I am sure that anyone who has been through the same will attest) we grieve in pieces, small parts and little private fractured moments. Those moments are interspersed with mundane feelings, elation and revelation, connection with my living family, and blank denial. There is a rhythm to it all that produces a sensation its own, not unlike the tide.

219

We are sad, but encouraged and drawn together, there is loss and gain. On one hand it seems natural in a way that is comforting, but absolutely tragic considering the incomprehensible purity and simplicity of such a tiny soul. The baby was five weeks and had a heartbeat.

Of course debates rage about souls, life, meaning, heaven and so forth, yet all of that feels so academic and unreal right now. Even well accepted, well-meaning and theologically exact platitudes fail to address something far deeper rooted in all of us, something more primal. I have lost a child. I am a father of four, one was barely more than a hope. I am the beloved of the most beautiful and wonderful woman alive. She has given a tiny birth through a scalpel. To that heartbeat, we say a tiny goodbye. The Lord gives, the Lord takes, blessed be the name of the Lord.

April 9, 2007

To my sweet baby,

It was only a week that I knew about your life inside of me. The week seemed like years, though, and I still feel like your memory echoes through me, I have to remind myself that you aren't there anymore.

At first the doctors thought you were just too small to see, and then they thought that I was losing you. Later they realized that I wasn't losing you, and they thought again, maybe you were too small to see! Maybe we just needed to wait. My heart soared with hope. On Friday we saw you for the first time, on the sonogram. I saw you. You were perfect, I heard your heart beat. I knew without needing to be told that you were in the wrong place, knew from the way the technician cocked her head, caught her lip between her teeth. From the way she wouldn't quite look at me. We looked at you together, not speaking, as she got all the pictures she needed, to be sure. You were so tiny, just beginning to form. And yet that heartbeat.

Things moved quickly after that, it was my Good Friday. I felt alone, I sat while doctors poked at me and took blood and I waited. They wheeled me away, into the operating room, and then I fell apart. I shivered and tears poured out of my eyes as I lay on my back under the lights. One of the doctors took my hand and I took some breaths and thought of sending you into pure beauty.

Since I woke up I have had peace. The first person I saw was your father, and I told him about where you had gone. My heart is glad, knowing that you are still alive, that you are in the Everlasting Arms. It was so hard to know that you were there and you were perfect, but that you couldn't live. But life is all around and you are alive and we are alive and the big thing, the big loss, which is the potential in you, the potential of who you would become, is not really lost. You are all that you are meant to be now, I believe, I think you are more beautiful that I would ever have been able to see here. I can't wait to meet you, to recognize you, to become all that I was meant to be when I shed this old self.

I know, without our loss being any less valid, that there would have been harder ways to lose you. I know many people who have lost children farther along, and in unfathomable ways, and my heart hurts for them. I pray for strength for all mothers and fathers who have empty arms. The doctors were afraid that I would be sad, being in the labor and delivery wing of the hospital, but they didn't realize that life was what I needed. I needed to remember that you are alive, and to remember that I have three very alive children who were born in the same way as all those crying babies in there. I have been blessed.

I joked with the nurses, afterwards, about how I avoided cesarean birth three times but still ended up with a cesarean wound. This scar is all yours, little one, I remember you with this burning pain in my gut, I will always remember that you were here, you have not passed without making a mark. I will always think of you, my fourth child, when I think of heaven. Heaven means meeting you.

All my love,

Mama.

April 13, 2007

I lost a post last night, and waved goodbye to it as it fluttered out my window and into that land where lost posts go. I've been doing this for too long to be losing posts willy-nilly like that, but there you have it. "Live and don't learn," that's my motto, to quote Calvin from Calvin and Hobbes.

It was terrifically interesting, too. Actually, not really, I think I talked about catheters and my bladder. You didn't miss much, but you'll be glad to know that my bladder is working okay again. And I talked about my desire to show people my wound, and how I have good friends who humor me, but how I still want a nurse. I like it when someone comes in to my room and checks on my incision and says, "Oh dearie, you're bruised. Poor thingy," and then clucks with her tongue and pats me on the head, and I gaze up at her patiently with so much strength, bearing the pain so heroically. I'm a good patient, a good heroine in my own drama. I also like watching the food channel with absolutely no guilt, because that's what you DO in the hospital. Watch TV, even in the middle of the day, even at 1:00 in the morning.

But other than the lack of Rachael Ray and nurses who coddle me, being home has been so sweet, and hard. Six weeks is a long time to not be able to carry anything over 10 pounds. The nurse told me the rules as I was being discharged, and I gave her a look that oozed, Come on, you are NOT serious, can you seriously expect that from me? Six WEEKS? She nodded, very serious. I don't think I'll make it, I keep forgetting to not pick up my kids. What are you supposed to do when a little missile in the shape of an edible baby comes hurtling towards you?

Unfortunately, not pick him up, in my case. So I've been sitting on the floor with my kids a lot, which the Leaf Baby loves, he always loves it when I sit on the floor. He thinks it's great fun. I honestly can't believe how this kid is becoming a kid. I know I wrote about it recently, but when he turns around and sits on my lap like I'm a little chair for him, and I can see on his face that he thinks that this is just so cool, I feel these twinges, these whispery feelings like please don't grow up. And then sometimes this brings a wave of grief and I feel empty again, missing that little baby hope inside me. I was looking at a recent photo of me, one from my Change series, I think, and I looked so happy in the photo that the grief ripples started up again. I don't feel like that girl. I feel curled up, protective. I feel wounded.

Mostly though, this grief has made me thankful. I've been given so much. I marvel over my kids, their bodies. I hold my daughter and trip out thinking about her limbs, arms and legs which are growing. I can't believe they're mine, can't believe I've been trusted like this. I guess I'm slow to understanding my own vocation. Sometimes I've whined about it. I probably will again. But I'm treasuring these days.

Last night we had a big bonfire, and a worship circle around it. The older kids love to be allowed to stay up late for these, we've been doing them weekly, and we had a bunch of guests at the Land, which was nice. There is a girl who will be living with us now, up till now she has been living in Golden Gate Park near our old home in San Francisco. Also some travelers who Chinua met in Arcata when he was taking photographs there. A couple of dogs, some more guests, our little community, and my children with me. Kenya sat in my lap and Kai lay with his head on my knee and the firelight made everyone beautiful and we all sang. I felt very blessed, like God has just opened his hands up and poured goodness into my arms, spilling around me like grain pouring from a chute. The feeling stayed with me even as Kenya pitched a mother of a fit when I decided it was time for bed. I smiled at my tired crying girl as I pajama'd her against her will and I thought— I know how just you feel, girl. But you'll feel better in the morning.

may

May 14, 2007

My birthday was amazing. After waking up covered in yellow flowers (courtesy of my Superstar Husband), I went out with my family. We played in the park, then we picked up pizzas and went to meet up with friends, where I thought we'd eat and then do cake or something. But no, I stepped inside the door and my friend Christy said, "I'm whisking you away..." and off we whisked!

I felt as though I was doing something illegal.

"Are you sure?" I asked a few times, until I was satisfied that it was going to be okay. And then I said, "I'm just wondering about the children," and Christy assured me that the children were well taken care of. So I gave myself fully into the hands of birthday whisking, which involved Sushi! and (joy upon joy) a SPA MASSAGE. I loved the massage. I was a little disconcerted by the way the lady acted as though I should know exactly what to do. "You mean I should take all of my clothes off and then get under the sheet?" I asked, sounding prudish but in actuality, I was just confused.

It was great! Of course, being me, I had to embarrass myself a little by emerging from the massage looking as though I'd mutated into a red-eyed tree frog. I was allergic to the eye pillow the masseuse had placed over my eyes, and they swelled up into flaming red balloons. The receptionist and the masseuse turned to look at me, and their serene faces quickly became concerned. I don't think allergic reaction was the result they were going for, but my body felt very relaxed, thank you.

I recovered as we drove to our final destination, a wee party at the home of some other friends. Once again, I began to ask about the children, and everyone conjured up a story about a homeless man who assured them he'd take good care of my kids. I finally cornered someone and forced the truth out of her. "Sara's watching them," she replied, and from that moment on, I could relax.

The highlight of the party was a song that Chinua made up from words that everyone in the room came up with to describe me. It turned out to be a little reggae ditty with the refrain, "You don't have club foot." There were lots of other sweet words that said nice things about me but that refrain was catchy as all get-out, and one of my favorite moments was the line "...and all your toes swing freely..."

We're home now, and I had a lovely day: cleaning, hanging my laundry on the line, moving furniture around. Renee and I drove into town this afternoon for dance class, which starts in a couple of hours. Looking on the bright side of things, I reflected, as we drove, that if we lived in town with all the benefits of grocery stores, herb stores, thrift shops and coffee shops, we would miss out on this drive that still takes my breath away, every time.

The wildflowers this year! The wildflowers! The late rains came and gave us the prettiest wildflowers I've seen. Hills of purple. Pink clover. Poppies, wild orchids. I gasp, I snort, I can't stop exclaiming

227

over the wildflowers. I mourn that they are so short-lived, that it
will quickly become hot and the sun will scorch them.

*

if I could,
I would weave you a ladder of wildflowers.
it would stretch straight into the air,
and I'm sure that your feet would scarcely bruise the petals
you'd feel them tickling that soft underside of your foot
as you leapt up my ladder, laughing.
you'd rise above all those things that nicker and nobble
the smokestacks, soot clinging to your clothes, the mounds of paper
bills and to do lists and, well, and all of it
you'd leave the freeways and the dust, the strip malls, as you held on tightly
poppies springing back under your feet.
lupin under your hands,
I can see you, eying that one cloud as a good resting spot.
the cloud that resembles your band teacher (from the seventh grade.)

May 21, 2007

I'm on the first day of a drive to Canada, to visit my parents
while my Superstar Husband is in Turkey. And whaddya know, the
best way to pack for a trip appears to be not at the last minute. And
I'm speaking from the better side of the coin, the winning side, the
one that isn't tearing her hair out and throwing loose socks in a torn
plastic bag from Safeway while feeding the kids meat on a spoon.

I had a really great time packing this week. I took the time to do
a good job, left my house clean enough for some friends to stay in
while I'm gone, and even have the van organized. (A little, I'm not a

different *person*, just more prepared).

I even put the jammies in a separate pocket of the suitcase so I could access them more easily.

So, as a first stop for my trip I decided to drive only 45 minutes north, to the ranch of some friends and rest up for the drive ahead.

While I was there I started crocheting a cowboy hat. I'll let you know how it turns out, because in my mind there is nothing cooler than a crocheted cowboy hat. Chinua disagrees, but he is wrong, WRONG. I drank Americanos, sat on a futon in the sun crocheting, chatted and laughed, and ate good food. My kids fed a bull, gave a horse some carrots, rode on his back, and played with the dogs. Leaf walked around and babbled and got into stuff and flirted with everyone, so he's probably had the least change in his routine, because that is pretty much what he does everyday.

I smelled roses, stared into the greenest hills, thought about my love far away, rested in the home of some very kind friends.

I guess you could say it has been beautiful so far.

May 28, 2007

Sometimes when I come back to visit with my parents I feel like I've turned into an adolescent again. I'm babysitting these kids, and I really need to get them to sleep because I have a report due tomorrow that I like, totally procrastinated on. And I'll probably have to pull an all-nighter. Or maybe I'll just read a book and then write it on the bus in the morning. Because, like I always say, there's nothing like a little procrastination to add some unneeded stress to your life! This was my method in high school. I don't know how pulled the grades off that I did.

Maybe it is this awkward-limbed adolescent feeling that has

curled into my spine and mellowed me right out. We get up, we eat, we get dressed. We may have baths, I will wash their soft chubby fingers and rub suds into their hair. And then, I will stare at the work I brought with me and try really hard to remember what to do with it. And, unfailingly, I will be stumped because my brilliant Superstar Husband is far, far away and he's got the gaps in my brain filled. And so we eat my mom's cooking again, we play, we pick up toys, we have story time, and we sleep well.

I miss him like a tree that has lost its leaves. I have gone into hibernation.

But hibernation can be fun! Last night I picked my sister up from the bus station and remembered what it is like to have a sister. I have a sister! We look and sound like each other! Except she's cuter, and I want to squeeze her.

My road trip was great, by the way. On the second day we drove for seven hours, which is a lot longer than forty-five minutes, but surprisingly it went really, really well. Even the Leaf Baby was pretty mellow. I think it was grace, that amazing strength that bathes you when you need it, when you need rivers and rivers of sunlight to wash over you. I felt it as I drove on beautiful highways. There were flowers everywhere, light everywhere, rivers running alongside the road. I love the first day of this drive because of the small highways. We stopped at Rebeca and Eric's house for a day and it was lovely and restful. Well, as restful as it can be with little kids playing. You know, that kind of highly socialized playing that you and I do when we go out for coffee and I decide I want yours more so I snatch it from you and you fall under the table screaming.

I have always felt so inspired by Rebeca and her kids. She has such a way of involving them with all the things she does, the baking, even cleaning. They eat it up. I come away from visiting with her wanting to be like her.

The second day of driving is not as nice, that boring I-5 cutting across the land like a blade. Now that I live on small highways, I don't wish to return to four-lane freeways. I feel as though the city has finally been sweated out of me. I look around the forest and green hills where I live and finally feel as though this is my home. Toes in the dirt, sweeping pine needles out of my house.

june

June 14, 2007

I woke up this morning feeling like a truck hit me in the night, when I was sleeping in my bed, next to Chinua. I swear, some trucker lost his way. Or maybe it's just a headache, brought on by the allergies that plague me night and day. Or maybe I spent too much time in the sun yesterday, and didn't drink enough water.

On Monday, Renee and I were sitting in my favorite little cafe in the tiny town to the north of us, ready to drive out to an even tinier town, west of the tiny town, for our dance class with the teacher we adore. I think I feel the same way about her that I felt about my kindergarten teacher. I remember being all five years old with my knobby knees and unruly hair and— Oh how I loved my beautiful kindergarten teacher. She was so BEAUTIFUL. I really have no idea what she looked like. But she was LOVELY. My dance teacher is over fifty and one of the most beautiful women that I have ever met. On the way home, Renee and I always talk about two things. How the dancing went, and how much we admire our dance teacher. ("She's so nice... did you see her skirt today? She told me that I'm

232

improving...")

But a funny thing happened on this particular Monday evening, and it has taken me this long to recover from it enough to write about it. I started out in a funk, determined to sweat it out of me, not understanding why my skin felt like it wanted to crawl away from me or something. We began our stretching time, which is *awesome*, probably my favorite part of the evening, with the drums going in the background encouraging you to *strrrreeeetttch* that muscle just a little bit more, and then we lined up to dance. Now, there is only one place that I hate to dance in this class, and it's in the last line. Basically, we follow the teacher, dancing across the floor toward the drummers in lines of three, and then we walk back. Being in the last line equals being pinned to the dissection board to me, because everyone watches you while they wait to dance again, and since on this day I was feeling about as intelligent as a worm, I really didn't want to be in the last line. I just wanted to be swallowed up in the crowd, but no, there I was, in the last line.

This is also an advanced class, and we are still beginners. So I fumbled, and I wobbled, and a couple of times I merely walked across the floor like cardboard (because, you know, cardboard *walks*) and I had a few breakthroughs, but somehow I managed to completely psyche myself out. The voice ranting in my head sounded something like this: *Step step arm arm, no! Darn it, you are such a loser. Okay, step step arm arm, Oh my word, you are never going to be able to do this. You should be better than this, everyone is sneering at you, just look at their lips curling, wow, you look like a chicken more than a woman, how terribly clumsy and big you are.*

Can you believe it? What a terrible voice! It was no wonder that I started to get tears in my eyes, and then, as the teacher picked up on the fact that I was getting more and more distraught, she began to really slow down the steps just ahead of me so that I could catch it at my pace. She encouraged me with signs to breathe, calm down, just follow her. When she turned more attention on me I realized that I was going to break down completely. Obviously, the only thing to do was make a run for it!

So I bolted. I grabbed my stuff and walked out the door and cried my way across the gravel parking lot and up to the top of one of the beautifully rounded hills. I sat down in the tall grass and hid up there, watching the tips of the grasses above my head, listening to the drums that I could still faintly hear. I cried and cried, and wondered what, exactly, I was crying about. It couldn't be about *dancing*.

From my point at the top of the hill I could see for miles, rounded hill after rounded hill, boulders and trees and clefts. The light was beginning to fade, the sun had already set. I lay back in the grass and watched the swathe of blue sky above me, listened to the bass of the drums pounding, and barely was able to calm down, despite all this calm around me. It was as though all the stillness could not seep into me, and I thought a lot about my whirling life these days, and how sometimes the smallest thing can trigger a rockslide, how maybe I've been waiting to cry.

Not being able to dance signifies a larger lack of ability that I feel, the crushing question, *can I DO this?* There are so many things whirling above our heads right now. We pray to pass through this with peace, with greater joy than before. But sometimes you just have to cry, you make a fool of yourself, you leave class, and you cry like a baby.

June 18, 2007

The time has come... to talk about *"good enough"*.

Last night I had a dream about our three rats. I dreamed that I was trying to transport them in their cage, (along with a baby jaguar that I had mysteriously befriended) and they all got free. I could see them jumping and running through the grass, and for the rest of the dream I frantically tried to grab at them, but they kept eluding me, their fat furry bodies slipping through my fingers. The night grass was wet, and for what seemed to be a very long time I stumbled through it, desperate to get my husband's three pet rats back before his heart broke.

What does this have to do with good enough? Everything, obviously. Or nothing. Depending on which way you look at it. But I seem to have a lot of dreams about *trying* to do something the right way, only to have something go terribly, terribly wrong, and then the blame cloud settles above my head.

Right now I am trying to make up my mind about whether I want to go to my dance class again tonight, or whether I want to go home and watch a movie. I know for a fact that if I go to my dance class, I will feel embarrassed (for walking out last week), but that the exercise will make my blood run through my veins a little more spunkily. It will be good for me. Humiliation, West African Style. I also know that if I go home and watch the kind of escapist movie that I desire to watch, pretty much nothing good will come out of it. One thing I'm learning is that this kind of rest doesn't really make me feel *rested*. I mean, every once in a while it does, but it's always better to take things in that will have me rising from bed a little more excitedly the next day.

What does this have to do with good enough? Well, the question running through my mind when I think about dance class tonight is, "Will I be good enough?"

I found this group of words about simple living the other day.

Simplicity is voluntary, free, uncluttered, natural, creative, authentic, focused, margined, disciplined, diligent, healthful.

Simplicity is not easy, legalistic, proud, impoverished, ascetic, neurotic, ignorant, escapist.

You can see the difference between the two lists. One feels like a sweet breeze, the other smacks of that dark gray blame cloud. I like the idea of defining my life this way, of creating lists of words like beads on a string, beautiful shining things that keep me on a straight line. These words would have nothing to do with good enough.

Because I think that the answer is no. I'm not good enough. I never will be. I'm not good enough for my own tyrannical mind, I'm not even good enough for the shining standard that I seek to be. (like God) But this is not the point.

In my Christian faith there are words like *redemption*. In redemption, every sad thing is brought to beauty and joy. Every slip up has sparkly grace mixed in with it. This word has nothing to do with good enough. The whole point is that we are not good enough, and that a true Man had to be good enough for us. This sets us free from our endless self-justification that is a badly behaved cousin of guilt, always whining in the corner, "At least I'm not like *Paris Hilton...*"

You know?

In a way, the specifics don't even matter. It could be my lack of decorating skill, it could be my dusty corners, it could be the way that I ignore things in my fridge that I know good and well are rotting. It could be a rough hand on my child's shoulder, it could be an envious glance, it could be not enough money, not enough time, not enough patience. The point is that we are told to take our eyes off our belly buttons and be filled with a different kind of motivation. Not to be good enough. But to craft a life of love. A life where God always has the opportunity to bust through the clouds with the answer for the day, to be THE MAN.

Our list of words as people, mothers, fathers, friends, ministers, whatever we are, should not be drudgery, obligation, guilt, mockery, envy, competition and resignation.

This is the list of words that my Great Rescuer has for me: Freedom, joy, mercy, servanthood (because hey, floor's gotta be cleaned, right?) mystery, courtesy, simplicity, beauty, rest, diligence, awe, and many more. Not to mention fun. Funnity fun fun.

June 20, 2007

After I wrote the last post I did indeed take myself to my dance class. I went! And it was awesome! It was fun and I had the right line, and I kept up fairly well, and the best part is that I'm not getting as winded these days, so I know I've gotta be getting stronger.

On a completely different note, do you know what my least favorite part of the whole bedtime routine is? It's brushing my kids' teeth. I hate it, it is excruciatingly annoying to me. And yes, I do let the two older ones "brush" their teeth themselves, but whatever they're doing with the toothbrush seems to have about as much effect as sucking on a Q-tip covered in high-fructose corn syrup would, so there I am, stuck brushing their little chompers and gums.

Do you know what my favorite part of the bedtime routine is? It's reading. I love it, I crave it, it's my favorite time of day with my kids and I could do it for hours. I've been trying to get them ready early so that we can read as many books as possible before it's time to crawl into little beds and lay little heads on little pillows.

I will become a reading guru, and live on the highest mountain top with many little children, and my asceticism will be reading without fail, and our brown teeth will eventually fall out of our mouths, but we will read on.

Yesterday I made soup for everyone here, and Kai helped me, pouring the chopped vegetables into the skillet, stirring everything around gently. I even let him chop, a little. He loved it, and it made cooking a lot more fun for me. Maybe we will cook on our mountaintop, too.

June 23, 2007

More from Annie Dillard:

"I do not so much write a book as sit up with it, as with a dying friend. During visiting hours, I enter its room with dread and sympathy for its many disorders. I hold its hand and hope it will get better.

This tender relationship can change in a twinkling. If you skip a visit or two, a work in progress will turn on you.

A work in progress quickly becomes feral. It reverts to a wild state overnight. It is barely domesticated, a mustang on which you one day fastened a halter, but which now you cannot catch. It is a lion you cage in your study. As the work grows, it gets harder to control; it is a lion growing in strength. You must visit it every day and reassert your mastery over it. If you skip a day, you are, quite rightly, afraid to open the door to its room. You enter its room with bravura, holding a chair at the thing and shouting, "Simba!"

The Writing Life

I love Annie Dillard because she makes me feel normal. She writes of being terrified of writing, of hating to write, of the danger and power and neurosis of writing. And I love it, because I feel all of these things, when I sit by myself in the early mornings and tap out a few more lines in my novel. The whole time I am so afraid.

Knitting is safe. It is rhythmic and soft, and I keep my knitting close to me while I write, so that when I come to the scariest parts I can grab it and soothe myself for a few minutes. It reminds me that there is order to the universe, that there are things that I *can* accomplish. I can turn a ball of yarn into a hat. Then I attack my keyboard again. It is perhaps not an accident that the one key that breaks occasionally is the backspace key.

Why the desire to write when it is so hard? So many things are more tangible. Chocolate is more tangible. Rocks are more tangible. Even a fish tank is more tangible. But a day is not complete without some kind of scrawling to record it. For me, a day without writing is merely that burning ball in the sky seemingly moving in an arc from one side to the other again. And again, and again.

It doesn't matter, but I have often wondered whether I can keep trying this, trying to write this book which is so uncomfortable for me, while I am mothery and soft the rest of the time. I mean, I leap straight from the somewhat intense things that I write about, into breakfast with toddlers. I think I can balance them, though. I think I can do it. I'm hedging a lot of bets on this.

June 28, 2007

Today I needed to go to the post office and Kai was playing with his friend who lives here. This friend is almost exactly the same age as him, and lately they have been inseparable. The social behavior of kids is so strange, you know? I mean, five minutes ago they couldn't play without fighting, and now suddenly it seems like they have a secret language.

Also, they make up songs.

They both wanted to come to the post office with me, and I can't blame them, since checking our post office box is the highlight of my day. You get to put the key in the little lock and then TURN IT and open that little door and maybe, just maybe, there will be something cool in there. Or maybe there will be four PG&E bills. More likely four PG&E bills. For some reason that I have never been able to fathom, we have four different accounts for different parts of our property. When I have politely inquired, Headquarters has informed me that it is in my best interests to *leave it alone. Laissez faire.* Okay, I get the point, I say, but do you really need to be all mysterious about it?

I was in a fun mom mood, so I threw a couple of booster seats in the back of the car I was driving and we drove up past the honeysuckle and around the corner and onto the highway. On the way there the boys amused themselves immensely by pretending we were driving off of the cliff and into the other cars and stuff. Great fun.

On the way home they amused themselves (and me!) by singing this song:

"Get up, stand up- stand up for your rice.

Get up, stand up- don't give up the mice."

I couldn't believe my ears. Not only was it a Bob Marley remake, it involved both rice and mice, two very cool and important nouns, which deserve more lyrical attention in my opinion. They sang it all the way back down the highway and kept singing as we took the crazy left into our driveway, past the sign, around the ponds, and back home.

july

July 5, 2007

Their exuberance kills me. They wake up jogging in place, their feet twitching before their eyelids twitch themselves open. They call to each other joyously, especially the baby, now that he can say their names, always with exclamation points or question marks behind them. They burst through the door to find me.

I am ready for them, sometimes. Sometimes I wish they'd sleep a little longer. Sometimes I fix them sippy cups of rice milk and pile some books in their beds and make them stay in their rooms a little longer. Sometimes we eat granola. Sometimes we eat fruit and I make muffins in the toaster oven. I cut them big slices of cantaloupe and little round pieces of banana and they coo like doves over them. Sometimes I stick some store bought cereal in a bowl and that's that. They always argue over who gets the red bowl. They take turns, but sometimes I forget who had it last, and that's never good. I usually have to urge them to eat, they are too excited about talking. The little girl climbs in and out of her chair seventeen times. They make silly faces at each other across the table. I suck coffee down like it's real energy and we're in a crisis.

We read together. We prefer the small couch, where we can sit in a pile. It's a love-seat, really, perfect for us. The baby changes his mind often about whether he'd like to sit with us and listen or not. They are still and quiet, breathing into my face, the girl sucking on her fingers. They laugh at the funny parts. They interrupt. They soak it in. We go to the library, and the librarians always smile at me. They love me for reading with my kids. I feel like I get points for doing something that I'm already addicted to, which is reading, myself. "A reading family," said one librarian last week, sighing happily.

They egg each other on. I am encouraging them to listen to me, and I am gaining ground until one of them sets the others into giggles and all sanity is lost. We sit on the floor in a circle and I explain to them that being good is really much more fun because time outs are not fun and being mean is not fun and fighting is not fun. "What things are fun?" I ask. "Being nice is fun," the older boy says. "And nice is nice!" the little girl adds, helpfully. "And inviting people over," I say. "And letting our friends play with our toys," the older boy says. "And kisses are love!" the little girl exclaims. We all agree.

Sometimes I am good at playing. It helps if I sit on the floor. We sit and play with small squares. "Get me five green ones," I say to the girl, and she does. The baby toddles over and snatches them and screaming ensues. Learning is always going on here. I am teaching them writing with the Handwriting Without Tears curriculum (which I love) and they wriggle themselves out of their chairs with excitement. They love the chalkboard. The older boy already knows how to write, but needs some help. The little girl doesn't know her letters yet, but wants to do whatever the boy is doing. "We're learning D", I say. Then I ask her what letter we are learning. She screws up her face and says "Ummmm." Then she draws a perfect D.

Sometimes I just lie down on the floor and let them swarm me. I have no energy for anything else. They lean their heads on my face and I smell their warm sweaty hair. We make ahhhhhhhhh noises. Then I pick myself up and start cleaning again.

We work together. They hand me clothes to put on the clothesline. They fight over who will get to give me the pair of purple pants. The purple pants become the Holy Grail. There is a meltdown. Nobody is giving me the purple pants. I will get the purple pants for myself. Dirt is thrown. Then they smile sweetly through dirty faces and hand me clothes again. We do dishes. The older boy carefully stacks them in the dish drainer. The girl moves them from the rinse water to the bleach water. I wash. The baby eats out of the scrap bucket and scavenges for food on the floor. I catch him and send him out of the kitchen, and he falls to the floor and cries.

We swim in the river. I put them in their swimsuits and we traipse down, my pale legs glowing. They are brown and sweet and nutty, and when we jump in the water they become incredibly weightless, like babies. Sometimes the older ones swim by themselves, with their life jackets, and I play with the baby as he floats in the inflatable hippo. Sometimes I hold on to them and we float down the "rapids" or the "rapins" as the girl calls them. We love this time of day best. The minnows nibble at us and the trees rustle above us, and the kids find me beautiful rocks to bring home for my beautiful rock "collection." Usually there's another meltdown when we leave, most likely from the little girl. We walk slowly home while she cries and pouts. It is nap time.

The younger two sleep. I make coffee and sit with it, nursing it. I take a minute just to sit, and then the older boy and I work together. Sometimes he plays outside with his friends. If he can't find them, he insists that he doesn't play by himself, so I get him to help me. If I don't mention the word "play" he usually starts playing with something. A couple of sticks. Some rocks. A truck. Sometimes he watches "Really Wild Animals" and sings along with the cheesy songs. I do office work or clean cabins or cook food or do all sorts of other odd piddly things until it is time to get the other kids.

We eat with everyone. We do more dishes. The Superstar Daddy takes photos or sings or does card tricks. We wander home (across the land) at some point. We have bonfires, with marshmallows. We read some more. I kiss them. I close their door and collapse on the couch. Then I get up and put a load of laundry on.

At some point they have become a force. We do everything together. They are my kids, there are three of them, and they take up 80% of my thoughts.

We don't own a lot of stuff. We have this family of ours though, and they take and give more than I could have imagined.

We may be moving soon. We are thinking out of the country. Out of North America. And I keep thinking, over and over again, that I am just so glad that we move together, that this thing called family will come with me, now, wherever I go.

July 26, 2007

The kids are shooting up. Seriously. I think it has something to do with the summer warmth; they are like the pea seedlings that I have in peat pots on my porch, stretching for the sun. They run around in our forest, on their feet which are constantly needing a new shoe size, pretending to be cats in Cat City, or werewolves.

(They have no idea what werewolves are- a friend of theirs brought werewolves into the game, and Kai and Kenya think that a werewolf is a nice kind of wolf-dog.)

The kids are shooting up, and their new favorite thing is gum. Especially sharing gum. Out comes the gum package and out come all the little hands, and then there are four little jaws moving, chomping away. I particularly like Kai's face as he's chewing gum. It's awfully grown-up, I guess, to chew gum, and he always seems pretty stoked on himself. He shoots me glances. *Notice how I'm chewing gum?* his glances say.

But yesterday there were some gum thieves that rustled through here, opened the drawer, and took the rest of the pack. They left their evidence- crumpled gum wrappers- on the floor of the house. I had a talk with the leader of the gum thief pack, about the evils of gum thievery. Also about how if you accidentally drop your gum out of your mouth while you're chewing it, you're just done. It's trash now. Okay? And there are ways of keeping gum in the mouth so that this doesn't happen.

*

I feel rested. I took a time of listening, a break from the online world. So I've been listening. I've also been gardening, and knitting, and contemplating the life changes that are descending upon my family. I've been spending time with friends, doing some sketches, and working around here.

I came out of my listening time sure of a few things. One is that I am an artist and a writer. These are the things that have always fed me. Soon I will be working on making more space for these in my life. Another is that there may never be the perfect balance that I'm (or any of us in this predicament are) looking for. Motherhood is a messy thing, it is relational. All relationships are messy, and especially ones with small people who have the social skills of raccoons: Always making a mess and grabbing your stuff off of the table. Parenting is an art, but it is an art along the lines of homesteading, or juggling, or being a street performer with a purple hat for change.

Writing requires solitude. It needs to be fed, there are breezes that need to come and tickle you so that your wells can be refilled, and it requires the kind of thought that is deep and hard to be roused from. Being a writer means being away, dreaming of another place, and mothering demands absolute presence.

And so. In my life there is a tension of away and not away, and I think that I need to learn to love it, rather than shrugging away from it all the time. It's something we do, isn't it? We try to get away from the things that pull on our muscles and make us work so hard. But these are the things that God brings us to shape us, and maybe I can learn to embrace that frustration that comes when I have the best idea ever, and can't find the time to write it down, or when I'm with my kids, but wishing I could finish that inspiring book.

Another thing I came away with is a really exciting idea for a story. It dropped into my lap, straight from heaven, or actually the seed of it came from the real story of a friend, which is still from heaven, in a way.

Meanwhile we are moving through summer and today I really need to get some of the seedlings replanted, and this baby blanket needs to be finished, pronto, and it's shopping day, and the kids are calling, not too patiently.

July 28, 2007

There is a little bookstore that sells used books, in one of the small towns to the north of us. It is *wonderful*. And I mean wonderful in the anthropological sense, with is something that has been at the top of my list of senses, these days. The raving anthropologist in me has come out to play, gibbering and scratching out diagrams and charts in the corner, while everyone else is just drinking their coffee.

We are moving. Much remains to be decided, and there are about—oh—twenty thousand details to be worked out, but this much is sure: it will happen. (How do you like that for surety?) And so my anthropologist is thrown into a flurry, binoculars out, notepad, a stack of books from the library.

I want to capture every little thing that I can about this unique place that I now live in. I have become obsessed with the culture of the back country of California, here in the woods, and the hills that were logged in the 40's and 50's, by the rivers and the ocean.

And, so, walking into the bookstore again, I was delighted. It was dark, very dimly lit. The bookshelves stretched to the ceiling. The books on them were labeled and categorized nicely, but books were everywhere. In corners like driftwood, stacked on chairs, stacked in boxes, propped against any available space. There were animals everywhere, too. The shop had the distinctive smell of many animals living together in a small space for a long time. There was a friendly dog who followed me around while I shopped, and put his head on my knee while I squatted to find something. And cats were flung around like the books, like something a wave dragged up on shore, only dry, and contentedly purring.

The desks at the front of the store were covered with papers and a couple of old televisions, more books and coffee cups, newspapers and pencils. I met the owner to buy my book and we talked to each other over the stacks of paper. He was older with a long white beard, wearing Carhartt overalls and a white t-shirt, a hat perched precariously on his head. Somehow, hoping that I would find a paperback edition of the book I was looking for, I hadn't brought enough cash with me, and I came up 50 cents short. "Oh, not to worry," he said. "This'll be fine."

In the center of the room there was an altar. Many, many religions were represented. It was the crowning touch to a quintessential moment for this region. The laid back commercial style, plenty of beloved animals, and a pasted-together collage of spirituality, set upon a formica table with a cat curled up on it.

The man was so friendly, joking with me about my many quarters, laughing about the shine his dog took to me. I love the people here, love their friendliness and I have been changed by living here. I took my book and one more piece of experience and left with a smile.

July 31, 2007

I love the mornings in my cabin. We have this great natural air-conditioning here, since it cools down so much at night. We open all the windows in the evening and when I wake up early to sit with my coffee and book it is chilly enough to make my toes cold. I know that soon it will be warm enough, hot, even, hot enough for a desert lizard, so I don't mind. I love the quiet.

I am mulling over the fact that the Leafy Boy is starting to really talk. He looks at me earnestly and tries to make sentences. "Mom-mee," he says, "Aww Dah, DAWN." Which of course means, *Mother dearest, I'm finished with the delightful banana you broke into pieces for me and would love to get out of this highchair contraption you have strapped me into.*

But really, this means that soon I will have *three* talking children in my life. Three children to call for me and tell me long and involved stories, and to say things to me like, "You didn't get my juice yet," in an extremely demanding (one might even say hostile) tone of voice, which is corrected continually but can't seem to change, in its three-year-old way. Where will I take my brain to rest it? Sometimes I just want to wring it out, you know? Or put it in the creek for awhile, to cool it down.

And Kai's stories. Don't get me wrong, because I listen with all the love that a doting mother can give to her son. But they—I don't know—don't seem to really go anywhere? We start out with a dinosaur, which is sad, or something, and we end with a dinosaur which is sad or something. But it seems to be important to Kai to get all of this out, so I will listen to these fifteen minute stories about the dinosaur who continues to be sad, but once again, where will I take my brain to rest it?

Or Kenya. Kenya is in a stage which I like to call the pure nether-regions of emotion. She is emotive in the most wonderful and terrible senses of the word, and she doesn't have stories that don't go anywhere, but what she does have is a mighty decibel range. She has a powerful set of lungs, that girl, and she isn't afraid to use them. I am helping her to channel her emotions into more effective ways of communication, but at the same time I am awed and impressed by her passion. She is everything I wish I could dissolve into when something doesn't go my way. And my brain is melting.

And Baby Leaf is talking, and he says his words with pride, because he can communicate, he can let me know what he wants. And he loves to babble, so sometimes he just does that. He is heartbreakingly cute. And when he kisses me he puts a chubby hand on each side of my face and leans in and puts a sort of raspberry on my lips in imitation of a kissing sound, and it is wet and scrumptious and I wipe Leafy drool away from my chin while my heart melts.

What do I need a brain for anyways? This is birdsong, an aria, a bow over the strings of a cello. Childish voices, singing and yelling and laughing. Distracted, absentminded, my mind is filled with the most beautiful clutter, and silence might be the emptiest luxury, after this.

THE THIRD YEAR

This was a momentous time for us.

It had been clear for a while that things weren't working out at the Land, though we were committed to being there. We saw that we were putting a lot of money and leg work into repairing buildings and had very little time to do what we knew we really wanted, which was building a haven for spiritual seekers. For around three months out of twelve, the Land was everything we dreamed of, with lots of travelers coming through, sunny days in the garden, and worship around the fire in the evenings. But during the other nine months of the year we seemed to be spinning our wheels, working in areas that had nothing to do with what we were genuinely gifted at. We worked on plumbing and chopped fallen trees. When we looked at how much we had done and how far we still had to go, we knew we needed to make a change. We knew we wanted to start a meditation center in the Christian tradition, but where? After a lot of thinking, dreaming, prayer, and even fasting, Chinua and I and other members of our community made the decision to move to India. We put the steps in motion fairly quickly, one of which was putting the Land up for sale. It was one of the hardest things we ever had to decide, and I'm so glad that we didn't do it alone, but that the other leaders of our non-profit as well as our board of directors were part of the decision. We saw God's hand even in the sale. We never advertised and the Land sold just months before the California real estate crash.

Still, it was difficult for people who had previously lived at the Land, as well as others who were emotionally involved. While most people were enormously supportive, there was some hurtful criticism of our decision from the outside, some from people who had never lived at the land, but felt attached to it for different reasons. This criticism really hurt, and in my writing during this time, you can read me working my way through it.

It was a hugely adventurous time. We packed up our things and moved to Sacramento for five months, just before leaving the US to live across the ocean. Things happened in this year that were more important lessons than any I had ever encountered. One experience (in driving) taught me that no matter how dangerous things seem, God's hand is with me. Another experience (with my house) taught me that often what seems safest is still a part of the unknown of life and that we can't cling to what seems safe. These two lessons still sustain me in the years since I've moved away from my home country and adopted country and have encountered many more unknown things. God is here. I am never alone.

august

August 14, 2007

Last night we returned from a trip to San Francisco and we are back in the forest. I love my shade. And my peas are doing very well. The broccoli? Not so much. Oh well, I am learning.

We stayed with some dear friends for a bit, which was amazing. The kids had a blast, and we drank coffee and talked for hours. And we caught glimpses of other friends who break my heart with their dearness. (I sound like my Grandma.) It was too short, too short. I mean, I literally caught a *glimpse* of my friend Curtis as he ran from work to sleep to school.

We slept on a church floor while we were in San Francisco. It was interesting to see what a wimp I've become. Ten years ago, I slept directly on the floor quite often. I even slept sitting up in vans, slept on the grass in the open at rest stops, slept on chairs pulled together and in backyards and sometimes I didn't sleep at all. Now my sleep is very precious to me and if someone points at the floor and says, "That's where you're sleeping tonight," it takes a few blinks before I can smile nicely and say, "Sure!"

We had a great time, it was fun and we met a lot of people. But it's so exhausting to take care of the kids under these circumstances—traveling from place to place, figuring out what to feed them, (and ourselves) keeping everyone busy and entertained. And I started thinking, *what is a home?* I mean, at home we do the same things. We eat, we sleep, we play. But at home it feels safe and relaxing, while when we were away it felt a little tiring. I wanted to go home, at the end of it, looked forward to being in my own place. What was I looking forward to?

I ask because we are moving to India. And things are moving very quickly now. We may be moving away from our home here within the next couple of months, and we'll be traveling for a little while before we settle into our new home in India, wherever that may be. It is vastly, amazingly exciting. We have been longing for this for years, since we last left India, right before we were married, and now it is coming to pass.

But what makes a home? I know that my longing for home springs from something eternal. I know that it is about more than four walls and a front door. I know that I am very simple in my needs. Give me enough space and some beauty and I'm fine. And enough space here, in this house, is about 850 square feet. But I need more than space, it is something more central than that. It is like a delicate web of security, and I'm beginning to realize that I have been placed here to weave this web for my children. Even as we move around.

Some things that come to mind are routine; a rhythm that pulses through every day faithfully. Not easy when you're traveling, but necessary. Familiar objects, maybe; a certain tapestry or picture that moves with you from a wall in your home country to a wall in a hot country across the world. I know that at this stage in the growth of my children *we* are their home. This will take more thought as we get ready to go.

september

September 6, 2007

We arrived home from a trip to Canada the night before last, after a day of driving filled with rain, cold, NPR podcasts, (many, many NPR podcasts) and our friends who drove with us. They were coming from the same direction to visit us at the Land for a couple of days, and we had fun playing with the configuration of drivers and passengers and vehicles. Girls in the van! Girls in the car! Boys in the car! Boys in the van! There are endless possibilities.

When we got home, I opened our front door and looked inside, and wow! I fell in love. Again. With my house. It was so beautiful, the warm wood everywhere, and Renee had cleaned it up for us (she was housesitting) and I felt so, so sad to be leaving. I went to bed happy to be home.

And then, yesterday.

I think it took me about two minutes to become stressed out. So much to do, finances out of control, (I say to myself, *I am about to have a heart attack*) weeds in the garden (despite Renee's valiant weeding while we were gone).

258

I have not yet complained much about living at the Land. But right now the burden of these ten acres is pressing down on me. We handle our finances with the combined contributions of the people who live together. Right now, as we leave, we have so few people living together that this isn't working. Neither is a shared work force, maintaining and improving, since it turns into a handful of us running around the Land in circles.

It's like a bad dream. I run and I run and I can't get it all done.

I've never wanted to simultaneously leave and stay so badly before. This is my home in a way that no other place has ever been a home to me. Driving back into the Redwoods was like driving into the womb, or something. (Bear with me.) But the situation has become unsustainable, and it is time for the next step. And this is breaking me, a little more, when I thought I had done all the breaking I can. There are so many other people who have history here, too, and our leaving has become symbolic to them of the end of something.

Selfishly, I feel like I can't carry their sadness along with my own.

There is no way to escape this, no other home I can go to, no possibility of getting away from doing what I hoped I'd never do, dealing with the end of our community being here after ten years, hurting with it. Leaving the river.

The only way over this is through it, we have to put things in boxes. We have to stretch farther than we've ever been stretched before, and this is no small thing. I fret about money and I fret about mess and it has no result.

And yet, God is here. He is calling us forward and we look for small miracles in the journey. I hear him in the rush of the river and think of being swept over, again and again. Once more, I am being combed through, and I pray that I will emerge a little more free of

259

burrs, of the stinky me that sometimes refuses to lie down. I pray for grace, for the ability to be more than me, more than what I am, because what I am doesn't seem to be enough.

September 12, 2007

Dear Checker at Costco,

Yes, you. The guy at the register.

The other day you and I were having a little conversation about why I didn't want to renew my executive membership. "Just give me the plain ol' plain ol' membership," I said. "Because we're going away." This is where our discourse became, well, ridiculous. Because you assumed that when I said *going away*, what I *meant* was going to *prison*.

You paused and said, "you mean, to the slammer?" And I scratched my head and thought, *what an odd way to joke around with a customer,* but I went along with your joke and said, "Yeah, what I should have said was, 'they're *putting* us away.'"

And you paused for even longer, then said, "that's terrible. When?"

I said, "Oh you know—soon."

And then you looked at me and said, "Wow. Are you serious?"

And that's when I realized you weren't joking.

I was having my own little joke there, all by myself. Because you thought that I was going to prison and that I was confiding it in you while I was buying my groceries.

Okay, so 1. If I was going to prison, I probably wouldn't tell you. I mean, I know we have history and everything, but I just don't think I'd be broadcasting it around the large warehouse store that sells Polish dogs and chocolate fountains.

2. If I was going to prison, I wouldn't be buying a huge bag of organic baby carrots and a huge bag of toilet paper. Why would I be stocking up on carrots and t.p.? You really need to think about this before assuming that people are going to be doing time. It would be better for customer relations, my friend. You need to know your target market. I'd probably be buying a giant pack of pens, for all my letter-writing.

So, I asked you, "Do you always assume that when someone says they're going away, they're saying they're going to *jail?*"

And you said, "Yes, when... uh... (pause) you come from a town like mine."

What? *What?* That little pause said it all. You meant, when *the someone looks like you.*

I mean, we know that people assume that we grow plants. That we have big huge marijuana forests. That's what people do, on land around here. But we don't grow marijuana. And I wish more people would ask, rather than just assuming, because then I could set them straight. But it isn't done, because it isn't *done*, you know, and that's what happens when you live in a county as secretive as ours. So I guess I can only say this:

Next time, if I'm going to tell you that I'm heading for prison, I'll be clear, okay? I'll say, "I don't want to renew my executive membership because they don't have Costco in jail."

And you can make sympathetic noises and think pleasantly to yourself that all your suspicions about me have been happily confirmed.

Signed,

The dready girl who buys all those carrots.

September 13, 2007

Yesterday afternoon, as I was enthusiastically, sadistically, and tyrannically pulling weeds in the garden, I was listening to an NPR "Story of the Day" podcast. It was a little story on the new corporate world, and how much different it is for the twenty-somethings now, who seem to want to climb the corporate ladder much more quickly than ever before.

The corporate world was as far from me and my gardening; our wonderful trees literally crippled with apples, the grapes on the fence, the weeds that I was ruthlessly, murderously, and determinedly ripping; as far as maple syrup is from the poison dart frog. But one thing the guest mentioned caused me to sit up in the dirt and listen.

She said, and I paraphrase, that she would not encourage twenty-somethings to attend graduate school because the twenties are a time for many relationships, for fun, for travel, for discovering yourself and who you are, not for responsibility, not for settling into something that will cause you to spend too much of your time working or studying. (Once again, my paraphrase.)

Well, I thought, *I don't think I got THAT memo! Rip. Rip rip rip rip.*

I am all about alternate lifestyle (in case you didn't notice). One of my mottos in life is "Do things a different way." Something not working? Do things a different way. Feel trapped or stifled? Do things a different way. There are so many myths of the way things have to be. The rules of conduct that North Americans have written for themselves are sometimes treated as the ten commandments. I'm reading a great book recently (about parenting) that suggests that sometimes the things we do, which we think are righteous, we actually do because we can *afford* them. Because we have more money than most people in the world.

And that is precisely my beef with the guest author (whose name completely escapes me) on this show. A whole *decade* for self-discovery?

How much time do you think we have?

We are all much more responsible than *that*. We have a say in the way things go on this big ball in the sky. There are so many possibilities, worlds of ideas, forests of actions that each person can run through, screaming with hope. We demean people if we put stock in the idea that a career is for making money, life is about climbing the corporate ladder. I believe that to truly radiate the potential that we are given, with integrity, we will inevitably make decisions about our lives that cause us to earn smaller paychecks, because we couldn't with good conscience earn the bigger ones. Corporations will have to make a few million less because they decide that they can't use sweatshop labor after all. It's not worth it to take the livelihoods of most people of a nation into subjection in order to make the stuff that another nation's kids will break and throw away. We need to stop building our empire on the backs of others.

Don't get me wrong, I'm not talking about graduate school. And I love to travel. And have fun. But I think that if we are assuming that our thirties is the decade where we start to get serious, it is only because we can afford to.

September 14, 2007

Lulu made a good comment on the last post about twenty-somethings burning out young.

She writes: "*Many have left demoralized. They have barely had a chance to learn the rules much less to learn how to work with unhealthy people. They are beat up all the time until they quit. Many of these kids would have been just what we needed to reform the system. And we've lost them. We don't allow them appropriate time for family, friends and life.*"

Whoa. I wanted to clarify a little, after I read this. Because "Ranter Rae" was on the loose, and might not have been as clear as she should have been.

I did what Lulu is talking about. I almost burned myself out. I told Renee yesterday that when I was in the community house in San Francisco, which was one of the hardest points of my whole life, I realized that I didn't know how to care for myself at all. I couldn't figure out how to take care of my kids and eat, also. You know, ingest food. I lost a lot of weight. I didn't know how to order my day in a sane way, and so skipped around between talking to people in the house, changing diapers, bookkeeping, and feeding people on the street. I also spent time yelling at people trying to park in our parking spot, and yelling at people who were trying to pee on our wall in the alley.

I was traumatized, when I came here to the Land. And then God and the Land began to heal me. I began to establish order in my days, to do one thing at a time. I hung my clothes on the clothesline and watched the river glinting at me through the trees, and I ate when I needed to. I swam in the gentle river.

When I say "doing things a different way", I don't mean burning ourselves out. When I say "responsibility", I don't mean carrying the weight of the world on our shoulders. I have to tell you that I am healing from over-responsibility, from feeling that anytime anything goes wrong anywhere, I am somehow to blame. It's a ridiculous idea.

This is what I mean: every person has a story, and I believe it is more than making money to live, to make money to live. There is a wild thread running through all of us, and I'm just beginning to discover what that means. My Superstar Husband and I have spent many years doing a lot of things that are not linked to our wild, brightly beckoning thread, and we are just now trying to rectify that.

Rest. Work. Play. Discovery. Giving, giving, giving. Creating.

I do believe that things are formed in us in our twenties. I can't count the number of times that I was crippled with angst over who I *am* when my Superstar Husband and I were first married. He is seven years older than me, and I was twenty-one at the time. He'd say, "Don't worry, it's your age," and instead of feeling patronized, I felt liberated. You mean, there might be an end to this?

And there is, I think. I am becoming more myself than ever. And thinking less about it. And the shaping of my twenties and the things I have had to learn are carving the way for the next decade, and the next and the next.

I think what I objected to in the statement of the woman on that show was the idea that experimentation is all we really can expect from that decade. And the idea that settling down is not for that decade. I have friends who have starting life-changing companies, coffee shops, ministries. All in their twenties.

I want to start with my kids even now, building into them a sense of giving and empathy, as well as playfulness, joy, freedom and creativity. To look at them and wonder, *what will they be? Who will they touch?*

But, really, and honestly, I have no idea about how it all works. So I definitely don't have all these solutions up my sleeve. And I am afraid. I have ideas of things I could start, things I could do, and I back down because I am afraid of failing. And I know, I *know,* that fear should have no place in me. I just think that we can do things a different way. Deconstruct.

Is it that way because that is the right way? Or is it that way because that's the way we've always done it? Because that's the way it was marketed to us? Because Fisher-Price says? Or Gerber? Or Oprah?

It's why I feel great about taking my kids from the Land of Plenty, into India. We'll just figure it out, build our own forests. Do things a different way.

September 27, 2007

A Somewhat ill-advised journey down Highway 1.

You are alone, headed south for a writing retreat in your van. Your first stop is in Willits, about an hour from home.

You look around you, as you walk down the street in Willits. You begin to think that you have seriously underestimated this town, this Willits place. You walk into a little organic burrito shop and eat a yummy breakfast burrito, which they allow you to order even though it is lunchtime! And then there is a little sign, thanking you for eating at a locally-owned restaurant. *Go Willits*, you think to yourself. You say goodbye to the nice girls who made you a burrito and some good coffee, and wander into a used bookstore to peruse its shelves, looking for an elusive book that you probably will never find. It's not there, although the store unfolds into room after room in an admirably magical way.

You turn the corner and find a little cafe called the Red Caboose. There is no reason for the way this cafe grabs you. Perhaps it is the unheard-of freedom that you are experiencing right now, the giddy head rush of no seat belts to fasten besides your own that grips you, or maybe it is the way that the front yard of the establishment is all grown over in a lush garden, with a wooden red model of a caboose heralding its front path. It somehow reminds you of Asia. And you are gripped with a desire for an adventure. A desire to explore.

You will drive down Highway 1. It can't take that much longer, can it? You consider consulting a local person or a map, but that is really not your way, you're not really into that. So you head down Highway 20 towards the coast and the legendary Highway 1.

There are almost no words to describe how happy you feel. The sun is turning the trees to gold and you are spinning along the kind of road that you like best; the curvy kind, the kind that takes you and turns you every different direction that exists on a compass, the kind that makes you grow a little taller as you resist the centrifugal force of hairpin turns. Not only that, but this is the kind of adventure that you like best; the kind that has travel and sunshine and trees and little towns with interesting people in them.

There is an old red Chevrolet truck in front of your van, so old that it has that narrow tailgate with the word CHEVROLET painted very seriously, in somber letters, across the back of it. It is the kind of truck you have always loved, and driving it is an robust elderly man with a Newsies cap on. There is another truck in front of him and the three of you take the curves together, keeping up, keeping on. You are heading to the ocean. You are friends, you and the man in the red Chevrolet.

The trees start to get scrubbier and more coast-like. Funny how it's only a few miles out, but because of the wild Northern Californian hills, it takes forever. You sense that the man in the red Chevrolet is starting to get tired of driving. He probably needs to get home to his wife. You observe some things, like the construction worker who is holding a stop sign with duct tape covering the word "stop" and black marker over the duct tape that spells the word "GO". Which is confusing. Because everyone knows what a red octagon means, even your five-year-old son.

You see a Confederate flag flying stubbornly in front of someone's yard. What could they be thinking? You don't have much patience for this, these Confederate flags so out of place in the Northwest that they can make an ignorant statement about the way they wish things could be. The way they wish everyone was the same.

And then you see a glimpse of the ocean, and the red truck is still persevering ahead of you. You are glad for the old man, that he gets to see the ocean today. In the distance it is shimmery and elusive. You are entering Fort Bragg, a town that you are barely on speaking terms with. You have tried to get to know Fort Bragg better, but it always seems to have a lot of hotels and you have not been able to connect. A man is holding up a sign that says, "ELK" and you are blank for a minute, blinking, *"Elk? What could he mean?"* And by the time you remember that Elk is a *place* you are past him, but you remember that it is probably not good to pick up hitchhiker dudes when you are by yourself, anyways.

You and the red truck keep driving on past the outskirts of Fort Bragg and then he turns off on road 409. You wave goodbye and feel a little sad. You were pals. It has been about an hour, since you started meandering to the coast, a whole hour of traveling with the ancient red Chevrolet. But you are cheered by the sight of the ocean below, so deeply blue and impossibly lovely and delicious that you might just have to drink the whole thing.

The little town of Mendocino. You and Mendocino have history. Here you fell a little more irrevocably in love with your husband, before he was your husband, before you were dating. You skirted around each other shyly in a music store, *Lark of the Morning*, and you tried not to stare at him too much, at his beautiful hands as he picked up a dulcimer guitar, a flute, an old hand drum. After you were married you came here together for a brief vacation, when your oldest was not yet one and shoveling sand into his mouth almost as fast as you could scoop it out. It's hard to believe that was over four years ago, those lovely days on the beach, the longing for a home as you gazed at perfect lattice work on houses with roses spilling out of their front yards.

You always long for home, no matter where you are. Beautiful things touch you with a sharp spike of yearning, and you have grown used to this as a state of being, rather than something you need to fix, or something you need to buy. The glimmer of sun on the sea, the perfect corners of beautiful expensive inns, these things make you hurt, in a sweet way, a way that promises a forever home someday.

You see a bush in a field and then suddenly think, *"That's not a bush, that's an alpaca!"* There are many surprising things like this, over and around these cliffs. You notice that the Navarro river is huge, compared to your little Eel, even at this time of year.

And then you are in Elk, the place, and you can see why that hitchhiking man wanted to arrive here. It is precious, tiny, with Inns that are perfect in their architecture, leaning prettily out over the ocean with their glass and corners and clean lines. They have names like the Sandpiper. Cute names.

You start to take notice of the Adopt A Highway signs. This bit of highway has been adopted by the Mendocino Medical Marijuana Group. The next one by the Irish Beach Planning Committee, which is mystifying until you realize that it appears to be the name of the town.

You come upon Manchester, which is nothing like Elk. This must be where the area stashes its poor people. There are no cute inns, only trailers that are moldering and leaning, junked cars and falling down huts. This is life on the coast when there is never enough money. Money flows on around these people and they may never get to jump in. A sign on a store advertises "Antennas and Chainsaws". There are satellite dishes on all the trailers. The highway here has been adopted by Dave's Plumbing.

And you drive on, and on, and here is Point Arena. You pass by another Catholic graveyard and another Catholic church. Are there more Catholic people on the coast? you wonder. No, wait, there are the United Methodists, representing also. Here the highway is adopted by Everything Under the Sun. This is a little hippie town, cute and brightly painted, not really a touristy place, but kind of, in its own way. You almost stop. Later you wish you had.

You pass a road called Gypsy Flat Road, and an Inn called the Whale Watch Inn. You wouldn't mind staying there, watching whales. It would be nice. Now you are coming into deep forest, and it is more like home. There are redwoods here, tall as mountains. A ferrari breezes past you, no doubt headed for the Whale Watch Inn. Look! There on the left is a Turkish house, with turrets and woodwork that must have taken years to craft!

You are coming into Gualala. In Gualala they have huge metal dinosaurs and condos! For so long now on this highway, you have only seen trailers and homes that seem to have been put together lovingly by hand, that condos jump out at you like eels. You are spinning through Gualala quickly, and you do see a supermarket that was probably made back in the days of the Old West. You like the name of this town.

Sea Ranch has golf. And you see a sign for a beach called Shell

Beach. You want some shells, so you stop, but Sea Ranch will not let you in. The County of Sonoma will, but they will charge you $5. You rustle up some old dollar bills and some change and determinedly set out for the beach. Unfortunately, someone lied. There are no shells at this beach. There is water, however, and sand, and marvelous miles of seaweed, covered in flies and smelling like brine. The sun is on your face.

The highway here is adopted by the Gleaners. You are beginning to regret your decision to take Highway 1. It sure is taking a long time. But you keep going, there is nothing else to do. The land becoming more scrubby again and it is covered with boulders. But some of those boulders are sheep! There are sheep all around you, and then you keep driving and cows are on the road. The truck behind you wants to pass you. He keeps honking, but you think he's crazy because there is a line of cars in front of you stretching as far as you can see, and all of you are stuck on this winding coastal road. You will probably be here forever. Still, you pull to the side to let him over, and then bemusedly watch him honk at the car in front of him. His life must be very frustrating, he's living a six-lane lifestyle on a two-lane road.

You are slumped over, now, with your elbow on the door of the van and your face on your hand. Will it never end?

Jenner. Wow, another town. But suddenly you perk up. You've been here before, you are near the highway that will take you back inland. You have reached the Russian River. You are exhausted. It has taken you four winding hours to drive what would have taken one. Still, you are so, so happy. There is an older woman on a bicycle, riding down a forested road beside the river and you can still see the sun. Suddenly you can think of nothing you would rather have done with the first day of your retreat. You made friends with the man in the red truck. You almost got shells on the beach. You lived in little towns in your mind, pretending the Turkish house was the house of a Turkish princess, and you even saw an alpaca. What a perfect day in September, a day of solitude, a day saying goodbye to the California that you love.

September 28, 2007

So what is it, inside me, that chooses the wrong things for comfort?

It's not that ice cream is bad. It's not. It's not even that I'm unhealthy, because I'm not. I eat well. I drink mostly water. My vices are usually too much pasta, brown sugar in my coffee, *coffee*. I don't smoke anymore, unless I'm with an old smoking friend in Canada and just *have* to light up for old times sake.

But sometimes eating ice cream feels like the smoking in the alley behind my house that I used to do, late at night, when everyone was sleeping and I felt that teenaged hollow feeling, the hurting that I just couldn't understand. I loved that house. We had just moved from the suburbs, where we were homeowners, to a rental in urban Edmonton. For my parents it might have been a sad move, but for fifteen-year-old me, it was heaven. Thanks to an understanding landlord, I painted my room a green called "Ireland's Pride." You can imagine the shade. I also ragged it off, giving my walls the texture of a ferny rainforest.

It was the beginning of my love affair with old houses and gardens and lit windows. At night I'd sit on my couch in front of my long, tall window, and gaze at the enormous house that I could see on the next block. I'd watch their windows with the lights pouring from within, thinking about towers and nooks and little rooms, and

I'd dream of the people who lived in that large red house. They loved books and cats. They ate yogurt for breakfast. They were professors. And then that ache would get to be too much and out I'd go to sit in the alley with a cigarette.

Last night I found out that my grandmother is very sick. I knew she was struggling with her health, but none of us had received any real diagnosis, yet, and the truth suckerpunched me in the gut. I sat on the couch. I called her. I cried. I called my husband. I prayed for a while, my hands on my stomach. I wrote a little. I turned on the television, then turned it off. I picked up my knitting, put it back down and then went for the food.

What *is* that? Once again, it's not that food is bad, it's just that it's not all that comforting. You're all shovel and chomp and then you end up burping. Baking is comforting, measuring out ingredients. Cleaning, reading the beautiful words of God. But nothing calls like the siren song of junk food. I believe this is called bingeing.

I did only end up eating about a third of a pint, hardly a binge. But there was some Pirate's Booty involved, and some peanut butter cups, also. Not many, but still. All designed to *distract*.

My grandmother is one of the strongest women that I have ever met, strong in that incredibly refined way, like the Queen of England. Except that she's Scottish, Scottish-Canadian, the kind of woman who enjoyed her childbirths, the kind of woman who gets tears in her eyes every time she thinks of my baby brother, who died, and yet who was the only member of my family I could bring myself to ask for the full details about him and several of the other family tragedies, because she processes grief by remembering, by talking about it. She is a woman of detail, the kind who remembers every single birthday of every person she's ever met, who sewed all of her own clothes and her children's clothes, the kind who retired at *seventy-eight*.

I can't think of her sick.

This troubling tendency toward distraction in myself is something that I'm working on. I bet we all are, to some extent. I've been coming up with a group of practices, harvested from different Christian traditions, different homesteading and artistic traditions, which I am using to reconstruct my life. I know what I believe, I feel rock solid in my faith. But what do I practice? How do I live this life, how do I reap the most out of it?

Probably not by eating ice cream and channel surfing. I don't want to be too hard on myself, and if you could see my little heart right now you'd see that it is tender towards nine-year-old me gazing glassy-eyed at the t.v. that she had previously ignored on this writing retreat.

These practices that I'm working on are almost like bookmarks, like things I can return to again and again. I hope to come to a place where I reach for the things that will truly comfort, even in times of great need. Even when someone I love so deeply is sick, when the idea of too much change threatens to rock me a little too hard and tip me over.

I will pray for my grandmother and keep calling her, keep telling her I love her and hear her trying to reassure me as she says, "I know you do, dear."

october

October 4, 2007

Oh Leafy,

You were sick yesterday, and snuggled ferociously in that hot-headed way that you have when you are feverish.

Before I realized you weren't feeling well, I told you that your pacifier, or Ny-ny, as you have named it, was for bedtime, and I put it away. While I was folding clothes and not paying attention, you took matters into your own hands, dragging a chair into your bedroom, climbing onto it so you could reach the dresser, and grabbing all of the pacifiers out of the container that I keep them in. When I next looked up, you were sitting at the kids' table with a pacifier in your mouth and two in your little hands, just in case.

You barely let me out of your sight, yesterday, sick baby that you were, you chose to hang onto my legs, or simply follow me around, and so we sat together a lot, you facing me on my lap, laying your head on my chest. If my attention was directed at anything other than you, you simply put your fingers on my face and turned my head back towards you. If I could replicate the feeling of your hot little hands on my cheeks, gentle but determined, or the sight of your very serious brown eyes above that little pacified mouth, oh Leafy, I would. I would just carry those memories around in my pockets to pull out when I was feeling sad.

We sat and tried to catch specks of dust, and it made you laugh, again and again, as lousy as you felt. The glittering air kept evading us, and you yelled, "Sparkles! Sparkles!" over and over. Your games last forever.

It's amazing to me, this talking that you do. The other day we were sitting around over dinner and you turned to me and said, "I love you, Mom-mee." And I thought, "It speaks in full sentences?"

You are some kind of guy. And I am one happy Mama, even when we are glued together all day, on a sick day, on a day that you need me a little more than most. Especially then.

October 11, 2007

I always feel sad when I come here.

I am in the City, in San Francisco, the only city that I have ever known intimately. I know many secrets of this city, especially secrets about the dark underbelly, the shouting that goes on at night, the faces that are slammed into fences and gates. I also know good secrets, like where to get the best coffee and pizza, and which streets to travel on when you are in a hurry. I know no other city in this way.

But it never did let me in.

Now, I am staying overnight in the big sprawling flat where I lived before I moved to the Land. I don't know what it is about a place that can get into me this way, I only know that I grip things, and my knuckles are tired.

I remember walking up the back steps, the old wooden steps that are ridiculously steep and that smell like pee, with Kenya, when she was barely four hours old. I was a little unsteady, but glad to be coming home from the birth center to go to bed. It was about 10:00 at night. I sat on the couch and someone fixed me some cereal, probably my mom. They all sat around me, all my friends and roommates, on the couch, around me and on the floor beneath me, and some perched above me, on the arms of the couch. They stroked me and touched me and of course, held tiny Kenya, who just hours before had revealed that she was a daughter, not another son.

These are the kind of memories I am gripping, here. And although now, years later, I have become so accustomed to the woods that I am sort of blinky and stunned in the City, coming here is sharp and poignant. This was home. It belongs to other people now, people who are kind enough to have me come and stay with them. But my memories of the last couple of years are not of here.

This is the way of things. And I want to hold on. But people are the same way, as elusive as the specks of dust that Leafy and I tried to catch on the day he was sick. You love them and love them, but you can't keep them. Even our children will grow up and go.

I have somehow entwined myself in the land under my feet. I feel as though small birds have pinned me to the ground, and when we break away, small pieces of us will break off, too. The other day I was talking with Chinua, trying to figure out how to bring the woods and hills with me. "Maybe a tattoo of a Redwood. Or a Madrone," I suggested.

"Definitely a Madrone," he said. "A Redwood would make a horrible tattoo."

Maybe it would and maybe it wouldn't. But I have to let go. Somehow.

And then I remember that I always feel this way. And I found a poem that I wrote, when I lived here in this house that I feel nostalgic for now.

*

you struggle
when you have left pieces of yourself
around the earth,
in this village
and that one. you'll find sometimes
that your edges don't meet
the sides don't match.
your skin doesn't stretch to cover
all of you.
  a slight ringing of bells is enough to
draw you halfway around the world
to call you away from your children
splashing happily in their bath.
or a stop at the curb
an otherwise annoying smell from
the sewer
  sends you rocking into boats
sends you into the warm air.
when you have left pieces.
tan faces, bits of amber
the rush of a crowd in the market
meat on a stick, the cockroaches
your hurriedly made bed
deep in the cold of air conditioning.
  when you have left pieces of yourself

with people, in this city and
that one,
you'll find that you can't
keep your thoughts with you
sometimes
they have taken you on a journey
a musing, winding road, many trees
thick forests. you struggle
to put a key in the lock of
your front door
with clumsy fingers.

    you trip, stand catching your breath
head down, looking at cracks
in the pavement. head in your hands
draw yourself back.
pieces of you, here and there
making small light patches
on a gray and rushing landscape.

   *

It is the same. I am the same, wanting to own what I cannot own, finding it difficult to say goodbye. And I will get through.

October 13, 2007

It is morning and I am writing with a little head snuggled into my shoulder. The other two kids are still in bed. Incense is thick in the air. I have begun the practice of burning incense while I pray in the mornings, in the dark, to see the rising smoke and know that

God hears my little words.

Kai sits beside me, he scratches his neck, where he still gets eczema, from time to time, especially if I am not careful enough with his diet. I remember how overwhelmed I was by feeding two kids with food allergies, back when I first started. Now it is simple to me. So much of life is like that.

Kai is wearing his blue jammies with the feet. Kenya calls hers her slippery jammies, and slips and slides all over the floor like a fish in them. I love Kai's eyelashes. Last night when I got home I felt exuberant, like I could float away because of the love that supports me. We played the game again, where we talk about what we like about each other, all piled onto the love seat like puppies. Kenya said that she loves the hugs that both of her brothers give. Kai said that he likes that Kenya is so bee-youtiful. Leafy ran back and forth.

I went to visit with some dear friends, and they showed me photos of the two lovely places that we will most likely end up living in, in India. One is mountainous and lovely, in the North. And one is beachy and tropical, in the South. And it hit me. I've been wanting to go back to India for so, so long. And finally, we are going. I felt wave after wave of happiness wash over me as I looked at the photos. Because India, also, is one of my homes. And I am returning.

My heart is busy storing up days that tell of God's faithfulness to me. How he stretches the line of my life like a ribbon, fitting it around the various curves and over the various mountains, lining it up in pleasant places, even in the midst of sorrow.

Today, we have even more evidence that we are being tenderly cared for than yesterday. So much of life is like that.

And now I have to look after the needs of this patient boy who is sitting beside me, the one with the nose that is so perfect I would like to have it framed.

October 16, 2007

I feel aware and alive this morning. You could chalk it up to dance class last night. I'm not sure if you remember my "give it a year" philosophy with my West African Dance class, but it seems to be working. It has been a year, maybe a little less. All I know is that when I started it was dark outside while we danced, turning the windows into mirrors that we could critique ourselves in, slightly. And the big barrel stove was going, turning the room into a sauna, making us slightly light-headed. And then when we drove home we shot through the dark on steep curves, under the trees that are as tall as mountains.

It's that season again. All the vineyards are turning, the ivy is turning. The poison oak is turning. Everything is beautiful, even the unbeautiful, and my year of dancing has made me stronger.

I wasn't as faithful about going as I would have liked. But a year later my feet can follow more often than not. And a year later I feel like I may just dance as long as I can find classes.

There are opportunities coming up that have put me into a state of awe. It seems that God has had our address all along. And although it still feels as though chunks of my heart break off when people come to look at the Land, mulling over whether they want to buy it, (just don't cut down the trees!) I am heartened by the fact that there is this dancing path ahead of us. And I'm allowed to take it.

October 17, 2007

1. It rains and rains and rains. This is good for the river.

2. I am in a little cabin in the woods with three children, ages almost two, three, and five. Use your imagination.

3. I am trying to get ready to move. Our community has been here at this Land for ten years. There are files in the office from 1993. I found a 1957 Ford truck manual yesterday. (Why on earth do we have this?)

4. Let's see. Yesterday at our community meeting we discussed: a) Dumpster vs. trash runs, which is basically money vs. pain. How much scrap do we have? We can get money for this, maybe offsetting the cost of the dumpster. b) The eleven vehicles that we still need to deal with. (Various people abandoned their vehicles at the Land over the years) c) What can we sell? Stoves? RV? Chainsaw? d) Which day should we go shopping?

5. Yesterday we also received a scathing letter from someone we haven't met, condemning our choice to sell the Land. Where have all these people who care so much been, the whole time we've lived here? I am amazed at the number of people who are popping out of the bushes angrily, like hedgehogs.

6. I love teaching my kids. It is possibly my favorite thing.

7. Also, my favorite thing is Leafy's new phrases, "HUG!" and "I love you _____" (name inserted) He yells "HUG" about eighty-seven times a day, and says "I love you" about fourteen times a day.

8. So, all in all, life is good. (Just, do you think it's cruel to make my kids play outside in the rain?)

november

November 1, 2007

Today is Moving Day. I'm still here, after an insane week of packing and sorting and purging and burning and cleaning. Do any of you clean under your couches? You really should, because then you won't be like me and be embarrassed when people pick them up and put them in the truck and it looks like a littered beach has been left behind on your floor. A beach littered with small toys. But who has time to move their furniture around, cleaning underneath it?

A bunch of stuff, including all seven pieces of our furniture and all of our strange instruments, are on the truck. It says a lot about us that about half of our belongings are cameras and the other half are odd musical instruments. We have more antique cameras than a camera dealer. Some people collect Picasso, we collect Russian medium format cameras.

A whole lot of stuff is waiting for me to continue sorting it. We really are in the middle of this, right now.

I have survived without having a heart attack, and Renee, who is also packing to move, is just barely surviving without having a nervous breakdown. I had to look at her quite sternly yesterday and say, "Renee, you need to calm down." She has too much going on, poor girl. And Mike and Julie, the other couple who live here, are busy being the sweetest people in the world, watching the kids for us, making dinner, helping us load the truck.

It's going to be weird, going away from community cold turkey like this. I'm going to be looking around at about 10:00 in the morning and scratching my head, thinking—*something's not right*. Because where's Renee? She should be at my house making coffee by now.

But in other ways, it will be delightful. Chinua and I have lived with other people our whole married life, and before, too! We hope that a community will form in India. But until then, we need a little break.

The surprising part is that Chinua is driving the moving truck South, to Sacramento, and the kids and I are driving North, to Eugene. I'm on my way to Canada again. We didn't plan it this way, but remember how I said my grandmother was sick? We got the news that she's really quite sick, and I need to go and see her. So I am driving to Edmonton.

This will be a month of journeying, since I'm taking another trip at the end of the month, this one a working trip that is so very exciting that I can barely contain myself. I'll tell you more about that one later.

As for now, I need to finish packing. The morning light is just beginning to filter through the trees and the kids are being crazy in their room. I think I'll bring some coffee to Renee's cabin, across the Land. Today we are saying goodbye to our home.

November 2, 2007

It's true that I finally melted down yesterday, standing in the midst of the debris of my life, melted into a tear puddle on the floor.

It's true that when my friend called, I answered my phone with the words, "You are so glad that you are not me right now." It's true that she replied, "Really? Because I'm pretty sure I would be glad to be anyone else in the world than me at this moment." And then we laughed. It's like when I was a kid and my brother and sister and I would argue over who was feeling "worser."

It's true that I waved goodbye to the Land yesterday, and that I did so in such a flurry of limbs and papers and financial issues that I almost forgot to blow a kiss.

But it's also true that my Superstar Husband is the most brilliant star in my sky. It's true that he sang love songs to me before I left, that he told me about twenty-six times to drive carefully, and that he took care of the rest of the debris, finishing up the packing that I couldn't even face anymore. He lovingly uncrossed my eyes and sent me on my way.

And it's true that on my way, I found strain slipping off of my freckled back, that when I reached the coast I saw the waves throwing themselves down in glee and thought, "The whole world is my home." It's true that the cliffs were etched against the misty pre-sunset sky like strong-armed guards, and I realized that even transition can be a type of home. That maybe I can let my bones settle into this change. That there is rest for me, there are homes everywhere, and that so many things that have piled on over these last years are now lifted. And everywhere I look there are houses with small people in them, sitting in their seats, walking to their fridges and back, playing card games at the coffee table. We are all looking for the same things.

It's true that we left too late yesterday. That I was not at all prepared, that I fed my kids convenience store white bread sandwiches.

It's true that Kai has reached the age of constant attempts at reasoning, that he can't let go, now, and let things flow. That he feels the need to check on our progress, say, every two minutes. That he whines a lot about how long it's taking to get there. It's true that this means he is becoming more of a person, and that instead of smacking my head against the steering wheel, I should admire his time-telling skillz, when he plaintively yells from the backseat, "MAMA! IT'S 7:14! Mamaaaaa, it's 7:16!" And ad infinitum until I die.

It's also true that we sang our way through the darkness last night, that we belted out the ABC song, that we transitioned seamlessly into Twinkle Twinkle Little Star, and then that I could hear Leafy singing "Winkle Pinkle DAR. Winkle Pinkle DAR," until I thought my heart would break from the happiness and love and rightness.

November 4, 2007

I am in Canada, at my parents' house. I'm up at an ungodly hour, which thankfully isn't really an ungodly hour, thanks to Daylight Savings (ending? beginning?), although I hate the fact that this means it will get darker earlier. *Wow, Rae, not a futile thing at all, there, railing against the shortening days year after year.*

But I have to get myself and children in the car for my road trip to Edmonton, to see my grandmother. So I will only say two things:

1. I hope I see a bear, or a moose.

2. I hate my passport photo. And I think it's time for some new hair color or something, something to liven my face up a bit, because if I look like the girl in that photo, well... that's totally not okay.

November 5, 2007

I guess you never really know how things will turn out. One moment you are driving along, listening to your kids talk in the back, watching the snow come down, and the next minute you are skidding out and you cannot stop yourself.

Two hours from our starting point, yesterday, the van we were driving skidded out on some slush and hit the barrier to our right, which propelled us back across the highway, where we flew over the median and across the lanes of oncoming traffic, plunging down an eighty-foot embankment and crashing down at the bottom. We flew. We literally left the ground and landed, eighty feet down, crushing the nose of the van and then landing on the passenger side.

And then our angels dusted themselves off and we all walked out of it. Miraculously.

I mean, it was crazy. There were screaming children and Kenya's hands were bleeding, and I couldn't get them out of their car seats, and the van was filling with the smell of gas, and we were in the snow, down a cliff, and I didn't know if anyone would find us. But then there they were, a group of male ballet dancers, on their way to perform in a ballet in the next town, 50 km away. They pulled us out of the van through the shattered back window, and ran up the hillside, each kid in strong arms. Then, at the top, someone who stopped happened to be an emergency room nurse. He checked the kids over. Someone else let us sit in his car until the ambulance came.

I was strapped to a gurney, with a back board, and a collar, until they could check my spine out. So the whole time I was in the ambulance I was strapped to this thing, and trying to keep it light for the kids.

"Don't you think I look funny like this, Kai?"

"No," was his reply.

Kai was really, really worried about the fact that we were borrowing Grandma's van to make the drive, and now her van was broken, and what was she going to do without her van? I had to work really hard to convince him that he didn't need to worry about the grownup problems.

Finally the hospital, and x-rays, and a doctor who wasn't so nice, and two victim services people who took care of the kids and were absolutely some of the sweetest people I've ever met. And Kenya's arm was bandaged, which caused some more trauma. When they finally let me get off of that board, I wobbled over to the area where the kids were and found them all cuddled on the bed together while Kenya was getting her hand taken care of.

I am still a bit bewildered. The whole day was so crazy, which is a huge understatement. Looking down, after, at how far we fell, I couldn't believe we were all okay. Seeing the van in the towing yard, when we went to get our stuff, I couldn't believe we were all okay. Seeing the window that was next to Kenya's all smashed in, I couldn't believe we were all okay. Finding her blankie with blood all over it- well.

There were mercies, mercies. There were angels. We came

bruised and shaken—and in Kenya's case, a bit cut up—out of a crash that could have been so much worse. There are so many things that were like pure mercy.

On Saturday night, before we left on our big journey, my dad felt uncomfortable about the seatbelt in the middle of the back seat of the van, where Leafy's car seat was going to be. So he put a piece of chain link through the seat belt, fastening it so that there was no way that it could budge. And other things, like the fact that I accidentally left our big camera at home, so it's safe, rather than smashed up.

I feel like I'm rambling, and I don't exactly know what to say, except that I'm thankful, so, so thankful that my Kenya girl is alright, that we are all alright. That I am only bruised. That there are no broken bones. That we are all alive.

November 5, 2007

I forgot to mention that the cause of the accident was unsafe tires. My mom had recently taken the van to the tire shop, where she requested winter tires. The man assured her that putting snow tires with studs on the back, while keeping regular tires on the front, was perfectly safe. However, everywhere that I've been researching this today insists that for safety, the same type of tire should be installed on both axles. As far as the guy advising my mom that what he was installing would be fine, I think it is a case of preferring what is legal, over what is safe. Since my mom was putting studded tires on her car, any employee at a large tire store such as this one should be aware of the dangers of uneven handling.

And there is my tire rant.

We are sore, sore, sore. I think everyone is recovering.

November 7, 2007

I am still writing my way through this. People have expressed surprise that I can write so soon after the accident, but writing is my way of making sure that I am still here.

I woke up this morning at my grandmother's house, to the call of "Breakfast is ready!" from my grandfather. It is like stepping back in time, being in this house. I've been longing to come back here for years, and haven't, simply because Edmonton is a long, long way from California. But here I am now. My sister and I flew out yesterday morning. Driving didn't work, but we still needed to come out to see my grandma.

The kids are with my Mom and Dad, and there is probably no other reason under heaven that I'd leave them at this point in time, but I'm always amazed by how secure they feel around their grandpa and grandma.

I have so much to say, but it will have to wait. I'm going to squeeze as much time with my own grandma and grandpa as I can out of this short visit.

November 11, 2007

Oh, I'm sore. My sternum feels like pigeons have found a home in my ribcage and are fighting amongst themselves in there. I trust that this isn't the case.

I found this quote in the book, *Walking on Water*, by Madeleine L'Engle, which I'm reading and loving right now.

"Unamuno might be describing the artist as well as the Christian as he

293

writes, 'Those who believe they believe in God, but without passion in the heart, without anguish of mind, without uncertainty, without doubt, and even at times without despair, believe only in the idea of God, and not in God himself.'"

These are good words to take to heart when living in a confusing and war torn world. Or after free falling in your vehicle. Or when you're five, and trying to figure out why we were allowed to be in the accident in the first place.

All I know is this: My driving may be a little bit white-knuckled, lately, and my baby may cry whenever he gets in the car, but I feel more than ever that my life is gently cupped in my Father's hands. We are like small smooth stones, warm and cradled and sure. No matter what happens He will not let go.

November 12, 2007

Has it really been only eleven days since the beginning of November? They have been eventful, to say the least.

Tomorrow we begin our journey back down to California, to our new home in Sacramento. I can't wait to see our house, meet it and move into the corners of it, and fill the fridge with baby carrots.

I kind of want to see my Superstar Husband, too.

It has been delightful, though, spending time with my mum and dad. They put up with me well, their daughter who just happens to come home and wreck their vehicle. It's so funny, really, I feel responsible and they feel responsible (because it was their car) but really, as my dad puts it, "You just can't even go there." They are so incredible to me, though, so giving and warm and I have been feeling really safe recuperating here. Now it is time to go home and behave like a grownup.

At the end of the month I have the incredible opportunity to be a part of writing about an amazing project with some wonderful people. This project is the reason for an urgent passport mission that I accomplished this past week. Which was successful, if by successful we mean having a passport that makes me look like a sunburned donkey. On the bright side, a sunburned donkey who can get on an airplane and fly overseas is happier than a sunburned donkey who cannot.

November 12, 2007

Today I found myself wondering whether I should do things in a different way before our big drive to California, in case the way I did things last time caused the accident. (!)

I am not at all superstitious, and I think that there is an underlying anxiousness in me that I cannot even reach with my awake mind. The kind of anxiousness that would have me *doing things in a different order* so as to not repeat the accident. Leafy has been crying a lot when we try to put him in his car seat. I bought him a new one yesterday (since the other one was involved in an accident, and can't be used anymore) and hopefully that will help.

Prayers of love and safety and oceans of grace will surround us as we drive south.

November 16, 2007

I'm going to Burkina Faso to do some writing, filming, and photography for the company that Chinua is working with here in Sacramento. I haven't traveled out of the continent since before

Chinua and I were married, back in the sleeping-in-hammocks-on-the-beach-on-an-Indian-island-days. I remember how for years I would grow covetous when I was driving friends to the International airport, how I longed just to get on a plane. I NEED AN INTERNATIONAL FLIGHT, I would think. And in recent times I have become much more content. I have learned the beauty of being constrained. As my friend put it once, "Lean into the restraint."

And of course, now that this new contentment is here, opportunities for travel are popping out of the cracks in the couch. (There is a lesson here, somewhere.)

And, the house. The house! I love the house. We're staying here for five months while Chinua works for some friends. When five months are up, we'll make the move to India. It makes me a little afraid, how much I love the house, considering how temporary this arrangement is, but I realize that everything is temporary, right? So you love things while they are there, without that compulsion to grasp.

I love the bead-board wainscoting in the kitchen, the quirky little doorways. I love the pantry that has the sink in it, so that I have to walk back and forth between the kitchen and the pantry to do dishes and put water in the pots. I love the water pressure. I love the world's biggest oak tree in the back yard. I love the funky falling down neighborhood, and the train that runs nearby, and the molding around the doorways.

Now if I can only refrain from injuring myself further, trying to get things in order.

November 18, 2007

Today I was sitting on my porch with my cup of coffee,

attempting to knit a baby hat (the second cup of coffee, after Kai knocked over the first one) and the yard guy was cutting the grass (he's employed by the company that owns the house).

It was late afternoon and the sun was at that sweet angle where the whole world is suddenly cast in its best light, and the oak leaves that are scattered across our porch steps looked like Martha Stewart put them there *on purpose.* This neighborhood for some reason reminds us of the South, and it also reminds me a little of Detroit, and never more so than when the ice cream man comes around in his rusty black van. Like he did this afternoon. I know, you're ready to kill me, right? Because the ice cream man is coming around in the middle of *November.* We'll just have our Thanksgiving dinner and then run out and get some Ice Cream sandwiches.

So I'm sitting there ignoring the ice cream truck, which seems to be hovering, and I'm not sure why, because I'm very deliberately ignoring him, thinking that my kids don't need treats right now, they are going to a party tonight where there will surely be treats (I was right, there were cupcakes). But then the yard guy calls up to me, and he wants to buy my kids popsicles.

So I change my mind, because have you ever heard of anything sweeter than the guy who is mowing your yard, who is only at your house because he is part of some landscaping company, running out to the ice cream truck to get your kids popsicles?

And then there we are, sitting on the porch. The kids tell me again and again how good popsicles are, and the juice runs down their chins, and it feels like this bit of extra summer ease that I did not have this past summer.

This world can be so beautiful sometimes.

November 24, 2007

It's too bad that we have to hang out in our own heads so much. My own experience of life would be a lot better if I didn't have this brain of mine to deal with. But here I am with these old eyes, and this spastic motherboard that processes all that they see, and this is what I get. These are the tools I've been given, fidgety and twitchy as they are. Can God do anything with poor old me?

Life is good. My children are my deepest blessing, and my husband is adorable. He's funny, he's smart, and he sings silly songs almost as often as he breathes. Our house is incredible, funny and Victorian and hilly and I love the friends who are around us and we had a wonderful Thanksgiving.

But my self is unsettled, and I haven't found the ground underneath my feet yet. I feel like I'm tripping, I'm not sure of where the boundaries lie. I'm not sure of what I am and am not allowed to do. That sounds stupid, doesn't it?

But for real, this is a big change. For instance, we have this fridge. It's really nice, I think someone wasn't using it anymore and kindly passed it along to us. (I'm not sure about all that happened before I got here.) It's big. It's nice. And everyday I walk over to it and open it and I think, "Is that really my food?" I mean, I have a fridge full of my own food. I'm twenty-seven years old and have never eaten in a non-communal way. In our last house, at the Land, we had a little half-size fridge. Up at the Big House was the kitchen, with the real food, not the juice and salsa that our fridge held. And the real stove was up there, too, while I had the single burner Coleman camping stove that I cooked the morning oatmeal on.

This is really different for me. I am not sure if I am allowed to be happy here, yet. I am a little nervous.

Maybe today is just a strange day. I've been having them, on and off. The victim services people from B.C. wrote to me the other day, sending me information about Critical Incident Response. The pamphlet shared all of the things that I may or may not be feeling or experiencing after having an accident like mine. I have to say, I'm feeling a lot of them, but what comes from the accident, and what comes from moving, and what comes from a major life change? And what comes from just being crazy ol' me?

It is a good time for a little journeying to West Africa, I think. The kids will be staying here with Chinua, and I will traveling with some wonderful women. We leave very, very early on Monday morning, which doesn't even really count as Monday. It's like the day in between Sunday and Monday.

Maybe somewhere along the way I will regain my rhythm.

November 25, 2007

Sometimes having dreadlocks is interesting. When Becca and I were at the airport, an older couple were obviously fascinated with our hair and couldn't quite believe that it wasn't "artificial". Even my grandmother barely believes that this is all my own hair.

Today I was at the big library downtown. (I think I'll be okay in the city as long as I stick to the libraries. I went into Bed Bath and Beyond tonight to buy a travel pillow and pretty much gave myself a hernia. I am afraid of *things*, especially so much silicone cookware and so many digital scales.) While I was in the library, a boy took a picture of my hair.

I was wandering by, minding my own business, and I semi-noticed him lifting his phone up and aiming it at me. Then, I heard that unmistakably loud fake shutter sound that cameras on phones have, trying to make up for the fact that they don't have shutters.

And then the boy (he was about fifteen or sixteen) kinda went *cough, cough* to make up for the fact that he had stolen my soul with his camera phone and his fake shutter sound had given him away.

It was all I could do not to bust out laughing, but I had some respect for the dignity of a teenage boy and acted like I hadn't noticed. Besides, there were books calling my name. All I can think is that he wanted a photo of some girl's crazy hair. I certainly wasn't wearing anything spectacular. Except, you know, it could have been that spandex glitter suit I had on.

November 26, 2007

I feel a little scared that the Leafy Boy might grow up in the ten days that I am gone. I really, really don't want that to happen. What if I come back and he's like, four? He's already learning about sixty-five words per day, I don't want any extra growth happening as well.

I'm probably worried over nothing. They'll all be fine. The dads will be fine.

In the meantime, Jessie and Cyndy and I will be boarding our flight early tomorrow morning, on our way to Paris, then Burkina Faso. The Paris part is crazy, I quite honestly never thought that I would ever go to Paris in my lifetime. It just goes to show you that maybe the darkest part of the storm really is right before the light. Or however that saying goes. I just totally messed that up, didn't I?

November 28, 2007

We're getting close to Paris and I've realized something for not quite the first time. I CANNOT sleep sitting up. I try and try, and no matter how exhausted I am, I can't get to that sweet drooling sleepy time place. I remember once, desperate on a Thai bus, when I simply gave up and laid on the floor among all the feet. The floor was hot and incredibly dirty and I slept like a baby. Now, knowing a little bit more about Southeast Asian cultures and their ideas about feet, I'm sure they were horrified. But they didn't show it, smiling and frowning sweetly at me.

I don't think that would go over as well here on Delta Airlines. Bummer. Anyways, it looks like my first day in Paris may be a little blurred by sleep deprivation. Which may be just what I need to get the courage to use my elementary school *Francais*. *Voulez-vous repetez, s'il vous plait?*

Do you ever have that incredible urge to leap up when the call for a doctor on board comes over the PA system on a flight? I've heard that call a couple of times, and tonight I'm really hoping that the person who needed the doctor is okay, but I also feel like dancing to my feet and yelling, "I'm a doctor!" Which would be a complete lie, since I'm totally not a doctor. Wanting to be a doctor is not the same as being a doctor.

Also, wanting to be a breakdancer is not at all the same as actually knowing how to breakdance.

November 28, 2007

Paris.

We have been meeting with the director of the non-profit we are working on, and all I have in my head is his accent. It is making it difficult to write in English, because I am composing my words with the understanding of someone who writes little English in mind.

We have mastered the Paris Metro. Yesterday it was not so good, but today, *Voila!* We glide from stop to stop with the greatest of ease. The subway is interesting. Let's just say that the way the French use arrows is very different from the way we use arrows in North America. But yesterday we were also suffering from lack of sleep. We went for 32 hours without sleep and then fell in our beds and slept for twelve hours. It's a good way to get on the right time schedule.

Now I need to get some sleep. Tomorrow we get up very early to fly to Burkina Faso.

december

When you go to West Africa...

You may find yourself in a small village market far away from any evidence of the twenty-first century. You might take photographs of women more beautiful than any you have ever seen, women who have never before seen a photograph of themselves. You will bless your digital camera again and again, because you will witness the disbelief and hilarity of women who find an image of themselves for the first time. They may grab you, grab their friends, laugh uproariously, direct you to the next person to photograph.

You may find yourself feeling completely, purely happy.

You will be invited into every village with hospitality that exceeds all limits. Your hosts will look for something for all your traveling companions to sit on- in the shade you will simply sit, and, not understanding the language, you will listen to the customary blessings with a smile on your face, because everyone understands the rhythm of speech, and everyone understands kindness.

You will see many, many, many children. You will exclaim over tiny babies on the backs of women, you will make toddlers cry with your strangeness, you will make the older kids laugh and shriek when you show them photos of themselves. They will yell out names as you flip through photos, and find other children for you to photograph. They will lift up the small ones so that you can reach them.

You may find yourself drinking moonshine gin in the morning, the tiniest sips of something you would never in your life drink at home, because you can't drink the water and your hosts must offer you something. You wouldn't dream of saying no. It tastes horrible and wonderful, because you are being honored. You will, however, draw the line at more than a few sips.

You may meet the kindest people you have ever met. You may realize all over again that possessions mean nothing, and that true joy is found in love and brotherhood. You may feel honored beyond what you deserve, again and again. You may share food with people who bring you their best, who bring you the rabbit because rabbit is the best meat they could find. You may close your eyes more than once, rather than looking at what you are eating. You may wonder more than once, what exactly you are eating.

You may have the best traveling companions ever; women who don't blink when asked to use a hole in the ground as *La Toilette*. Together you will laugh and laugh and laugh, almost more than you have laughed ever in a five day period. Because these people who are hosting you sure do believe in laughter.

You may arrive home and be incredibly sick, running to the bathroom more times than you can possibly count. You would go back to Burkina Faso again if you could, sixteen times if you could, even if you had to be sick like this every time.

You may arrive home and wonder who those kids are, and then

realize with a shock that they are yours! And that though ten days is not a long time, you have traveled light years away, and coming back is like coming from a long, long distance. You will hug them and cuddle for hours. You will look around at your incredible wealth and feel undeserving. You will never be the same.

December 8, 2007

You think that you won't forget, but you do.

When you are there you feel that the red dust has crept all the way inside of you, that you will never look again at your world of wealth with the same eyes, that your ribcage holds a whole new heart.

You feel that this new music is yours forever, that the drums have found their way inside your bones, that the voices will never stop ringing, that the laughter will continue and you will always see white smiles flashing, that you will be able to bring some of this joy back.

You *know* that never again will you waste food or water, that a simple thing like a grocery store will always feel like a palace, that you will not forget the bad millet harvest, the fact that the well goes dry for four months a year. You will remember. You will not settle back in.

But you don't. And you do. And quickly wealth is normal again, and you are not sitting under the shade of a tree in a village with red dust and chickens and children all around you. You are not drinking Nescafé, you are speaking English naturally again, and you are forgetting, you are settling, you are giving a cursory nod to the teller at the grocery store rather than shaking his hand and greeting him.

December 12, 2007

Do you know when you have those days? I was having one
yesterday. Tomato cans were falling off shelves all around me, I
almost started sucking my thumb, I felt self-conscious and insecure
with a ferocity that was sickening and pitiable. These days have not
been totally infrequent lately, in adjusting to this new life, outside of
the strong gravity of the Land, the structure of my days there.

Actually, because of my fairly major problems with anxiety, these
days have not been totally infrequent during the course of my life,
but that's beside the point.

Do you know how, when you attempt to talk to your husband
about how you're feeling, and you're all- *Please tell me I'm not crazy-* he
looks at you like he's wondering which boulder you overturned to
crawl out from the bowels of the earth and pretty much says- *No, you
really are crazy?*

(This is not to put down the absolute caring and overwhelming
love of your husband, who would stand on coals to help you, either
that or just juggle work and kids for eleven days so that you can take
a trip to Africa, all without ever mentioning a word about the
sacrifice he's making, which, you should mention, is soooo much
better than you would do or have done in his place. It's just that he
doesn't always understand your particular brand of insanity.)

So then, misplaced and feeling abused, you drag your feet
around your carpets and then finally call your good friend Tammie,
that friend who lives on an incredible ranch in your old stomping
grounds to the north. The Tammie who gave you a new espresso
machine- which arrived in the mail right before you left for Burkina
Faso, replacing the one that died in the car accident.

307

And you have been using it every day but because you couldn't upload the picture of it when you wanted to blog about it, you didn't mention it to her until she asked you yesterday (YESTERDAY) whether you had received it. And you know that you are a lout (LOUT!) because *good golly already.*

But the point is that you tell her all about your feelings and it is as if you have been trying to speak French all along, and things keep getting missed in translation, but now you have found someone who speaks the English you speak, or maybe the Russian you speak, if you speak Russian, and she understands! And she tells you that you are not crazy, which is important, or maybe it is that you are both crazy, but there is kinship there, which is the most important. It's that kinship of women who have a language that is unintelligible, at times, to the men who love them. It emotional, it's not logical! Sometimes it's not even right, but it's *understood.*

December 15, 2007

It's strange how sometimes all we know of an entire continent is what is given to us by the media. We only hear of war, atrocities, tragedy, famine, and epidemic disease. Where are the people in all of this? Are they lost? Do we understand that they have stories?

I remember that we were driving in the Land Cruiser, packed in cozily with that same red dust working its way into our eyebrows and our teeth. The 4x4, or *quat-quat*, as they say in Burkina Faso, was being given its exercise, helping us travel along roads as pocked as the surface of the moon.

Through the roar of the air outside and the laughter of the people inside, we talked.

All we have is our feeling, he told me.

Your feeling? I asked.

When we see a poor man, we think- that could be me, he said. *Or if it is a rich man, we know that maybe next year we will be in his place. Everyone can put himself in the place of his brother. It is why we help each other.*

Oh- like empathy.

It is all we have, he went on. *We Africans, we have no power in the world, we have no product, no money, nothing. We only have our feeling.*

I see this feeling. You treat every man like a brother.

If it is taken away we will have nothing. It seems that people want to take this away- I don't know why... He shrugs, hands out. *I don't know why. But we can't lose it, or we will have nothing.*

December 18, 2007

Hard truths.

Sometimes people you love get sick and don't seem to get better.

Please please please please please please please please please please please please

Everything you work for erupts underneath your feet

I didn't mean to I didn't mean to I didn't mean to I didn't mean to I didn't mean to

You leave your beloved home- you have to say goodbye

I loved you I loved you I loved you I loved you I loved you I loved you I loved you

You reach out for support and find anger. You will never make it. You will never be enough. You have a fatal flaw.

I am done I am done I am done I am done I am done I am done I am done I am done

Things will never be like they were. You need to close that door.

I am sorry.

December 19, 2007

There are ten thousand beautiful things surrounding me, visible and invisible~ I shuffle along in their midst, the days trickle in and out with a cloud of joy, children are always laughing around me.

The joy of service, the service of love, the fact that love can cover and comfort and remove those black marks that end up covering our bright blue skies.

Christmas, the lights, the making of gifts and cards and my children are writing books and I am free. There is love, there is wonder, there is love. I can't say enough about it, it is the kind that will welcome us home. Birth, rebirth, the shooting star wonder of Life entering the world~ we turn our heads with tears in our eyes, look back when we can to see blinding hope.

December 20, 2007

Honey, can we talk? -
Of course we can talk.
Good.
Wha-why are you acting so strange?
Just look into my eyes and try to read my mind.
(Significant Pause)
NO WAY!
Yes way.
WHATTTT??!
I know.
But HOW?

Damned if I know.

But we-

I know.

Are you SERIOUS?

Totally serious.

When?

This morning.

Whoa.

(Hugging and Kissing and Staring in Disbelief.)

You're pretty good at reading my mind!

December 20, 2007

There were so many points along the way that I probably should have figured it out.

Like when the women at the airport in Burkina Faso said to me, "You are pregnant?" and when I shook my head and acted a little offended they craned their necks to see my belly better and discussed it amongst themselves, obviously not believing. I mean, I know I need to work on my belly a little, but jeez.

Or then, crying when I was talking to the head guy of the project I'm working on.

Crying when I was talking to my employer on the phone.

Crying when I bumped our van tire into the curb.

Crying in Burkina Faso when I felt like I was lost on a long road of translation errors.

Or the fact that my belly just kept expanding. Or meeting another old friend who happens to be a nurse at my friend's party and becoming offended because he pointed at my stomach and asked me if this was baby number four.

Turns out everyone's smarter than me.

I'm ecstatic. It's not exactly what I would have picked, but I'm not in charge. And yes, we were being careful. Like that ever works for us.

But now that I'm pregnant, (I'm pregnant!) I can be so so so excited about another little roly poly to curl up on my belly.

December 22, 2007

Does anybody else ever feel tempted to go and buy more pregnancy tests, after you discover you are pregnant, just to have the thrill of seeing that little line magically show up? Or is that just me?

*

Things I still have:
Pregnancy vitamins
About four pounds of pregnancy tea, made of alfalfa, oat straw, nettles, and raspberry leaf. I can't extoll the benefits of this tea enough. However, it takes like food for horses.
Things I don't have anymore:
Maternity clothes.

*

I am so big already. None of my pants fit. I can't believe that I went from wondering vaguely if there was something weird going on, a few days ago, to undoing the button on my pants repeatedly, only to do it back up when they fall down when I stand up, now. I look pregnant. There's no other word for it. I think I may have been in a strong form of denial, assuming there were other reasons for every symptom I had.

*

This seems like perfect timing. I think that if I had discovered that I was pregnant a few months ago, I would have stomped around whining, "It's my body! I'm not ready to share it again!" But now it's like my organs are telling me, "We were getting a little lonely in here anyways..."

December 23, 2007

I have no idea how far along I am in this pregnancy. Which is a result of my poor memory and lack of cycle recording skills. I found myself looking through my planner, thinking, *Thanksgiving... someone had cramps on Thanksgiving... nope, that wasn't me, that was a friend of mine... I think it was before then...*

If I had to guess, I'd say that I'm probably six weeks along. But it could be five. Oh, I really have no idea.

As for my expanding belly, let's just say that with Kai, it took four months before you could even tell that I was pregnant. But with Kenya? I was hounding the doctor at six weeks because I was sure, I was SURE that I was having twins. But no. There was just one little baby in my belly. And then with Leafy the same thing happened. Also I gain more weight every pregnancy. Also I weigh more pre-pregnancy this time than after I had Leafy. I attribute some of it to my hair. But let's not focus too much on weight gain, shall we?

We are flying to Detroit tomorrow to spend Christmas with Chinua's family. It promises to be a rocking late-night, good time. I never understood my husband's leaning toward the very late night until I started hanging out with his family, and noted people casually hanging out at two in the morning like it was the middle of the afternoon.

We are pretty excited, since we don't get out there nearly as often as we would like to. They require an arm and a leg and your lips and a few eyelashes if you want to purchase a ticket. I did find an incredible deal if only we would fly on Christmas Eve, to which I replied, sign me UP. And I've already been told to bring an extra suitcase. For gifts. I don't think I need to worry about the kids this year.

So, it may be a while before I get to see anybody about this pregnancy. This would not have gone over well in the past, but I've learned a little about babies in the womb. They usually do pretty okay if you just forget about them and eat really well and sleep when you need to and read to your kids.

December 26, 2007

I have to admit that I was a little worried about my Kenya girl. She is- how should I say it? demonstrative? particular? insanely aware? about and over and around her desires and non-desires.

For example, when I woke her up early in the morning the other day, so that we could, you know, *get to the airport*, she shrieked, "I NEED SO MUCH SLEEP!" and then scrambled back into her bed again and again while I repeatedly dragged her tiny behind out. She also charmingly stiffened her legs while I tried to get her dressed. I was stoked!

She's right, though. She needs a lot of sleep. If she has a lot of sleep, the sweet, wonderful, amiable girl that we love radiates like a small star. If she doesn't, well, I'm sometimes afraid. It's one of the reasons I'm glad to be homeschooling. If I had to shovel this child onto a bus at 7:30, like my mother did when I was in school, well, I whimper thinking about it.

But after a day of flying with a small sprite who seemed to be slightly offended that we were traveling without consulting her, (I should mention that all the kids were really good, even if Kenya was slightly offended) I was a little concerned about her reaction to SO much family. We haven't been out here since she was a little over a year old.

But I didn't need to worry. She is wonderful and she is herself, and she is having the time of her life with her aunties and her cousin (the one who looks like Kai, she says) and the little dog who lives here whose name is Harry and who sports a "King of Karaoke" shirt. ("He's the King of Karaoke?" Chinua's brother asked. "He really is good," I said.)

They all are taking to Detroit like ducks to water.

And this, in no particular order, is a list of what I ate yesterday:

- Banana pudding (Amazing with a capital A)
- Dressing
- Fried corn
- Greens
- More greens made by someone else
- Curried chicken
- Turkey
- Gravy of course
- Green beans the likes of which I have never tasted
- Macaroni and cheese the likes of which I have never before tasted in. my. life.

- Yams
- Potato Salad
- Sweet Potato Pie
- Pumpkin Cheesecake
- Peach Apple Cobbler

Leafy had three pieces of Sweet Potato Pie. And I only had a bite of some things. I think my tendency to visit Chinua's family in early pregnancy is going to lead to some wild rumors about the size of my appetite.

December 27, 2007

I've written about some of the obvious signs that I should have noticed earlier; signs that I'm a raving pregnant woman, and thus, my erratic actions are completely normal. One more that I've noted is my obsession with matzo ball soup. Because it is very pregnant of me to crave Jewish food like I will absolutely die if I can't have some bagel with lox already. It's a three times proven pregnancy symptom of mine.

And so the other evening, the kids and I were making the matzo balls, which means that I was making them and they were just kind of mucking around in the matzo mix. Don't you want to come to our house for dinner now? I promise that we washed our hands.

Kai then asked me, "Is this going to be enough matzo carnage?"

I paused in my ball rolling and stared at him. "Matzo *what*?"

He looked back at me, a little hesitantly, but still fairly sure. "Matzo *carnage*. You know, what you make matzo balls out of. Carnage is something you make bread and cookies and matzo balls out of."

I resumed rolling. "I'm not totally sure, Kai, but I think the word you're looking for may be *dough*."

December 29, 2007

One thing that I'm loving about being pregnant this time is Kai's special attention to it. He's always been *encouraging* about having more babies, this one. Kai is possibly the most socially oriented kid that I've met. He just wants to hang out with people, all the time. And since Kenya was born when he was nineteen months old, he doesn't remember not being a brother. So, every day, the child is asking me whether we can have ten kids. Sometimes he asks me if we can have 3211 kids, a show off number. To which I reply, "NO, no no." Obviously.

But I was happy to be able to tell him that we really are going to have another baby. To say that he is excited would be like saying that he *likes* mangoes. He adores mangoes, and he is coming out of his skin about the baby.

Every day, he asks, "Do you need to rest, for your baby?" or "Do you need some food, for your baby?" All this chivalry is making me swoon.

Yesterday he asked, "Are you going to have milk in your num-nums again, for your baby?" We've always called breast milk ";", and I have no idea where in the world the kids got the idea that the vehicle(s) for milk were the num-nums, not the milk itself. Kenya will hold up one of my bras and say, "Is this for your num-nums?" and I just say yes. I guess it could be embarrassing later on, if they continue to believe that breasts are called num-nums, but for now, it's just really cute.

But then, yesterday, I also realized that we should probably talk a little bit more about the technicalities of it all. We've talked about how the baby is swimming like a little fish, and how he doesn't breathe, because he has an umbilical cord and how when he comes out, he'll take his first breaths, and the kids stare at me with big eyes.

But yesterday, Kai thought about it for a while, and then asked, "So... are you going to, like, *poop* the baby out?"

january

January 1, 2008

In Ontario
close to Toronto
we are visiting the family on my side.
Snow everywhere, piles of it just waiting
but we have no snowsuits
because we live in California.
I remember snow, I remember freezing
I remember mascara running off of my thawed eyelashes
on the bus, the fourteen year old embarrassment.
I am nauseous and pregnant now
but I remember my thin gawky body covered in overcoats that
were too big
as I sit in this parking lot,
covered in snow
hijacking wireless
on a New Year's Day
that somehow snuck up on me

like this pregnancy, like being an adult,
like my children growing up away from the snow.

January 3, 2008

To say that I am exhausted would be a vast understatement. But exhaustion seems to be normal, right now, just as feeling as though I've been scrambled and put on toast seems to be normal. And we did get home last night at 2:00 in the morning, 5:00 in the morning Detroit time.

However, not to brag or anything, but the kids were angels, ANGELS, on our flights home. I mean, they were quiet, they slept, they sat and entertained themselves, they read the Sky Mall magazines and the safety manuals dutifully. The seventeen-year-old behind Chinua was a lot louder than my kids were, that is, until my husband turned around and asked, "Excuse me, are you going to be THAT LOUD FOR THE ENTIRE TRIP? Because I think you could bring it down a few decibels." And then I died, because it was not at all Canadian of my husband to do that. But he justified it by saying that everyone on the flight would be happier as a result. And they were. And they broke into song.

I felt some concern for Kenya as she sat next to me and amused herself for about an hour by eating one side of an apple off and creating a perfectly flat surface. She chiseled away tenderly with her little tiny teeth, humming to herself the whole time. Then she ate the skin away and made little faces, with eyes, and noses, and mouths. And then she named them. It reminded me of when she was at my grandma's condo and she ate the skins off of the grapes while murmuring softly over them, "There you are, little baby..."

But then, as she held her apple in her hand, as the flight

321

attendant finished announcing our landing in Minnesota, she shrieked, "Mommydaddymommydaddymommydaddy! She said we're in MINI APPLES!" And I thought, okay, now I'll die of love.

Yup. The kids were great. Chinua and I, now. Well, I think we did pretty well, and it was all because of pheromones. We were doing that thing, you know, when we start bickering at each other and picking fights and sighing, and then we talk in fierce whispers for awhile about which one of us is being meaner. But the whole time I was thinking, "I don't want to do this right now, this makes for bad memories, I have had enough travel bickering to last a lifetime, no more..." So, when my Superstar Husband came up and hugged me, I did what I knew would cure me for the rest of the night- I smelled his face. And then I sighed for a long time. And he smelled the top of my head. And he slumped and leaned his head on mine, and said in the sappiest voice, "I love you." Pheromones. I'm telling you.

Maybe it sounds silly that I love the smell of my husband's face, but I DO. Especially around his jaw. Try it, the next time you're bickering. People around us may have wondered about us, but I think they usually do anyways, so the fact that we were sniffing at each other probably didn't faze anyone too much.

January 4, 2008

I'm out.

Well, no, not really. But don't you wish sometimes that you could just say, "See ya," and then find yourself a nice cozy world where it is not storming and there are no assassinations and nobody is asking you for anything?

I think it's the kind of day I'm having. It's a day when every movement makes me even more nauseous. It's a day when suddenly being pregnant and expecting my fourth child, who will be born before my oldest turns six, seems overwhelming. When nine months seems vast. When I can't get comfortable. Already.

A day to be a whiny child. Along with my whiny, not-quite-feeling-well children.

Today is a day when my to-do list is slapping me in the face like a wet fish, when I am ignoring it and procrastinating, lying on the floor trying to feel better. (Have I ever mentioned just how much I love lying on the floor? Sometimes I wonder if I'll still be lying on the floor when I'm sixty-five. Probably.)

Today is the kind of day that reminds me of days in the past when I used to hole up in my room with a book and a large bag of chips. Or maybe a cake. I would love to do that now, minus the food. But now I am a mom, and I'd better get used to it. And now I have work to do.

I'm trying to resign from being a bookkeeper, and in doing so, I seem to accumulate even more work—things that need to be done before I can fully lay it all aside. It's killing me. I feel like my life is one big deadline. For example, right now I somehow need to magically open up a high-interest bank account. I have no idea how to do this. I need to get tax receipts out. I need to get my computer fixed. I need to send out some communications. I need to work on updating a website.

I feel like I'm having a panic attack.

Maybe what I really need is to pray.

Breathe into me. I'm lost and lonely. I'm growing to hate numbers. I want nothing to do with this.

It's you that I serve. This is not for nothing. You are not harsh. You bend me but don't break me. You made life and we are glad. We are safe. The storm hasn't killed us. We have so much.

I'm tired. Please make me free again.

January 6, 2008

One thing that was hanging over me since we got home is the fact that we had no FOOD in the house. And that we've been eating nothing but eggs because we have no *food* in the house. I babysat for a friend yesterday and when she came over I asked if it was okay if her daughter had eggs for lunch.

"Well... she's actually already had eggs today, but that's fine, I guess," she said, kindly.

And I was like, "IT'LL HAVE TO BE OKAY, BECAUSE THAT'S THE ONLY CHOICE." But I didn't actually say that. But it was true.

So, today I went shopping, blissfully alone except for the little butterfly in my womb, and first of all I had to plan my meals.

Ever since I was eighteen I have lived in community, and in most of our communities there has been meal sharing. In the last one, at the Land, Renee practically begged to be the cook, the whole cook, and nothing but the cook, so help her God—so we let her. And I scrambled my brain on taxes. But anyways now here I am and there are SEVEN (dinner) MEALS A WEEK! I'm so new at this. I love to cook, let me just say. Love it.

But what do I *cook*? I mean, good gracious, how do I feed my family? I don't know how people do it, night after night. Maybe it's partly because I'm using up so much energy right now, incubating this baby, that about half an hour after I eat, I'm STARVING, but it just seems like overkill, eating everyday.

So, today, wracking my brain, I called my mom to ask her for her lasagna recipe. She gave it to me over the phone, in a kind of sketchy memorized fashion, since she's been cooking for decades.

Then, later, at the store, I called her again. "You said ground beef. But how many *pounds* of ground beef?" (What did I think she was going to say? Four?) She told me one, and then we hung up. Because it costs me about a million dollars an hour to call Canada on my cell phone.

Then, later, when they found my phone in the freezer, next to the frozen juices, the grocery store people called the last number that I had called, which happened to be my Mom and Dad. (It says, Mom and Dad. We're not on a first name basis.) And they explained to my Mom that they had located my phone in the freezer and that when I came looking for it to please let me know that it was at the grocery store. But not in the freezer anymore.

What a day of phone calls for my Mom. There's nothing to let you know that you're still connected to your daughter like ground beef and lost cell phone notifications.

I'm sure she laughed.

January 8, 2008

This morning when Chinua and the kids and I got into the van, to drive him to work, it looked remarkably disheveled. Enough that I remarked on it. I said, "Were you tearing through stuff in here?" And my Superstar Husband shook his head and looked innocent. And then I saw that everything had been pulled out of every pocket in the van, including the glove compartment. "SOMEONE WAS IN HERE!" I said. And so it seems that someone randomly decided to go through our van, looking for what, the Lord only knows. And the Lord forgives. And so do I, especially since it seems like nothing is gone. The Lord would forgive even if the van was gone, but if that happened, I know it would take *me* a minute.

Last night my little Kai slept over at his best friend's house. I can't believe that he is old enough to sleep over. And he kind of isn't, really, except at the home of some of my most trusted friends. When Elena called me last night to ask if it was okay, I said, "Is it okay with me? You're the one keeping my kid!" She was wondering if he would miss me. I said, "Heck no. He isn't that kind of child."

And I was right. When I went to pick him up today, I hugged him and asked him how it went. He looked at me and said, "I didn't miss you." And I didn't say, YOU ARE NOT AT ALL CHARMING, YOU UNGRATEFUL WRETCH. But I thought it. It didn't help that he cried all the way out to the car because he didn't want to come home. Why do kids have to be so immature? How about a little credit, kiddo?

We then proceeded to have an awesome afternoon doing school and reading and baking bread. Because life at home REALLY SUCKS, and we hate to be here.

And then I thought about it, and how Kai had plaintively said, "I don't want to go home and be all by ourselves!" And I responded, "You have TWO siblings and one on the way and you're ONLY FIVE." Elena added, "You don't really know what it means to be by yourself."

But I realized, as I was driving home, crying for about the seventh time today because of my intense longing for the Land, that we are all transitioning. This boy of mine has lived his entire life with other people in and around and through and on top of all of the different houses that we've lived in. No wonder he feels like he's all alone. This is very different. We all need grace, here. GRACE! GRACE! Like that.

Tonight I made white bean and butternut squash soup. I loved it. The kids weren't wild about it, but I made them eat it anyways. And we made bread to go along with it. It was actually really easy, and I used dried white beans that I cooked all day in the slow cooker, rather than canned beans. A word to the wise, though, from a learning cook. If it says 19 oz of canned beans, that is not the same as 19 oz of *dried* beans. Because, you know, they grow. So, I think we may have this soup again soon, since I have these beans and half of a butternut squash left. I put parmesan in the soup, and toasted the pumpkin seeds, just like the recipe said. And I did not regret it.

5. Chinua is working late and after the kids go to bed (in twenty, no, nineteen minutes), I'm going to knit and watch "13 going on 30" because I deserve it.

January 9, 2008

Leafy is learning to talk at a speed of about a hundred miles a minute. He's also a little confused about which phrases are appropriate for him to use, and which are not. For example, he has told me to "obey" more than a few times.

As I came out of the bathroom today, he said, "You STAY OUT DA BAFROOM!"

It is something he's heard again and again. Mostly because of his habit of finding a cup, scooping some toilet water into it, and then offering it to our guests.

January 10, 2008

Do any of you have a middle of the afternoon slump? Because I sure do. I get regular house stuff done in the morning, and we do school, and then the afternoon is supposed to be the time of day where I do other projects, or organize stuff, or write, or paint! (Although I'd drop dead with amazement if *that* ever happened.) But now, I push through the slump and I write! I write. Because it keeps me sane. GRACE! GRACE! (GRACE! is sort of my version of Serenity Now!)

A wise woman once said that if you can go through trials without letting them embitter you, they will refine you. That wise woman probably heard that somewhere else, most likely it's a paraphrase of the Bible, maybe the whole Bible, since that seems to be a great deal of the message, and that wise woman is my *other* personality.

Because, my friends, I'm feeling BITTER. I'm feeling bitter, like with a raspy smoker's voice at eighty-two, imagine it with me if you will- BITTER. Maybe I'm thinking the voice of Marge Simpson's sisters- BITTER.

It's a sucky way to feel. It leaps up out of me at the slightest provocation. Bitterbitterbitterbitterbitterbitter.

Bitterness will suck you dry, it will take the joy out of your life, it will rob you of the lessons that the trials you have gone through are meant to offer you- a good gift, a gift from a Father who loves you. It might make you sick to your stomach, like it does to me. It might make your heart race with anxiety, cause your attention to wander from your children to inner rants and raves. It might cause you to accidentally crush a can of tomatoes with your bare hands. Or not, if you're not all that strong.

I believe that bitterness comes when we think we deserve more than we've been given. I think it also can fester when we don't know how to grieve and let go. Often it seems like grief demands a reason, like maybe I moved away because everything WAS SO SUCKY. Or maybe, just maybe, I moved away because it was simply time to go. A season passed, and love is everywhere, love is around the corner, love is right now. But we aren't where we were. *That doesn't mean that where we were is bad.*

The question of whether we deserve more than we've been given is an interesting one. Maybe, in a perfect world, some of us would make more money for our hard work. Maybe in a perfect village, we'd all let each other know how much our contributions meant. If I was perfect, I'd certainly be a better friend.

But today I was reading about Joseph with my kids. Joseph with the coat of many colors. One thing that hit me was that after Joseph was sold into slavery by his brothers, (totally didn't deserve that, I don't think) and then he worked his way up in his slave owner's household, he gets thrown into prison for leaping out of the lusty clutches of his owner's wife. Totally didn't deserve that, either.

And then, in prison, what it says about him is that he was such a *great prisoner* that he was put in charge of the other prisoners. Actually, what it says in my kids' bible is that he didn't whine and pout about being in prison. You know, like "poor me, my brothers jumped me when I was seventeen and sold me into slavery and then I got thrown into prison because some woman who is already married tried to hit on me and I ran away." You know? That would be totally lame of him, to object to that, right?

But somehow he still gets the award for being a good citizen. (I got that award once, a long, long time ago. I think I was eight.)

So basically, maybe some stuff has happened that makes me feel like crap. Maybe it was a raw deal. But, here we go, into a new year, and I want to get the good citizen award. Or not. Maybe I just want to be sweet, salty, curried, pickled, but not bitter. Maybe I want to leave this stuff behind. And be the best damn prisoner that I can be.

January 11, 2008

Today I believe I will be able to take the past and roll it between my palms, and blow the pieces backwards, where they can't touch me. I want to remember the beautiful things, so many beautiful things. I want to remember the things that have changed me.

I think that deciding to step away from what we were doing was one of the most courageous things that Chinua and I have ever done. I really believe that. And I see how God has continued to allow things to fall into place, again and again, perfectly. I have received gifts, this past year, like the trip to Burkina, like the ability to be here still, even after a major car accident. And I see that it has not been without trials. There has been turbulence. We have had to fasten our seat belts, a few times. So maybe the unlocking of emotion right now is not without cause.

I know, however, that Joseph eventually became a prince, in Egypt. He got sprung. So tomorrow I think I will write a little about the next year. Maybe it will be ridiculously hopeful. I'm not planning to lose weight or start jogging. But I would like to shift a little closer to that rightness that I see there, off on the horizon.

January 13, 2008

I think in 2008 I'd like to turn 28. That'd be cool!

Also, I think I'd like to have a baby. I'd love to gain a bunch of weight! And then lose it.

And I'd like to move to India with my family.

But there are other things, also, things that I can dream of. I'd like to begin taking doing more writing and photography for advocacy.

I want to write my book.

I want to publish a book of portraits.

I would love to paint more. I have a painting that I'm about to start working on, and I'd love to make it one of several, this year. I didn't paint anything in 2007. There is this sleeping part of me called Painter, and she has retreated behind mother, writer, blogger, pregnant person who needs to eat a lot. But she wants to come back out to play.

I'm going to make quilts for my kids, with fabric I bought in Burkina Faso.

I'm going to put the finishing touches on the hat I knit for Chinua, finish knitting the sweater for my mother, and the shawl for Renee. I'd like to knit without that niggling feeling that I should jump up and do something else.

I want to find ways to practice my faith that are sturdy and rhythmic and true. I've become more and more intrigued by the idea of practice, and the knowledge that people all throughout the years have put prayer, true song, service, and meditation into practice, until the truth of God simply flows through them. I want a safe space to return to. I want to throw myself into discovering my own ways of practice- maybe writing has something to do with it, maybe brushes and paint.

I'd like to be a better listener, this year, to practice silence while people are talking, rather than jumping in with stuttered interruptions. I'd like to know the right questions. I'd like to take myself out of the center of my universe (except, maybe, on this blog- it seems inevitable, here).

I'd love to learn to truly value every single moment with my children, rather than trying to speed things along a little. Oh- I'd love to have more patience. And find ways to be more creative with them, and learn to teach them more responsibility, and bring them a little farther into living.

I want to pay more attention to my husband, to treasure him and listen to him (see above). To give him my mind, when we talk, rather than allowing it to flit hither and thither every single second.

I want to see more stars. To swim in more large bodies of water.

I want to grow things.

I'm going to be more decisive. I will grow up and make up my mind and decide what I want and ask for it. I will not apologize, again and again, for having needs.

And, I want to learn how to carve a bear out of a piece of burl with a chainsaw.

Okay, maybe not that last one. But I find I miss the plethora of burl wood bears that reside in the Redwoods. Oh, kooky woods people, how I love you.

So, you know, not that much. It never hurts to dream, I don't think.

January 14, 2008

This just in.

That big storm that just happened? The one that raged the West Coast?

It absolutely obliterated our old house at the Land. Four big Douglas Firs fell, and at least a couple of them fell into the house, crushing the roof to the floor. IT'S GONE.

If we had been living there, we would have died. If we had happened to be away, all of our stuff would be destroyed. Our friends Mike and Julie were living there while the sale closed. They moved out two weeks before the storm.

It's working out okay for the people who bought the Land, because they have some nice insurance. No one was living in the house at the time of the storm. The man who bought the land was sleeping in one of the bedrooms while he prepared the house for rental and left THAT DAY to go back to his house in Blue Lake, because he was frustrated with the rain. THAT DAY. The room he was sleeping in was crushed. It was our old room.

Sometimes a few things are clear. Once again, I hear from God that no matter what happens, we will be okay. Just like in the case of our car crash.

And sometimes you find that things are just finished. I feel that it is now beyond the shadow of a doubt; this timing of our move. We discussed whether to stay another winter. We discussed whether to wait on the sale. It was absolutely perfect timing- the timing of the sale. It was absolutely the right person to sell to, someone who has the ability to bring contractors in immediately, rather than another non-profit who would be more devastated by the loss of that building.

We are affirmed and stunned. We are so thankful.

January 15, 2008

I find myself wanting to know *which* trees fell, and how they fell, and what it all looks like. I wonder if it was that group of three that the kids used to call the castle. Flowers grew out of the base, in the spring. Wild orchids and some kind of blue flower that I never really identified.

It really is true, that you can't look back. And my pining for my little house in the woods is useless. Especially now. But there is a crazy lesson in here somewhere, about the finality of change, and the strength in looking forward and going on.

The most crushing accusation that I can imagine being made against me is that I wasn't listening. Listening to that small voice of God's—the one that I have been trying to follow for most of my life. It has been one step after the other, leaning in his direction. To be accused of disobedience is a weight on my shoulders that I almost haven't been able to bear. And it has happened, recently, these accusations. Many more people have been supportive than accusatory, let me say. But still, I feel as though I have been under a dark cloud. It has been heavy on me. I wish I had a thicker skin.

It is maybe just coincidence that immediately after I made that decision, to turn away from the hurt and into the new day, I got the news that there isn't even any reason to be looking backward. Because here is God! And he is saying that he really did put things into place the way they needed to be! And if it had happened any other way, ANY OTHER WAY, this could have been horribly tragic.

And I feel different. Something, some dark shameful thing, has slipped off of me. My world, the one where you pray, and believe, and then joyfully make your choices without fear, that world is falling back into place around me. I wish I was more certain, all the time, of what I know to be true. I wish I didn't need a reassurance of this magnitude. And I didn't really ask for it, but then it was there. I don't think it gets much more clear than that. Maybe one day I will be like the oak tree, here outside our house in Sacramento. The one that *didn't* fall.

And yes, we say thank you again and again and again and again. I should say, too, that I don't mean to say that we are invincible, or that suffering will not enter our lives. Everyone dies. But the timing is God's. I hope that if suffering comes to my life I can accept it, also.

January 17, 2008

Here are my rules for how NOT to write.

1. Jiggle your leg really fast for five minutes while you lean your head on your hand. Jump up every two minutes to wash one dish. After you sit back down, think for two minutes, write one word, and then get up to wash another dish. Maybe you need to put a load of laundry on. Maybe you really need a pickle. Oh, yes. You need that pickle. Get the pickle. Now you need another one. Sit down and jiggle your leg again. Pull up your shirt and examine your belly. It's *bigger*. Gosh. Maybe you should Google "am I having twins" again. But first, there is something between your teeth. Go on, go to the bathroom mirror, and while you're there, tweeze your eyebrows because face it, they're getting out of control.

2. Think about all the great writers you know of. Compare yourself to them. Admire their PhD's maybe, or just their solitary madness. Tell yourself that you had better not write any crap. No crap at all. Every word must be a jewel, a twinkle, a star in the deep darkness that covers the earth. Then try to begin. When nothing comes, lie on the floor and sob. Notice that the carpet needs vacuuming. Go in search of the vacuum cleaner.

3. Sit at your computer, open up your word document, and write a few words. Then put your chin in your hand and daydream about what it will be like to be on Oprah. And think about sending a copy of your bestselling book to your Writing teacher from the twelfth grade. Maybe you should include one for your Literature teacher,

too. She was always nice to you, wasn't she? Then think about money for awhile.

Rest assured, if you employ the above methods, you will have no problem NOT writing.

Here are my tips for writing: I'll give you a few and then share some of my favorite quotes from writers who rock and happen to all be women.

Mine:

1. Find your rhythm. Feel the words, taste the sentence. Run it over in your mind. Is there a cadence? A rhythm? If you have no idea what I'm talking about, go get your favorite book of all time and read it aloud. There will be a natural flow to the words. Find your flow. Make it musical.

2. Sit your butt down. Sit down like you are glued to the chair. Turn your WiFi off, so that you can't access the internet. Then write as fast as you can. Or as slowly as you want. Just remember, you are building. You take a little piece of beautiful writing out of a bunch of crap, then another little piece out of tomorrow's crap. The sad news is, you will have to write crap. The happy news is, you will find the jewels inside. (Don't follow my imagery too far, lest it make you queasy.)

3. Carry a notebook everywhere. Because if you are like me, your mind is like a sieve. So write it down, when you see it, when you hear it, when you think of it. Think like a detective. Become a spy. Make use of your position as an observer.

That's about it. Then there are the more ephemeral pieces of advice from writers. When I first started writing, I really didn't like this kind of advice. "Just give me a time of day, type of pencil, and how many words, and I'll do it," I thought. But lately, slogging through my own insecurities, I find these people to be incredibly encouraging.

Here's Madeleine L'Engle. *"If the work comes to the artist and says, 'Here I am, serve me,' then the job of the artist, great or small, is to serve. The amount of the artist's talent is not what it is about. Jean Rhys said to an interviewer in the Paris Review, 'Listen to me. All of writing is a huge lake. There are great rivers that feed the lake, like Tolstoy and Dostoyevsky. And there are mere trickles, like Jean Rhys. All that matters is feeding the lake. I don't matter. The lake matters. You must keep feeding the lake.'"*

*

Annie Dillard says, *"A well-known writer got collared by a university student who asked, 'Do you think I could be a writer?' 'Well,' the writer said, 'I don't know... Do you like sentences?' The writer could see the student's amazement. Sentences? Do I like sentences? I am twenty years old and do I like sentences? If he had liked sentences , of course, he could begin, like a joyful painter I knew. I asked him how he came to be a painter. He said, 'I liked the smell of the paint.'"*

*

And of course there's Anne Lamott. *"The writer is a person who is standing apart, like the cheese in 'The Farmer in the Dell,' standing there alone but deciding to take a few notes. You're outside, but you can see things up close through your binoculars. Your job is to present clearly your viewpoint, your line of vision. Your job is to see people as they really are, and to do this, you have to know who you are in the most compassionate possible sense."*

february

February 5, 2008

I feel the need for some therapeutic writing. Bear with me. I have issues, as we always liked to say in my community. My friend would always say, "Graaaaave issues." Or, if someone was being all nuts or whatever, we would say, "*I*-shhues," because banter makes everything better.

But anyways. Oh dear, where do I begin?

I am afraid.

I am not afraid of just anything. I am afraid of people. I may have told you this before.

Let me tell you what I am not afraid of. I am not afraid to travel. I am not afraid to meet a hundred new people in Burkina Faso and spend five days with them and attempt to make myself understood in a language I don't speak.

I am not afraid of flying, I am not afraid of new and foreign food. I am not afraid of germs and sickness.

But I am deeply afraid of my responsibility toward people. I am afraid that people will ask more of me than I can give, and I will inevitably disappoint. This is a debilitating fear, when you live with the values and convictions and life work that I do.

Lately I've been living without this fear. It has felt very freeing, and I've been able to relax a little, pursue some interests, settle into myself, figure out what I really want out of life, and begin to make plans for projects and receive a slight hint of our future direction.

The difference has been that I am not doing what I normally do, which is accepting the stranger, offering hospitality, offering help to weary travelers.

Don't get me wrong. It is all I want to do with my life. But it fills me with fear.

I realized that it still lives with me, slightly buried under an outer peace, last night. Someone who needed some help and friends to meet with called us up and asked if we could get together. We said "Of course!" and set up a time to have her over. And she was wonderful. It was a beautiful night, and we talked for hours, and we prayed together, and it was good.

And still? And still.

At the end of the night I was left questioning whether I had been enough, had done enough, whether I had disappointed. My fear was so great that my shoulders were hanging up by my ears, where they had been edging all evening, and my Superstar Husband was forced to sing me a little song about how I did a good job, to make me smile again.

It is a scenario that is all too common in my life.

Maybe it was exaggerated by the fact that I have been so alone, lately. (Not that I necessarily even want to be alone, I mostly want to be with people that I have deemed "safe". They are the ones that I know won't ask more of me than I am able to give.) People have tried to help and have asked me what I thought would *happen*, if I disappointed people. I have no answers for a question like that. It has nothing to do with what will happen. This anxiety is so deep rooted that I have no idea where the root lies. It really makes no sense. But it is still there.

But it made me fear the future, a little, which is never a good thing. Sometimes, someone with my temperament, my particular social anxiety, may retreat and just be an artist and a writer for a living. I've always known that this is not for me.

But, I realized, last night, that I am moving to India. Land of need. And there needs to be some kind of adjustment, man, some kind of healing, some kind of miracle.

Or maybe just day by day I will be moving through this incredible crippling fear, the fear that makes me dread the phone, the fear that makes me ask my husband to talk to people for me, and I will bit by bit overcome it, with the help of songs, with the help of a few inner prompts (sometimes I have to ask myself what I would tell someone in my situation) and with the help of Jesus, who is fairer, who is purer than every beautiful thing I have ever seen.

He is much more tender with me than I am with myself.

February 6, 2008

How did I find myself sitting on a table wearing "clothing" made of paper yesterday?

I had my first prenatal visit. I really don't have any intention of giving birth in this hospital, but prenatal care is prenatal care, and prenatal care is good. Especially when you can't remember when your last period was.

So, when the nurse practitioner did the ultrasound, and we saw the wittle baby, (just one) and she pronounced him/her to be 12 weeks 1 day old, well gosh. I was flabbergasted. Fastest pregnancy ever.

I'm heading into my second trimester. WAIT! Didn't I just find out that I'm pregnant? I'm heading into my second trimester? Time for a new chapter in my Pilates for Pregnancy book?

This means, I realize, that I was fully seven and a half weeks pregnant by the time I thought to run out to the neighborhood Safeway and pick up a pregnancy test. I honestly don't know what happened. Why didn't I know that I had skipped a period? Why did it take me so long to figure it out?

All I can think is that I kept attributing all of my symptoms to something else. Nausea? Well, I got pretty sick in Burkina Faso. Exhaustion? Must be jet lag. Stormy weepiness? Jet lag? Trauma? Culture shock? My general emotional instability? I think I just sort of hurled all my symptoms into a plethora of categories and was content to leave it at that.

Anyways. Now we know. And wow, I'm already a third of the way through. And the wittle baby sure is cute.

February 9, 2008

Last night I started piecing a quilt for Kenya. (Do you like how I wrote *piecing*, like a real quilter? Pretty snazzy, I know.)

I couldn't help thinking of my grandma while my machine hummed away. I think she gave me my sewing machine when I was about thirteen or fourteen. My grandparents owned a fabric and notions shop for most of my life, and to this day, the smell, when I walk into a yarn shop or a fabric store, the smell conjures my strong and creative grandma.

It was quiet last night, since everyone was gone. I got a lot done,

343

for me, for the first time I've tried this in, let's see—fourteen years. I could see my Grandma, sitting at her machine, talking through a mouth full of pins. She always holds her pins between her lips while she sews, and if you think it's hard to understand someone who is brushing their teeth and talking, you should try interpreting for someone who's trying not to be stabbed in the lip with a pin.

I pinned and sewed and cut and ironed. I could smell their house, feel the coolness of the basement, that summer when Grandma decided to help my sister and I put together log cabin quilts. It gets hot in Edmonton in the summer, and her basement with the cool air and our lemony iced tea was a good place to be.

It seemed magic to me, then, following the instructions to pin this piece to that piece, and sew this to that, and then you iron it and there before your eyes is a quilt piece, built like a log cabin, turning around itself. It still seems like magic.

One of the worst things about my Grandma being sick is that she can no longer sew, like she has all her life. Last night I thought, maybe I can show her my quilt as it progresses, across all these miles. So, I'm going to show Grandma my quilt as I make it. I emailed her two photos today, and I almost can't wait to send her more.

February 15, 2008

Here's the setting: We are at the post office, applying for passports for our kids, which requires both of us and all the kids to be there. It's a happy family outing in a Federal Building in the Capitol, where the security guard, who is a senior citizen, tells us he is heading to Hawaii on Monday.

While we singlehandedly cause the line to stretch about a mile, we lounge around with our elbows on the counter, trying to keep the kids from wrestling, letting Kenya know that fifteen kisses is probably enough for Kai to handle (she always gets very affectionate when we are out together), joking with the post lady about how much money this is costing us. "My favorite thing!" I say. "I love spending hundreds of dollars on paper!"

Then I notice the Stamps for February poster. "Hey Chin," I ask in a lowered voice. "Is that guy black?" He looks where I'm looking, at the Black Heritage stamp.

"Well, remember, back in those days it was all about 'passing?' He looks like he's passing."

I'm not so sure. "Yes, but... I don't know." This man seems to be doing a lot more than passing to me. He looks white down to his large mustache and the part in his hair.

"Well, I don't have my glasses on," Chinua tells me.

"Here, use mine." He takes them.

"Oh no. That dude is not black." The (black) post lady overhears him and laughs. "I know," she says. "I've had other customers asking me about that."

"Do *you* know who he is?" I ask. She shakes her head.

"I have *no idea*."

Chinua and I finish up and walk away with our miniature entourage. And got sillier and sillier.

"For Black History Month, we've decide to feature *white people*!"

"Due to the unnecessary controversy surrounding black people, we've decided to have white people featured for Black History Month!"

"In the spirit of non-discrimination, we're going stop honoring Black People for Black History month! Now all races will be represented!"

"It will be National Everybody Month!"

After doing a little, you know, what's that called... RESEARCH, I realized that Charles W. Chesnutt is indeed PASSING. Go and read about his life— it's really interesting, and reveals more again about how strange and complex the racial undertones of the day were. And I really mean no disrespect to this man, who seems to have spent his life bringing awareness to black issues and decided not to live as a white man, passing or no passing.

February 18, 2008

There are few things that make me happier than the fact that the tree outside my house has turned out to be a cherry tree.

It is for its beauty that I love it, nothing else. We will not be here long enough to eat the cherries. In fact, we are in the homestretch now. So soon we will be airborne. So soon we will be over the clouds.

I remember that I am writing my story, that this is my own adventure. I remember that adventures are not often easy. Often you find yourself hiking wearily along, looking forward to the campfire and bit of hard ground at the end of the trail. But sometimes adventures burst out at you with a shower of sparks and you get to see your kids' eyes get really big at their first sight of a camel outside of the zoo. Or you find yourself drinking Turkish coffee on a side street that you've never seen before.

It is this that I look forward to. I am waiting for these blossoms to unfurl, the tightly held travelers to burst out in the sun. I look forward to who we become, because this is our adventure.

February 20, 2008

Kenya and Kai have some rules in the car. Their rules, not mine.

All the cars driving beside us are our "friends". The ones not beside us (I'm assuming on the other side of the road, but it might include the ones behind us, since we always seem to be *fleeing*- "Go faster Mama! Watch out, Mama!") are "bad guys."

Also, lately, when we've been grocery shopping they pretend they're grownups! Getting their groceries!

"Let's get some fruit!" Kai says.

"I think I'm all done with my list!" Kenya chirps. "We love and love all this food, don't we! Because we're grownups!"

Meanwhile, I shuffle along beside them, barely lifting my feet, wearily checking another item off of my list. My uterus is weighing on my pelvic bones with a pressure that makes me sure that in a minute I will have to pick it up off the floor.

Maybe I should pretend to be a kid pretending to be a grownup.

February 21, 2008

Tonight we drove out as far as we could to see the eclipse. It was wonderful, except for the occasional whine from a child who was JUST SO COLD. I would love to see these children in an actual winter climate. Although they would probably be ecstatic, contrary beings that they are.

Even Leafy said, "The moon is so boodiful!" And we saw Saturn. And I showed Kai and Kenya Orion, which has always been my favorite constellation, ever since it was my connection to Chinua, when we were thousands of miles away from each other, long before we were married. I would sit on the beach in San Diego and listen to the waves and when I saw Orion, I would breathe a prayer for my friend, the man who would one day become my husband.

I have never been more proud of Kenya than I was today. She wore a sock on her hand all day.

She has sucked the two middle fingers on her left hand ever since she was about four months old. We have numerous pictures of Kenya as a baby, Kenya as a toddler, Kenya as a three-year-old, sucking her fingers. She does it ALL. THE. TIME. Not just for bed, not just for consolation. ALL THE TIME.

But I have this funny list of things I need to do before we go to India. Things like, Find storage, Find a good shipping company, Train next bookkeeper, Buy sleeping bags, Buy kid back packs, Buy stroller. And then these odd things like Help Kenya stop sucking her fingers, Potty train Leafy.

And now you know which one we are working on today.

I really didn't know how it would make me feel. I didn't realize that my rush-in-and-protect instincts would swarm all over me and smother me and almost make me say "Never mind! Just joking! You can just keep those fingers in your mouth until your boss complains!"

I didn't say it.

It is time, and my brave, strong girl met the time to quit head on. Her teeth are visibly shifting. And I don't want her to touch things on trains and buses in India and then put her fingers in her mouth. Nope.

I also didn't know that I would almost burst with pride. That I would see her thousand little reflexive moves toward her mouth, and then the stifling of the reflex, and then the hand that didn't have a place to be and so tentatively lay in her lap, and her mouth moving self-consciously around itself, that I would see all these things and my heart would melt, for her strength.

I don't know that I've ever witnessed as much determination in overcoming something so deeply ingrained, in any of my kids before. This is no small thing. She doesn't remember ever not having this habit. It's all she's known. When at rest, left fingers go into your mouth. When you are hugging your mom, when you are reading a book, when you are watching a movie, when you are walking through a crowd...

This is her mountain. I love to be here to see her climb it. (Even though I am a nervous twitchy wreck.)

February 22, 2008

Some questions:

Is a pickle with a slice of Jarlsberg cheese wrapped around it considered food?

Why is my eyelid twitching all the time?

What will help me stick to my schedules instead of writing them out and then ignoring them?

Does googling endless queries about mosquitoes and shipping containers count toward preparing for a big move?

Why do my children take great joy in pretending their basmati rice is a pile of little maggots while they eat it?

What does it say about you if you realize that the only piece of furniture you don't want to leave behind is your mattress?

Speaking of sleeping, how does one rid oneself of crazy tormenting dreams about mean people?

Why does the movie Anne of Green Gables soothe me so? And why did I think the acting was perfect when I was a kid?

Where did Kenya's other pink sock go?

Why does Leafy swing from cuddly saint to terror child?

Why does Kai swing from melancholic tyrant to sunny delight?

Who poured my glass of juice down the drain?

Where do those tiny K-nex go?

Why is exfoliating so delightful?

Why are my dreadlocks so linty? (I'm going to write a song called lint in my dreads. It goes, Lint in my dreads, Lint in my dreads, I've got lint in my dreads, lint in my dreads, like that. Maybe I'll add a verse that goes Trying to get it out, trying to get it out...)

What it is about a down comforter?

Do I like Chinua's face better with a beard? Or shaved?

How tall will my kids be when they're done growing?

Why is it so hard to find a decent cup of tea in a coffee shop?

How do people find time to style their hair? Maybe they choose to do it because of the lack of lint?

How many years will it take me to knit this sweater?

Am I the only one who is repulsed by sweets when I'm pregnant?

Did you know that my friend Chad is turning eight this Leap Year? Which means he's really thirty-two? (I could actually be wrong about that. I *think* that's what's happening.)

What's the funny sound my van is making?

And finally, whose idea was it to put cheap plastic toys that are really candy dispensers next to the cash register at Target, causing me to have to have a discussion about what is cheap vs what is quality every single time we go?

February 25, 2008

This has forced its way out of me. I have to write it.

To the people who have shared air with me, laughed, cried, been friends, been family, been iron against my iron. To the ones I've hurt, to the ones who have hurt me, to the ones who have given and given, to those who were enemies, to those who cut deeply, to those who offered their cupped hands filled with water, to those who gave sustenance, I want to tell you this:

I wish you nothing but good. The good that sustains you and is something you can lean against, like the tallest, thickest tree. The kind of good that feeds you when you can't feed yourself. I wish you good.

I wish you kindness, the kindness that sends you a loving glance rather than a reproachful one. Someone to kiss your forehead when you are tired, and then to kiss you on that one spot on your cheekbone just because. I want someone to put their hands on either side of your face and tell you that you are so, so beautiful. That they will never leave you.

I wish you puddles of sunlight on wooden floors. Thick rugs. Tea or coffee with friends, or just by yourself, with a book, maybe a crossword puzzle. I wish you afghans to keep you warm, down comforters on the coldest days, hot water for your tired feet. I wish you calm and peace.

I wish you a clean home at the end of the day, firelight in deep winter, fields of flowers in the summer. I wish you wildness, the tangle of the ocean, hot sand and craggy rock formations. I wish you singing. I wish you dancing. I want to see laughter in your eyes, I want to think of you smiling.

I wish you small children who will pat your arm and smile up at you, or hug your knees really hard, grown children who will lean over you and kiss your head. I wish you warm rain that you can wade through with soaking clothes, I wish you flowering cacti in your deserts.

I pray that the good will keep you. That you will be safe in the midst of danger. That you are taller than you were yesterday, even if you are a bit scarred. I pray that your dark places are not lonely, that you feel sheltered, not stifled, that your legs will be strong from running. I pray that your tears are not bitter, that your heart is always soothed.

I wish you courage. I wish you home.

February 26, 2008

Today was a long, weary day, but I won it over and made it mine. I pinned it down and tickled it. I slapped it in the butt and made it laugh. I was bigger, somehow, than the day that almost overcame me.

I woke up to the sun, which would have been lovely after yesterday's storm, except that the sunlight stabbed me in the eye, where a large snake curled around my skull. I have had this headache for a couple of days, and it doesn't leave me. I can feel it pressing on my cheekbones and it hammers me in the temple when I stand up.

But I dragged myself out of bed. Point one.

Then I snuck out of the house for my appointed writing time, leaving before anyone was awake and returning when my husband needed to go to work. There were cherry trees blooming. At a local cozy coffee shop I had mediocre tea. But my breakfast was a naughty and much needed chocolate chip scone. And I had a nice conversation with the owner about Bill Bryson. Point two. I wrote as much as I could before my headache threatened to crack my skull. Point two and a half.

At home I finally gave in and took some tylenol. Usually I have no problem with pain medication, but I tend to hold out a little longer when harboring a fugitive in my uterus. I was grumpy because the house was messy and it was past time for me to start working on school stuff with the kids. And there were crocodiles slashing at each other with their teeth in my head, which also made me grumpy. I barely said goodbye to Chinua, but at the last minute, we shared a long hug. Then I said, "Did you know that the guy who played the brunette Mormon brother in the Ocean's Eleven movies is Ben Affleck's brother?" because 1) I'm slow to catch stuff like that 2) I watched the Academy Awards at my friend's house last night (Did you notice that Denzel shaved his head and grew a handlebar mustache? What's up with that?) and 3) I'm deep like that, in hug sharing moments. Score point three for hugging my husband and no nagging.

I noticed that the kids were playing really well. They wanted me to help them build a fort in their room, and then they sat and read library books in there for a long time. Instead of starting school, I took the opportunity to slowly and meditatively clean the house. My headache started to fade. My home became more peaceful. I lit incense and made sure all the blinds were as open as they could be. The kids were still in their fort. Kai was reading to the other two. I drank a second cup of tea~ totally not mediocre this time. Four points for me.

When they and I were done, we sat down to do reading. Kai read to me and Kenya and I went over a vowel song to the tune of Old MacDonald. The vowels made the sounds, instead of animals.

We were all singing, even Leafy, and I realized that although it seemed unlikely before, we were all having fun. Point five.

Lunch was healthy. Point six.

After lunch I folded laundry and vacuumed and then we did some math work and I knitted a few rows in the sweater that I am making for my mom. Leafy was taking a nap. Kai finished the last page in his math book. Tomorrow he starts another one. I told him that he's halfway done with kindergarten math. He made his eyes really wide in that way that he does. He worked on a bit of handwriting, and then he and Kenya sat at their little table and played with Play Doh. It was Kenya's heavily influenced choice for her "stop-sucking-her-fingers-reward". I say heavily influenced because I kind of steered her that way when I realized she was leaning toward Disney Princess stuff.

I knocked some stuff off my to do list while they rolled the colored dough into worms. They are a little obsessed with worms these days. Later I stuck Charlie and Lola on for them while I knocked even more stuff off my to do list. I was on a roll. More points. I've lost count of points by now.

Around dinner time everyone began to melt into the carpet. I realized that they all had low blood sugar because I didn't give them a snack in the afternoon. We sat down to eat, and Chinua was working late and I didn't complain. Another point. I tried to convince the whiny kids that if they wanted to be happy they should eat because their bodies were saying, "We don't have enough food to make us happy." When Kai continued to be sad, and more sad, and whiny, and more whiny, I tried an old trick of Chinua's, making my hands into ducks who talked to him. He turned his head away and said "Dumb, dumb, dumb, dumb," and instead of telling him that HE was the one being dumb, I just started washing dishes. Then I grabbed him and sat with him on my lap and we were quiet and swaying for a long time, until suddenly he was happy again. Endless points.

As much as I wanted to simply dump them into bed, I read. I read them loooong books, the kind that I opt out of at times, saying, pick another one, a shorter one. We probably needed to read the long string of words, tonight, and let it draw the kinks out of us. We probably needed some good stories.

The day was long and weary. But at the end we prayed together, and sighed thankful sighs, and I kissed them. And you get a lot of points for gentle looks when you are seething, and kisses when you are withdrawing inside. These points aren't exchangeable, and you can't cash them in, but at least you can know that you didn't let the day put it's tire tread marks on you.

February 27, 2008

I am still fighting with this monstrous headache, so in the interest of keeping it positive, here's my list of why this pregnancy rocks.

1. I'm sleeping through the night. Didn't happen when I was pregnant with Kenya, or Leafy really, for that matter. Sleeping through the night when you are pregnant is a nice perk. And I guess I should say, *mostly*. There is the occasional bad dream (Kai), wet bed (Kenya), or lost pacifier (Leafy) to deal with. But I didn't sleep through the night a single time from the day Kai was born until the day we moved to the Land when Kenya was fifteen months old and she decided she liked the quiet of the woods. Of course, at that point, I was almost ready to have Leafy.

2. We don't live in one room. This is the first pregnancy that I've

355

experienced where I haven't been sharing a room with my snorkly kids. (Snorkly sounds like this: *snorkle, sniff, cough, snorkle.*)

3. I have a comfortable bed. First time, yo! With Kai we slept on a futon that had the delightful springiness of cement. Why we did this for so long I cannot fathom. Oh yes, we had a blank space instead of a bank balance. But still, the floor would have been more comfortable. And then there was the bunk bed with the quarter inch foamy on top of metal rails. Oh, you don't really want to know. But now. Well, I've already told you how I love our mattress.

4. My Superstar Husband is amazing at being the Superloving Husband of a pregnant woman. Emotions? He can handle them! Do I need space? Take the space you need, Baby! Dying and you can't move another inch? He'll pick up tacos on his way home! This is not to say that he doesn't still need reminders. Or that he has in any way improved in the Valentine's Day sector. But then, neither have I. And everyone needs reminders.

5. I have a washer and dryer *in my house*, that I am not sharing with twenty people. This is a first. This is not undervalued by me.

6. I'm not changing diapers. JUST KIDDING! Ha ha ha ha, ho ho hee. Not changing diapers. Chuckle.

7. Spiced tortilla chips from Trader Joe's. Today I bought three bags of them. *Three bags.*

I'm bearing in mind that this is all short lived. Soon I will be quite possibly sleeping in a tent on the ground with my entire family, wondering why I complained about that futon. Then again, I have been longing for this kind of travel for years, so maybe reason 8 that this is the best pregnancy so far is that I will walk through this one in many different countries. I'll remember that when I am craving salsa in a country where salsa does not exist.

February 28, 2008

Yesterday a tragic loss was suffered by our dear friends; the loss of a life~ of a son, a brother, an uncle. The grief is immense and deep and torrid. The community is shaken. I know that everyone is so thankful for this community at this time, for those who are so kind, for those in cars or planes or who fly across the world to be with the family. Many of us have lived together in the same house at one point or another, we have intertwined lives, and the family who is in mourning is a beloved family, a family who has touched many, many people.

I don't know what more to say. This is beyond any of us. I don't think we will ever be the same. But underneath are the everlasting arms.

march

March 2, 2008

There is something that happens. It makes it possible to keep for hurt people to get up in the morning.

The something is a rallying, as to a long, high-pitched call from a mountain-top. Clusters of people circle around. They touch one another. Forehead to forehead, cheek to shoulder, hands gently rubbing in between one another's shoulder blades. We touch each other to make sure we are all still here.

Food is made, piles of food stack up on tables, the help pours in, the people keep coming, they fly from across the world.

Maybe tomorrow is possible.

We call each other, just checking in.

And then, the singing. So wounded, but so brave, slow hymns, wavering song in deep sorrow.

This something, the people who drift into each other's arms. Maybe there will be a way through.

March 3, 2008

You know that kind of weariness when you are emotionally cracked and leaking, physically exhausted, and your brain doesn't work even enough for you to figure out what to make for dinner?

That's the kind of weary I am. Yesterday was the service for our friend. It was beautiful and terrible. I am in the strictest awe of his mother, brave and still herself, no matter what.

There are so many friends around, right now, a strange blessing.

Maybe sometime soon I will have more to write.

March 12, 2008

Things I don't know:

I don't know what it is like to love a child who has grown up.

I don't know what it is like to lose something that I treasure above all other things.

I don't know what it is like to be the remaining spouse.

I don't know how to grow old.

I don't know how tall my children will be.

I don't know the depths of my husband, despite our years together.

I don't know what will happen tomorrow, despite my plans, despite my ideas. I definitely don't know about next year. And I don't know what the consistency of my friendship is, whether it helps in grief, whether I am as clumsy as a pup, or slightly okay.

I know that I love so much, clumsy as I am.

March 18, 2008

I had an interesting weekend. I was able to get together with some friends, right before developing a sickness that caused extreme crankiness as well as the sensation that a large person is sitting on my head. But I mused this weekend, as much as any woman with three young children with colds can muse. I thought about life, and calling, and writing, and time. I thought about my idols- those things that I feel like I can't be happy without. I thought about dryness, and drought, and long stretches of desert. And I thought about displacement, about moving, and about the rule of displacement- how if there is too much sand in the bucket, the water cannot fill it.

I didn't mean to fill my well with sand, but I believe I have. Somehow bad habits have crept in, and I haven't been reaching my source. Habits like starting to work the minute I wake up, rather than meditating on the Words of Life and breathing prayers into the morning air. Habits like aimlessly surfing the internet. Or filling my mind with books or movies, afraid of silence, afraid of listening.

It was good to re-evaluate.

I am really afraid of change, and all my bravado can't really cover that. I'm starting to admit it. My dreams tell me, like they always do, as they show me every fear played out, and I wake up sweating and shaking. People in my dreams leave me, they get lost, they die.

But thankfully I don't live by my fear, and perfect love casts out all fear, and today has enough trouble of its own. Right?

So it's one foot in front of the other, oceans of grace, wide open spaces, hugs and kisses and phone calls, waking up to prayer, and playing with my kids.

And, of course, packing. And eating pickles. And smelling my husband's face. And vacuuming. Just life.

March 19, 2008

I didn't sleep too well last night, worrying about a friend. This morning I found out he was safe, which was a huge relief. I'm sure you've felt something like this before. I can't tell my brain to stop at night, when it's moving so swiftly, and even when I managed to drop off into sleep land, my brain was going. In Technicolor. So it could have been a rough day.

But then my friend Jessie called and asked me if she could drop by with lunch. Since I'm still somewhat deaf (or just a bad listener) from my "someone sitting on my head" illness, I didn't hear the "with lunch" part, so I was pleasantly surprised when she brought treats. We had a sort of picnic inside. And the kids didn't fight! It was awesome.

During the afternoon, I worked on our Indian visa applications, and somewhere along the way, our UPS guy showed up. Can I just say that I love our UPS guy? He is seriously one of the nicest people-he acts as happy about packages as we are. "Looks exciting, it's Bed Bath and Beyond!" he'll say. Or, today, he said, "Must be something good, I need a signature!" And he's bubbling over while he says these things. Maybe it's the cool uniform, or the rockin' truck with no doors that makes him so happy.

But the package was a good one. Our new camera, a little Canon Powershot G9. I'm ready for India now. Ready for all the shots I'll ever need to take.

March 21, 2008

Things have been rough around here, lately. Our little Sacramento community cluster has been taking some hits, the latest

361

of which is our friend in the hospital.

So, today, my friend Joy (the wise-cracking one) came over so that we could pray together. I think she also came over so that we could hang out a little, too, and so that she could chew on my kids for awhile... but I'm not sure. All I know is that I'm just telling people to come on over, because I am locked down in my house until further notice. (Until my remaining things are contained in a few totes.)

I was on the phone when she arrived, so she just came on in and started cooking some food that she brought with her. In my kitchen, with my pots. Just making herself right at home. Can I just say for a minute how much my delicate heart LOVES THIS? I love it when people come in and start cooking. Especially when they give me some food. Like Joy did.

Anyways, after some food and some inevitable banter, we sat down to pray. I was sorting through photos also, and we paused to ooh and aahh over some of our long-time friends looking oh-so-young, like babies, in some of the photos. And then we realized, we really must let some of this worry and angst out, we needed to pray!

So we started to pray. It's a mysterious thing, praying together. You sit and talk, not to each other, but to someone you can't see. And you mm hmmm and uh huh, if you're into that sort of thing. Whatever you say, you're pretty much baring your deepest heart in front of some other person. It's a little awkward. And it's holy ground.

We had just gotten started, when Kenya came running inside. This is what she had to tell me:

"Mama! Kai accidentally peed on my foot!"

So, I'm all, *alright. What on earth?* Why right this second does Kai have to pee on his sister's foot? And how did that happen? And why

362

is he peeing outside, anyways?

"How did he *accidentally* pee on your foot?"

"He was making mud for us, and he accidentally got some of the pee on my foot."

OH. Okay. My son was making pee mud. For them to *play in*. In the front yard. And he missed, a little, and got some on my daughter's foot. Which doesn't really matter that much, since they were planning to play in it anyways, but that hasn't occurred to either of them, because that's not how they think. They don't think like that. Like sane people.

Anyways, Joy and I pressed on, amidst *washing the foot, and I need new pants, and get some out of your drawer, and I need the ones with the belt, and they're in the hamper, and these ones? and Kai, stop touching the negatives, and Leafy stop touching that photo, and I want it! That's DADDY! and you still can't touch it...*

Sometimes I am just so glad that God can hear our squeaky voices, even through all the din.

March 22, 2008

Yesterday I had some discouraging moments, as I couldn't work out some details with our shipping, and I'm just so tired of dealing with *logistics* for my whole entire life.

But now I take a deep breath and let it out. I have about fifty hundred things to think about. And the wild children are asking me if they can take down the walls in our house and plant thousands of dandelions. (?!)

Yesterday when we were sitting at the table eating, Chinua was telling me about his first experience in Israel (we are going to be in Israel en route to India) and I listened with my chin resting on my hand.

"It's so strange, because you get there and it's the most familiar place in the world to you, because you've heard about these places *forever*. But you know nothing about it at the same time, because you've never been here before."

While he was talking I thought about Moses and Mt. Sinai, and the Jordan River, and Jesus and the Mount of Olives, and I thought -about Jesus-, "Oh... I miss him."

It was such an odd thought, but one that I've been having a lot lately. He is the man that I've decided to follow forever, sometimes dejectedly, sometimes with singing, sometimes barefoot, sometimes with hiking boots on. I just wish that when I arrive in Israel I would find him one day, wandering on dusty hills with a bunch of people running behind him, hoping to see something amazing. (Like that kid in *The Incredibles*.)

Oh I miss him. He is with me, but I never read John's words, *"That which was from the beginning, which we have heard, which we have seen with our eyes, which we looked upon and have touched with our hands..."* without feeling a little bit envious. I had a dream a while back, that I was with a group of people, and we had found out that Jesus was going to visit us in the flesh. I was so, so, excited, and trying to figure out what I would do when he arrived. Finally I stationed myself by the door, figuring that I could touch his feet as he entered. But then someone picked up a guitar, and I realized that I had got it wrong, and that we were going to sing together, Jesus wasn't going to walk in.

But even getting it wrong was beautiful. *One day I will see my wandering teacher.* That is the belief that I write the story of my life on. *He sets the lonely in families.* That is the theme.

Traditionally, today is a day that he spent lying cold in a grave, and because we get to know the whole story, we know it gets better. But at the time? They were thinking, *Oh- I miss him.*

"He was despised and rejected by men; a man of sorrows, and acquainted with grief; and as one from whom men hide their faces he was despised, and we esteemed him not." Isaiah 53:3

March 25, 2008

Last night my beautiful, beautiful, beautiful grandmother passed away.

I don't know how to say how much I'll miss her. She was a force in my life that was grounding and true. She loved me fiercely.

I know my Grandpa will miss her beyond words (they just celebrated their 60th wedding anniversary). My parents and all our other family will miss her as well. She was an incredible woman, with a red-headed temper and the most loving arms. She loved her family fiercely. You could *feel* her love, from way, way off.

I wouldn't want her to come back and be sick again. I just wish sometimes that everything could stay like it was before.

March 26, 2008

Today we pack up the truck.

Yesterday I finished training a new bookkeeper, got rid of a table and highchair, and drove to San Francisco to pick up our visas. About halfway there I realized I should have taken the train.

I am halfway numb and halfway hurting. We lost another friend on Monday night (the friend who was in the hospital) and I've never experienced anything like this- three dear people in the space of a month. We have friends (multiple) who have lost not only their brothers, but their best friends, once again in the space of a month. My heart breaks for these families.

The people who have left us I know are not gone. But they will be missed, here where we still touch things that are dirty and get up to wash our faces in the morning, here where people go into the hospital one day and a few days later leave their bodies behind.

And in the midst of it, we pack up our moving truck. Nothing feels quite normal. Thank God for the wild children around here-drumming and dancing, demanding food three times a day. They keep things on the right track.

Today, as I work, I'm going to think of the wildflowers that will be exploding across the landscape in Humboldt. Maybe I will lie in a bed of them, maybe I will be able to cry.

March 27, 2008

Understatement can speak volumes. When my Grandma got sick, and I used to call her to talk to her, we had a sort of ritual. She had leukemia, and thankfully had almost no pain, except for the yucky tests they had to put her through.

But she would get really tired if her white blood corpuscle count was particularly low, and often she would need blood transfusions to help her. My grandmother was possibly one of the most energetic people on earth, and hearing her sounding weak and tired made me feel as though someone was holding back the sun.

We would talk about all sorts of things. Mostly the kids. At a time in my life when Grandma and I were in danger of running out of common ground, I started having kids. And from then on there was no shortage of things to talk about. It's nice to have someone who could hear you tell stories about your kids ad infinitum, without ever getting sick of it. My parents and grandparents can always be counted on for this.

But we would talk. I told her about my knitting, and quilting, since she was an avid sewer and knitter. And she of course expressed alarm about my plans to move to India.

And then, always, when we talked about her sickness, I would say, "I really don't like this Grandma. I just don't like it."

And she would say, "I know you don't, dear. I know."

March 28, 2008

Here's some advice: Moving is stupid. Don't do it. Unless you want to end up lying on your carpet on your back trying to blow up an inflatable mat, because all the beds are moved and you don't have the right inflator thingy.

You may also find yourself contemplating setting things on the various lawns of your neighborhood, just to get rid of them. Or at least putting garbage in the trashcans of your neighbors. And you will ask yourself whether the local thrift store accepts condiment donations. And you will cry, but not really. You will threaten to cry, but then nobody will rescue you because surprise! You're the Mom! Lucky you.

So stay put, people. Just stay where you are. And when you think to yourself, maybe it would be fun to go somewhere, remind yourselves that it's actually a not-good idea. And you'd better just take a walk around the block.

March 30, 2008

We are almost all better now.

I say almost because there is that great lump of grief waiting to pounce on me when I can finally make myself vulnerable to it.

But, after yesterday, which was one of the most insane days ever, and the two days before, which were also insane, we are done with this part of our move. We got to the ranch last night just after midnight, after finally finishing and then driving for the five hours it takes us to get here.

I could barely walk this morning. But this is one of the happiest places in the world to me, and I am recuperating.

March 30, 2008

There are so many kinds of losing. It seems that grief takes many forms.

There is a wild pain that wakes you up in the night gasping for breath, a panic that makes your heart skip a beat. There are dreams that leave you weeping into your pillow. There can be screaming, anger and striking and tearing. It is the grief for the untimely, for ones who shouldn't have left the earth so quickly. I've never felt this kind of grief, but I've seen it and I've cried along with those who wake up in those nights with the darkness sitting heavy on them.

There is grief that has you lying in your bed, curled in a ball. Your tears leak into your pillow, you don't want to eat. Food seems pointless. You don't know what to do with the days that stretch on ahead, but you know that you need to be brave, sometime, somewhere. Soon. But now you will just curl up into yourself and cry into the softness. You miss your dear brother, or your husband. You weren't ready to let him go. I haven't been there, either.

And then there is grief that takes you gently. It is the longing for someone who will never be there again, but who led a long and full life, who had many days, many memories. It is a sharp pang when you look in the mirror and see your curly, curly hair- the hair that didn't come from nowhere, the annoying ringlets that you inherited. It is when you remember your special nickname, the one that your grandma used for you; "Pet Lamb." It is when you think, "Oh please can she come back? Just so I can hug her and smell her one more time? So I can hear her singing while she washed the dishes? So I can write down her stories?"

It is when you stop in your tracks on the way to walking somewhere, stop dead midway, stand staring off. You wait for your heart to feel okay again and then keep going the way you were, toward your kids who are waiting for you. This is the kind that is mine.

april

April 2, 2008

We're still on our journey north to Canada, taking it very, very slowly. I'm feeling wandery and content to look out of the van window. Chinua and I are having a good time, giving each other loving looks in the car, and the kids are amazing, as usual. I love my kids.

My eyes fill with tears at the oddest of times.

Will we reach Canada tonight? Tomorrow? Right now we don't even know. Today I had the incredible chance to visit with a friend and her hours-old baby. There is nothing like the smell of the newest of children.

April 3, 2008

In Portland we call some friends (one good thing about the diaspora of our community is that we have friend in many cities) and drop in. We meet at the park. The kids have glowing halos around their heads as they play on the swings. We ooh and aah over how much their kids have grown. They ooh and aah over ours. It is chilly in the shade so we shift around to get into the sun~ our eyes are happy to see each other.

We decide to stay for the night. Dusk is close, it is the golden hour and Chinua's camera shutter is never still. Our friend bicycles away toward his house and we follow him in the van.

Food and wine happen, we talk and lounge on the floor. I'm not feeling so great so I ask if I may take a bath. My friend pours one for me and when I go into the bathroom, there are candles lit and bamboo towels on the rack.

Time has passed, but not much time has passed. Our kids speak in full sentences, they are a little taller, but our hearts are the same.

April 22, 2008

Pregnancy update: I've reached the point in this whole pregnancy schtick where I have two companions who make themselves known at many moments during the day.

The first is, of course, my little baby. *Tap tap tap*, he/she says. *Tap tap wriggle.* It's code for *I love you*.

The second is heartburn. And it burns burns burns, the ring of fire. It's code for *you are going to regret eating anything at all. Ever.*

April 24, 2008

I have no idea what our next house will look like. Maybe it will be tall and leaning, with curved staircases, like a house from a Dr. Seuss book. Probably not.

Maybe it will be round and chubby, with thick earth walls and a hole in the ceiling. Probably not.

371

Brick? Cement? Stucco? Wood? Tinfoil?

I'm hoping for a garden. I still miss the earthiness of the Land, the blanketing screen of the trees with the sun coming through the leaves. I want to sit in the dirt and smell flowers all around me. The herb smell of warm weeds. The metallic smell of the sun.

I'm hoping for doors and windows that I can throw open.

I guess we'll see.

may

May 2, 2008

We have about four more days to get ready to fly away.

FOUR DAYS.

FOUR. DAYS. Until I move with my family to India.

What do you think the chances are that I can have Leafy fully potty-trained by then?

No, I thought so too. Bummer.

We fly to Turkey, and then Israel, and then from Jordan to India. Because moving with your family is not enough when you are six months pregnant and everyone is still five and under. We have to throw a little backpacking and rustic camping in the hills of Turkey in there too.

But the truth is that I'm looking forward to this more than almost anything in years and years. And then at night before I drop off to sleep I start thinking about moving away from EVERYTHING AND EVERYONE.

And then I ask Chinua to hit me over the head and knock me out.

May 3, 2008

You do things a different way. You find new things that comfort you.

A cup of tea in the perfect spot by the window. The notebooks from the stationary store down the street. Breakfast at that one restaurant with the really good lemon pancakes. You find new ways to breathe, different clothes to wear, new ways to look at people on the street.

You can change. You can see things with eyes that have not seen this before. The sun sets in the sky oddly. Slowly it becomes a familiar orb, foreign no longer.

You find the perfect market stall, the one with the piles of glowing fruit and the man with the superlative kindness. You make friends with his wife. You find new ways of cooking things. These are the things that I know to be true about traveling, about moving to new places.

*

It is 3:00 in the morning and I can't sleep. It probably isn't surprising, but what is surprising is that I haven't been all that nervous before now. It began with the packing. I have pared our things down to the very basic, the most special, the smallest things, and yet, as I pack, I see how much we will have to leave behind. We will give more things away, and the most special will be waiting for us, one day, in a box that we will open and exclaim over. But they are only things.

I remember my sense of loss when I moved to California from

British Columbia. It took me years, and I went through the loops, around and around the culture shock trails, before I came to where I am today. How amazing, that we can have more than one home.

It is the parenting parts that have empty spaces. I'm not sure exactly how this works, how we adjust together to the new tastes in our mouths. But in a way, it is like every part of parenting; there are always gaps, you are always figuring it out as you go, it is always a different child's month for testing you in ways that make you reach for the farthest bits of strength because you need to be stronger than the days ahead.

*

You find the paths that everyone loves, the new birds and flowers. You play in the waves. You find new soap, new types of clothing. You color together on paper that feels different than the paper at home. You watch excitedly through the window of the train, counting camels, sheep with long tails, elephants.

You listen to each other, you kiss and hug relentlessly, you write and you draw and you tell stories while everyone is drifting off to sleep under a different night.

May 6, 2008

Today we finished packing up all of our backpacks, taking things to the thrift store, and returning electronics that we needed to return. Then we drove for a few hours to Seattle, leaving Canada and all the new growth on the poplars behind.

Goodbyes are the hardest part. My parents have been so incredible during this time that we have been staying with them, and it's so hard to go farther away. Thankfully technology has reached a point where we can be in touch like never before. But still it's hard.

I'm sitting in a hotel room right now, a really swanky one that we practically stole online, in a bit of a daze, wondering how many new things I am on the cusp of. I feel as though we have reached the top of a really long hill, are just about to pull up over the crest to where we can see the other side. We're not there yet, and as I sit here in a strange city in a strange hotel room, I am wondering what exactly it is that I am on the other side of.

Tomorrow our first adventure begins. We are flying to Istanbul, Turkey, ready to join a bunch of brothers and sisters from all around the world on a camping adventure. The theme of the gathering is Peace in the Middle East.

Tomorrow we crest that hill, and perhaps our legs will run away with us as we head down the other side. All I know is that I hope I'm not going to be doing a whole lot of actual *carrying* of my backpack, or I will be literally rolling down that hill.

And... right here, just before the plane journey that will change all of our lives forever, I'll stop. But of course our story doesn't end here.

Our family did reach India and of course it wasn't anything like we imagined it would be. (Nothing ever is.) The move was both harder and better than we could have imagined.

If you are interested in seeing photos from this time in our life, you can check out the small gallery I've created which includes photos of the Land, the kids, and the house after the trees fell on it — http://racheldevenishford.squarespace.com/trees-tall-as-mountains/

I'm working on the next book of the Journey Mama writings, all about our time in India. Until it's ready, you can read about India and all our current adventuring at http://journeymama.com .

ABOUT THE AUTHOR

Bio

Rachel Devenish Ford is the wife of one Superstar Husband and the mother of five incredible children. Originally from British Columbia, Canada, she spent seven years working with street youth in California before moving to India to help start a meditation center in the Christian tradition. She can be found eating street food or smelling flowers in many cities in Asia. She currently lives in Northern Thailand, inhaling books, morning air, and seasonal fruit.

She is deep in the revisions of her second novel and the compilation of the second Journey Mama book.

Other works by Rachel Devenish Ford:

The Eve Tree

Reviews

Recommendations and reviews are such an important part of the success of a book. If you enjoyed this book, please take the time to leave a review at Amazon.com or your site of choice.

Don't be afraid of leaving a short review! Even a couple lines will help and will overwhelm the author with waves of gratitude.

Contact

You can contact the author in a plethora of ways:

Email: racheldevenishford@gmail.com

Blog: http://journeymama.com

Facebook: http://www.facebook.com/racheldevenishford

Twitter: http://www.twitter.com/journeymama

Instagram: http://instagram.com/journeymama

Thanks so much for reading.

ACKNOWLEDGEMENTS

To Chinua, who makes space for me to write, to my mom and dad, who are simply full of love and care, to Candace, Elena, and Renee, for being perfect partners in crime, to Julie who taught me how to knit, to Amelia, who taught me how to make fudge, to Jessie and Levi, who took me to Burkina Faso, and to the people who worked so long to make the Land such an amazing place to live. Thank you.